A Treatise on Possibility:

Perspectives on Humanity Hereafter

A companion guide to the album
Nothing Is True & Everything Is Possible

Rou Reynolds

FABER *ff* MUSIC

© 2021 by Faber Music Ltd
First published by Faber Music Ltd in 2021
Bloomsbury House
74–77 Great Russell Street
London WC1B 3DA

Text © 2021 Rou Reynolds
The right of Rou Reynolds to be identified
as author of this work has been asserted
in accordance with Section 77 of the
Copyright, Designs and Patents Act, 1988

Lyrics by Rou Reynolds
Music by Enter Shikari
© Universal Music Publishing Ltd.
All Rights Reserved

Album artwork by Ian Johnsen & Stuart Ford
Photography by Tom Pullen & George Perks,
Vada Studios, Warwickshire, UK
Orchestral session photographs by Ian Coulson
Smecky Music Studio, Prague, CZ
Book art by Ian Johnsen
Typeset by Kenosha Design
Edited by Lucy Holliday & Hamish Ironside

Printed and bound in Turkey by Imago

ISBN: 0-571-54178-X
EAN: 978-0-571-54178-2

Reproducing this book in any form is illegal
and forbidden by the Copyright, Designs
and Patents Act, 1988

To buy Faber Music publications or to find out
about the full range of titles available please contact
your local retailer or Faber Music sales enquiries:

Faber Music Limited
Burnt Mill
Elizabeth Way
Harlow
CM20 2HX
England
Tel: +44 (0) 1279 82 89 82

fabermusic.com

Introduction

Nothing Is True & Everything Is Possible is Enter Shikari's sixth studio album. The 16 year old me would have never believed you if you'd told him that his band would make six albums and feel like they are only just getting started all these years later. Over the years, I've had such great opportunities to explore the world and distil my experiences into rhythm, pitch and poetry. I'm eternally grateful for this continued chance to create and analyse life through music.

I am honestly more thirsty than ever to learn and to create, and so thankful for the freedom to continue to do so.

Rou Reynolds, 2021

THE GREAT UNKNOWN

Is this a new beginning?
Or are we close to the end?
Now my ears are ringing
It's getting close

Is this a new beginning?
Or are we close to the end?
Now the room is spinning
It's getting closer now

I've been waiting for the great leap forwards
I'm so impatient, yeh, I want to cut corners
I stare at the skyline
Reach for a lifeline
I shout into the great unknown...

If there's anyone out there
Just give me a sign!
I shout into the great unknown...

Oh the beauty of the twilight glow
Oh the delusion of Vincent van Gogh
A red sky at night
A shepherd's flashlight
His beam sweeps like brushstrokes across the sky

Crossing The Rubicon

Now we're crossing the Rubicon
We tried everything under the sun
So we're crossing the Rubicon
'Cos it's too late

Fill me out a prescription
For this existential dread
I woke up into a nightmare
And I'm hoping that you'll take me back to bed

But we can't turn back it's a labyrinth
Now the die is cast my friend (we endeavour)
Christ what a mess
I think Beckett said it best –
Try again, fail again, fail better

Fill me out a prescription
Can you free me from this curse?
I woke up inside your compass
And you're navigating us from east to worst

Something's got to give
We've come too far to turn back

{ The Dreamer's Hotel }

Outrage!
That's it I'm going on a rampage
Don't waste my time with any context
I'm gonna ruin all your prospects
I'm gonna pick all your pockets

Fury!
I am the judge and I'm the jury
It's dog eat dog and I'm a pure breed
I'll work you up into a frenzy
But God this baggage is heavy

Meanwhile...
Back at The Dreamer's Hotel
5 stars but all rooms are vacant

Meanwhile...
I can hear alarm bells
Outside they're losing their patience

Cheapshot!
Another tempest in a teapot
I am King Arthur in Camelot
Connected to the hotspot
For 8 days on the trot
Fighting the trolls and the bots

Students!
Nuance ain't nothing but a nuisance
You're either good or you are evil
You play a prick and there's no sequel
And that's the will of the people

Meanwhile...
Back at The Dreamer's Hotel
5 stars and rose-coloured windows

Meanwhile…
Back at The Dreamer's Hotel
5 stars and courtesy disco

If love is blind
Hatred is deaf
And well fed

Waltzing Off The Face Of The Earth

Regardless what you feel
This song isn't real
And the earth isn't sphere
And you're not really here

You can't trust your own eyes
And you only hear lies

Our future's been denied
And there's nowhere to hide
Now that nothing is true
And everything is possible

Regardless what you feel
Here comes the big reveal
Darling, you were a mistake
And climate change is fake

You must dream of being rich and famous
Only then will life be painless
We all start to twig
From pig to man, from man to pig

There's been a shooting in a Walmart
So put guns on every shopping cart
There's dead kids on the beach
Bigoted parents now decide what teachers teach

modern living...

I'd like to welcome all my people here
But listen, everything you love is about to disappear
I feel it coming there's something in the air
But this is living, oh it's modern living, yeh

How can you never be nervous?
How can you never consider the risk
Consider a hideous end?

On every face a filter
Masking weakness, masking woe

You're the picture of composure
You're tossing a coin, getting heads twice
And then expecting it thrice

We're Apocaholics Anonymous
Our fear is bottomless
Now God's forgotten us

We're Apocaholics
Drinking gin and tonics
Lying in the flowers
Counting down the hours

The Pressure's On

I step out the door and it's dark and I'm on my own
I breathe in the scent of the pine and the conifer cones
I feel like I've fallen down a staircase
And broken my bones

You better figure it out now
You better figure it out now
The pressure's on

I can't quite believe the time that's gone flying by
You try and tell me that everything will be fine
I appreciate your belief
But I'm not sure you're right

You better figure it out now
You better figure it out now
The pressure's on

And this isn't what I planned
I wish you could understand
I throw myself into the day
But I just seem to ricochet...

T.I.N.A.

"There is no alternative
Take my hand if you want to live"

No, I feel it coming in the air
You can enter if you dare
It's the essence of humanity
To build an infinite reality

F16's flying overhead
The present is the past
That we cannot shed
Umbilical cord
That we cannot cut
A secret trapdoor
That we cannot shut

I never noticed you were in disguise
But now I see you T.I.N.A.
You were a barrier around my mind
Yeh I see through you T.I.N.A.

It's a crisis of creativity
We've forgotten our ability
A glimpse of light from another sun
But you block it out, now we're on the run

Marionettes
(I. The Discovery of Strings)

Master,
I think you owe them an answer
You've become so complacent
And they're becoming impatient

Vandal,
You left their strings in a tangle
Since you turned to the liquor
Their eyes are starting to flicker...

Thunder,
They look up and they wonder
Are they controlled by the heavens?
They start to question their essence

Get it together
You know there's only one minute
Or they're gonna discover
They're gonna uncover

Sober,
Oh god I wish this was over
After dark and it's lights out
They can't believe their own eyes now ...

Marionettes
(II. The Ascent)

Looking up and gripping their strings
They ask "Where do they lead?"

"Climb! Climb!
Search and seek!
We will test this 'truth' you speak!"

By the sweat of one's brow
Thou shall eat bread
But curiosity began to creep
From underneath the bed
Of toil and doctrine
And the marionettes awaken
Into a nightmare...

Now we see the warning sign
We'll disobey our Frankenstein
I keep my focus, keep my cool
The higher we go, climbing up to heaven
Or a hell or maybe something inconceivable
It used to be unspeakable
We snatch back our strings
And as the freedom bell rings
They start to sing

"Reveal yourself, reveal yourself
The world that you created
is not mightier
than our means to remake it!"

Our minds are firewood
And now we spark the match
We set ourselves alight
Escape this childhood
And now we spark the match
We set ourselves alight

Oh, truth hurts.
Now you know – truth frees.

satellites* *

I wish I was a comet
Burning up into the night
I wish I was a comet
But I'm just a satellite

I don't like the limelight
So we don't hold hands in daylight
I still drag the closet
All my limbs, they ache inside

And surely all my family and my friends,
My god and my ends
They cannot all be wrong
So I play along:

We refrain from touch
We are satellites
In a cosmic dance
Amongst the northern lights

And we orbit fast
But I wish we could collide
I'm sick of concealing
I'm sick of the feeling
I no longer want to hide

'Cos I think it could be love
But I can't show you enough
I wanna burn through the atmosphere
Soar like a meteor tonight

All the gravity between us
Someone bring me down to land
And write a prayer to Venus
What is life without affection?

Now online they discuss
Whether I exist
And in the court they decide
Who I can kiss

thē kǐñg

I used to be the king
But they took everything
They even stole my crown
I'm gonna track you down

Watch your back my friend
I'm about to kickstart a cycle
Of never-ending revenge
And this time it's primal, it's tribal

All our drawbridges are up
Is this a wind up?
I used to be a charmer
But now there's holes in my armour, fuck!

I can't walk away, I can't walk away
I got all this pride, all this shame, all this anger to obey
"Well if it's revenge you seek,
Then be sure to dig two graves"
Why? One for my enemy
And fucking one for you, preferably

I just want to be adored
And I'll die by my own sword, thanks
I trust no one, as I prowl under the amber streetlamps
All our drawbridges are up
Is this a wind up?
I grab my sword and swing
But I go and pull my hamstring, fuck!

A Treatise on Possibility:

Perspectives on Humanity Hereafter

A companion guide to the album
Nothing Is True & Everything Is Possible

Rou Reynolds

Contents

Preface

If you've read (or are, at least, familiar with) my previous books, you'll know them as pretty much straight-up explanations of lyrics.

This book is not that.

You've had the lyrics in the preceding pages, but now we're going to get into 'proper reading' territory. Though this book once again revolves around my lyrics, it's *more* of an analysis of the world in which the Enter Shikari album *Nothing Is True & Everything Is Possible* was written. I'll guide you through my thoughts and feelings on that world, with the lyrics acting as convenient signposts along the way.

In an age of tweets, soundbites and headlines, where deeper thought and analysis are rare (certainly true of the world I inhabit for my 'day job' at the coalface of – broadly speaking – 'rock' or 'pop' music), I have taken it upon myself to dive into the deep end. Into *detail*.

This. Book. Gets. Dense.

A lot of research went into its pages. It goes in hard. It is my attempt to step back, take a broad perspective on human life, and ponder upon the precarious position we find ourselves in, here in the early stages of the 21st century.

Before we get into it proper, and to avoid any confusion, let me clarify a few things about myself ...

I am not a *doomsday prophet.*

There are points in this book that *are* quite bleak and kind of scary, but they're just an analysis of our current systems and the behaviour they encourage. Pessimists, defeatists and doomsday prophets will tell you that catastrophe is *inevitable*. That is not true. So long as there is a willingness to understand what is happening. This is not a pessimistic book and I am certainly not predicting the end times. I'm simply looking at where we're headed if we stick to business as usual. I don't revel in the 'thrill' of possible human catastrophe or destabilising civilisation, and I'm not looking to terrify or numb you. I am just exploring what is possible, in order to avoid the *worst* possibilities.

I am not a *salesman.*

I'm not here to persuade you of anything or tout any quick fixes, like some sort of snake-oil vendor or spin doctor. My goal is to present information, and show you what links I have made with that information. In an ideal world, I'd like to think I can broaden your perspective, and hopefully spark calm and compassionate conversation.

I am not a *scientist*.

But I *have* researched the most up to date science, as best I can, and I'm relaying what I've learned here, along with my own thoughts and conclusions. I've tried to avoid biases as much as possible, and I'd like to think I do not have any ideological allegiances. I only have curiosity. I strive only to understand our world further, and I hope to persuade you to do the same.

I am not a *politician*.

This book favours no political party or ideology (as George Orwell said, 'no writer can be a loyal member of a political party'[1]). In fact, within the pages that follow, I actually argue against the entire current socioeconomic system itself, along with other archaic ideologies we cling to or take up arms in the name of. I'm not invested in any political identity or historical ideology. I'd much rather view the world through the eyes of the bird of prey, circling high above, instead of from the perspective of territorial rabbits fighting it out on the ground.

I am not a *specialist*.

Philosophical and scientific inquiry are extremely fragmented fields. A person trains in, and then goes on to specialise within, a specific area. They then zoom in further still, and research within a small portion of that specific area. This shows the amazing human capacity to build upon shared knowledge – the detail at the forefront of science today is truly *awesome* – but this also means that interdisciplinary thought is not encouraged anywhere near enough. Specialist bubbles create blinkered and narrow areas of expertise. They limit exposure and communication between disciplines.

One of the major benefits of my position as a free and enthusiastic researcher, is that I am not bogged down in one area, enabling me to spend time investigating the wider trends and discoveries, and piece them together like a detective. It is in this style of investigation that this book has been written.[2]

I am not *beholden* to any *company* or *organisation*.

I have no corporate allegiance or sponsorship. I have no reason to 'hold my tongue' to avoid ruffling the feathers of some board of directors. I'm lucky enough to be in a position where my income is solely derived from the work that my friends and I create. I'm blessed with relative independence. And in an age where *Nothing Is True*, I think it's especially important to be able to say this when hoping to present factual information with any credibility.

I'm lucky enough to be a regular traveller. Through touring, I get to meet people from different walks of life and experience different cultures. I get to experience ideas, ideologies and perspectives from all over the world. I think that this learned cosmopolitanism helps me achieve a broad perspective.

To quote Mark Twain on the subject: 'Travel is fatal to prejudice, bigotry, and narrow-mindedness, and many of our people need it sorely on these accounts. Broad, wholesome, charitable views of men and things cannot be acquired by vegetating in one little corner of the earth all one's lifetime.'[3]

This is not intended to throw shade on people who do not or cannot travel. Not at all. I understand perfectly well that I am profoundly lucky to have experienced such a wide range of culture, and it's just one reason why I feel compelled to write. Time and time again, my experience has proven that the majority of people are good and kind, and it is our systems that cause corruption and obnoxious behaviour in humans. If this seems an unrealistic, or just an odd worldview to you, then I encourage *you*, more than anyone, to read this book.

This book is an analysis of our world today, and that analysis ultimately presents a stark warning ...

We *must* change the fundamental direction of society, and quickly.

We must change our *selves* and change our *systems*.

Wilfred Owen, my favourite poet,[4] had a narrow and short-lived writing career, covering his experiences as a British soldier in the First World War, during which he died. In a preface found, unfinished, among his papers, he wrote; 'All the poet can do to-day is to warn, That is why the true Poets must be truthful.'[5]

Thankfully, I haven't ever found myself on a battlefield, 'bent double, like old beggars under sacks, knock-kneed, coughing like hags', 'blood-shod' or 'drunk with fatigue', but I *have* seen the equally unnecessary pain and adversity that our socioeconomic values and structures can cause.

All *I* can do today is warn. And hopefully, I'll be presenting you with a more truthful lens through which to view the world than you will find in most corporate media.

In *Nothing Is True & Everything Is Possible* I hold a mirror up to society, with the aim of revealing our shared experience, the bigger picture that is so often covered by mists of complexity and everyday toil.

So, here, in the pages that follow, I present the bigger picture. This is my treatise on possibility.

1 Introduction

Nothing Is True & Everything Is Possible

As 2016 drew to a close, I was about halfway through writing the fifth Enter Shikari album. *The Spark*, as that album would eventually be known, was inspired by personal hardships, but I certainly wasn't alone in considering 2016 to be the worst year of the 21st century so far. From Brexit, and the divisions it created in the UK; to the death of David Bowie; to government cuts that continued to cripple the NHS[1]; to the electing of a misogynistic, narcissistic reality TV star to the most powerful office in the world; 2016 was a total bastard. So much so, that people began trivially anthropomorphising it and 'blaming' the misery we endured upon the year itself. Like I did there by calling it a 'bastard'.

'FUCK 2016!' became the online dictum.

Perhaps the most pervasive and defining characteristic of 2016 was the increased penchant for political dishonesty and, more so, the bold tenacity in which the lies were communicated.

I was dumbfounded as the UK Leave campaign plastered a devious oversimplification of the economics of Brexit on the side of its campaign bus to mislead the public. 'We send the EU £350 million a week, let's fund our NHS instead' was flagrantly deceptive for two reasons: the £350 million figure was false,[2] and all the prominent Leave campaign MPs seemed ideologically opposed to a well-funded Public Health Service in the first place. (Their voting record since then seems to further prove their disregard and disrespect for the NHS too. In 2017 they all voted against a fair pay rise for nurses[3] and all voted against conducting a precautionary analysis into how Brexit will affect the NHS.[4])

(Now, don't worry, that's the last you'll hear of Brexit in this book (well, almost), I'm just using this as a prominent example of political dishonesty which, yes, was apparent on both sides, but this was the most conspicuous example.)

Oxford Dictionaries declared 'post-truth' to be its 2016 International Word of the Year, reflecting what it called a 'highly charged' political 12 months.

> **post-truth** *adjective* relating to circumstances in which objective facts are less influential in shaping public opinion than emotional appeals.[5]

'BRING ON 2017!' we all impatiently cried.

We were longing for the same motivating, fresh-start psychology that a new year brings to us as individuals. We were longing to compartmentalise and move on from recent events with a sigh of relief and revitalised enthusiasm. We were clinging to *possibility* for liberation.

Unfortunately, unlike *self*-improvement, when it comes to widespread *social* improvement, we have very little apparatus in place to achieve progress. 1 January came around, and with no structural New Year's resolution in place, it was just another day in the never-ending political shitshow.

On 20 January 2017, Trump took post-truth to a brazen new level and began his presidency with a barefaced lie about the size of his inauguration crowd. It didn't matter that we could all see the pictures and video, his authority now supposedly transcended reality.[6]

2017 saw a surge in terrorism in the UK with the Westminster Bridge, Manchester Arena and London Bridge attacks. We learnt – via the #metoo movement – that vast, heinous instances of sexual misconduct had been committed over the years. Trump's continued lies and petty, spiteful attitude accompanied a new zest for science denialism as he withdrew the US from the Paris Climate Agreement – an accord set in place to keep the global average temperature increase below 2°C, (perhaps his most sadistic attack on the future of humanity during his presidency).

'FUCK 2017!' became the updated online dictum.

This was usually accompanied by the cliché 'surely things can't get any worse!' and would be delivered with a nervous laugh, because in an increasingly post-truth world, everything was now seemingly possible. The full dichotomy within the word 'possibility' was becoming glaringly apparent. That is to say, 'possibility' was not so much a safe haven of hope and comfort anymore. It had increasingly become something sinister. For me, it was beginning to be bloated with existential dread.

I won't continue listing the further shocks and examples of post-truths that we saw in the intervening years between 2017 and now, as that's a whole other book in itself... But, increasingly, we saw individuals, governments, and the media, all twisting truth, disregarding context, exaggerating, sensationalising, and appealing to emotion to promote and protect their identity or ideology. Establishing actual truths had become like grasping a particularly slippery, writhing salmon, while stood barefoot on an oily, freshly trawled mass of mackerel. In short ... very, very difficult.

'FUCK 2018! ... FUCK 2019! ...'

/ / / / / / / / / /

'Possibility', as a word, more often than not, has positive platitudinous connotations. For example:

- 'Anything is possible if you put your mind to it!'
- 'You too, can achieve the impossible!'
- 'Redefining what's possible!'

In discussing possibility, we are usually addressing the optimistic *promise* of infinite human potential.

But the innate dichotomy within the word 'possibility' has become more apparent recently. We've witnessed events we previously thought inconceivable. From Trump and the global resurgence of nationalism, to climate change denial and ecological decline, our experience during the last few years has encapsulated what we could define as not the *promise*, but the *threat* of infinite human potential.

I'm a slut for semantics, so let's dig into the title a little further. The positive phrase 'anything is possible' has an evil twin – 'everything is possible'. I say 'evil' because this phrase triggers much more of an apprehensive state than a motivated state. Why? Well, this is to do with the implication of control: 'anything is possible' or 'any of the things are possible' implies within it some kind of choice. It is basically saying: 'Any of the things that you choose, are possible'.

The focus is on the singular actions that *you* choose to implement.

This gives you a sense of ultimate control, and hence, safety.

Conversely, 'Every of the things are possible' means 'All of the things'.

Everything is possible, *regardless* what *you personally* choose to make possible ...

The focus is on the infinite. And you do *not* have ultimate control.

So if *The Spark* was essentially an exploration into human *vulnerability* – both its unifying effects (when we *acknowledge* our innate fragility, i.e. when we speak to each other and care for each other) and its damaging effects (when we *ignore* our innate fragility, i.e. when we bury our feelings and act tough), *Nothing Is True & Everything Is Possible* is essentially an exploration into human *possibility* – both our creative and our destructive potential.

(That's the longest sentence in the book, by the way, so well done if that all went in first time, I was grappling with it for weeks. It'll be nice and manageable sentences from here on out, don't worry, I don't have the capacity, patience, nor desire, to write sentences as long as the writers of the past – the above sentence was 71 words; in philosophy, Locke holds the record with 309 words,[7] and James Joyce – the bloody sadist! – holds the record in fiction with 3,687 words from his epic *Ulysses*. No. Just no, James.)

/ / / / / / / / / /

There is now so much danger woven into our capability as human beings.

Since the Industrial Revolution our technological accomplishments have advanced endlessly and at a speed that has overtaken our ability to ethically and rationally use and administer those technologies. Our constantly improving, yet still primitive, grasp of causality and morality has made our technological advancements hazardous.

So where our ingenuity has certainly reduced our *interpersonal* risks (e.g. crime, famine, infant mortality), our ingenuity has *also* increased our *existential* risks. For examples of these, let's start with an obvious one; our nuclear capability.

Here's Albert Einstein writing in a telegram from 1946:

> Our world faces a crisis as yet unperceived by those possessing power to make great decisions for good or evil. The unleashed power of the atom has changed everything save our modes of thinking and we thus drift toward unparalleled catastrophe.[8]

I must say, I can breathe a little easier now that the world's largest nuclear arsenal is out of Donald Trump's hands, a man whose rationality and morality are at levels that would insult toddlers everywhere if I was to compare his to theirs. (And yes, by the way, a president does not need a second opinion, and congress play no part in the decision, they have absolute authority to unleash the equivalent of 10,000 Hiroshimas in a matter of minutes.[9] I sincerely hope we do not have another Trump, or an equally petulant individual in the White House ever again.)

A second example of existential risk is anthropogenic climate change. The processes involved in our energy, transport, food and production industries all have a detrimental effect on our ability to sustain human life on Earth.

Thirdly, our increased interconnectedness has given viruses the ability to spread more quickly and more broadly, making pandemics infinitely more possible and civilisational meltdown a complete reality (COVID-19 was just a dress rehearsal for what is possible in terms of the infectiousness or lethality of viruses).

Lastly, our communication technologies (specifically social media) have increased strident political tribalism and hostility and sent social trust plummeting.

These are all cases where our technological advancement has had effects that we did not foresee or understand. Or that we did see, but simply ignored. And now these advancements – nuclear power, fossil fuel power, global transport and social media – all bring a degree of risk to organised human life on Earth.

It is, of course, *not* our technological ability *or* our inventiveness that is the problem here. Instead, it is the socioeconomic system they are implemented within. These developments have created such danger because the most powerful among us, and our most influential institutions, are motivated by baser instincts: self-preservation, lust for power and short-sightedness. And they're motivated by those baser instincts because it is *those* aspects of our nature that our economic system rewards!

This is a core thesis running through this book: the way we structure our world brings out some of the *worst* in our human potential. What are we to expect as an outcome if we construct an economic system that rewards – through monetary profit – short-termism, self-absorption, greed and the destruction of our habitat?

The philosopher Will Durant summarised Aristotle's ethics like so: 'We are what we repeatedly do. Excellence, then, is not an act, but a habit.'[10]

We are what we repeatedly do. And what our system *encourages* us to repeatedly do is act in self-interested ways.

It is impossible to achieve excellence when the structure of our civilisation predominantly rewards habits of self-interest. It's like expecting a dog that was brought up in an aggressive pack of wolves to be a loyal and affectionate pet.

We know we are an incredibly mouldable species, one that is bent and shaped by our environment and our experiences. The erroneous debate between human nature and human nurture is best debunked by Robert Sapolsky: 'Our behavioural biology is usually meaningless outside the context of the social factors and environment in which it occurs.'[11]

So simply, within a socioeconomic structure that rewards self-interest, we will likely *learn* to become increasingly self-interested.

Right now, human possibility has been hijacked. It has been rigged in favour of division and destruction. That may sound bold or grandiose, but it is clear that many of the best aspects of our nature are not encouraged or honoured within our socioeconomic structure. And overall, if we want to be excited again about human possibility, instead of worried sick, we need to design a society that coaxes out the *best* in our nature, not the worst.

I've jumped straight in at the deep end here. If this all seems quite intense, well... it is! But don't worry, I go through it all in more detail as the book goes on. This is the general argument that I've been making throughout Enter Shikari's lifespan, and I think *Nothing Is True...* may address the idea with more perspective and clarity than I've achieved to date.

The Pandemic Of 2020/21

I started writing this book at the beginning of 2020. It was never meant to be the hefty piece of writing you hold in your hands today, but as I was writing, and unweaving the concepts, it grew and grew. The COVID-19 pandemic provided me with more time off tour than I can ever remember having! That enabled me to live the more solitary, isolated life that was needed in order to research and properly take on writing this book.

But oh what a miserable bit of irony the virus has brought: we release an album concerning the alarming possibilities that we all face, a warning of the innate failings of our value systems and our economic system, just before we experience a global pandemic that, at time of print, has killed over three million people. For our purposes here, we can think of the pandemic as the latest addition in a long list of other socially destabilising events that this album explores – an addendum.

We can read through these lyrics and find lines that are seemingly relevant to, or even predictive of, the global pandemic, but as with any case of *confirmation bias*, this is just us looking for evidence that confirms our opinions or hunches, whilst ignoring that which disproves. I was just as unprepared and unaware as anyone else. I mean, we knew that pandemics were a possibility – well, actually, an inevitability – as virologists and epidemiologists had been warning us about the next one for years. But unfortunately, it is a flaw in our thinking that we rarely envisage something happening to us that is radically outside of our own normal, everyday experience. This is another human bias, one called *normalcy bias*: 'Nah, that ain't gonna happen' or the slightly more self-absorbed: 'nah, that won't happen to me'. This ignorance or disregard for what is possible makes us very poor at being ready for 'black swan' events like pandemics. (Though I should point out that pandemics will probably become *more* frequent, *more* deadly and *more* economically damaging,[12] as we continue exploiting our planet's land and wildlife, so they will become less and less of a rarity.[13])

Another factor to consider; our economic system requires a constant cycle of production and consumption in order to function. It simply cannot deal with being put on hold (i.e. during a pandemic, when we go into a lockdown), and it reacts with a debilitating recession. This is not comparable to a war in that we won't have cities and supplies destroyed – our capacity for production has not dropped and neither has our purchasing power. The system simply can't deal with being paused, it requires an uninterrupted cycle of production and consumption or else it reacts in the same way a toddler would react should you press pause on the *Peppa Pig* episode they're watching. With a hissy fit.

Imagine how our economy would fare if COVID-19 had been a more stubborn and easily transferable virus. It would be obliterated. Our economic system was designed at a time when we had little understanding of viruses and disease, and now that they will likely become more frequent, it is simply unequipped and incompetent when it comes to global pandemics.

The lyrics for *Nothing Is True & Everything Is Possible* do not predict the 2020 pandemic by any means, but they do highlight the systemic shortfalls in our socioeconomic structure, the shortfalls which led to our drastically ill-prepared position in relation to COVID-19 and the economic woes it leaves in its wake.

/ / / / / / / / / /

Nothing Is True & Everything Is Possible is an album inspired by the recent political shocks over the past 5 years. It is about the obstacles to truth, trust, creativity, cooperation, compassion, and true communication. And it is about realising what our species is now capable of, both destructively and creatively.

This book dives deep into these subjects, far deeper than one can within the 4-minute confines of a song. I wanted to do this because now is the time for detailed analysis, for confident and thunderous criticism. And ultimately, for rebellion.

2 An Overview Of Our Predicament And Our Emotional Response

2.1 *The Great Unknown*

> Due to our own actions or inactions, and the misuse of our technology, we live at an extraordinary moment, for the Earth at least – the first time that a species has become able to wipe its self out. But this is also, we may note, the first time that a species has become able to journey to the planets and to the stars. The two times, brought about by the same technology, coincide – a few centuries in the history of a 4.5 billion year old planet.

> Carl Sagan (from *Pale Blue Dot*, 1994)

To Be, Or Not To Be

Nature is being destroyed at such a rate (tens to hundreds of times higher than the average over the past 10 million years) that many of Earth's vital life support systems are now in total decline.[1]

The effects of climate change are now no longer just projected but experienced.[2]

Democracy itself is under intense strain from post-truth politics, populism and creeping autocracy.[3]

We have an accelerating worldwide refugee crisis, and due to the COVID-19 pandemic, yet *another* economic crisis.

Maybe the tragic effects of the pandemic and the recession it leaves behind will push us to reform society and industry, finally setting us on a more sustainable path. It is often in times of crises that most political transformation and progress takes place ...

Or maybe the end *is* actually nigh ... It certainly feels like we are watching a perfect storm of crises bubbling up on the horizon, each one influencing the other, further destabilising our existence. Don't just take it from me; Nafeez Ahmed, a social scientist that specialises in complex systems theory, writes: 'Civilization's breach of planetary boundaries is now triggering multiple interconnected crises which are shrinking the safe operating space for human survival. And it could either result in breakdown – or breakthrough.'[4] It is these anxieties that motivated me to open the album with the line:

Is this a new beginning, or are we close to the end?

But before we depress ourselves too thoroughly, let us pull on the reins for a second. People have *always* banged on about the end of the world, haven't they? Perhaps we're wrong to feel apocalyptical again now?

Maybe it's simply in our nature to believe that we're on the edge of disaster? Certainly, throughout the annals of history it's quite unremarkable for people to claim they are living at a similar crux, a point where the past appears rosy compared to a frightening future ahead. Even just looking back to the 20th century, there were numerous moments where disaster was forecast, from the Cuban Missile Crisis, to the Cold War, to Y2K.

My favourite example of a false apocalyptical prediction was the return of Halley's Comet in 1910. Comets have long been hailed to be signifiers of doom, and the French astronomer, Camille Flammarion amplified that anxiety further when he announced that 'cyanogen gas would impregnate the atmosphere and possibly snuff out all life on the planet'.[5] People panicked. Many rushed to purchase gas masks and 'comet pills'. In Atlanta, Georgia, one man 'armed himself with a gallon of whiskey' and requested that friends lower him to the bottom of a dry well, 40 feet deep.[6] (I can sympathise. Haven't we all considered retreating to a cave with a vat of gin at least once after contemplating the state of the world?)

Of course, there is a clear difference between 1910 and now, though. We live in a world with *more* potential for catastrophe, in that our current threats include the *man-made*, instead of just the *astronomical*. The main phenomena with the potential to 'snuff out all life on the planet' are not celestial objects plummeting to Earth, but a plethora of dangerous human activities, tendencies and technologies. But still, perhaps it is a standard of human nature to be preoccupied or fixated on the negative, regardless where the threats come from? Maybe, as humans, we've always been gloomily prophesying a disastrous future, where, in reality, everything has been chugging along just fine?

The English historian Thomas Babington Macaulay (a man with a name so splendid I demand you read it out loud) certainly believed that fevered predictions were a staple of human behaviour, when in 1830 he wrote:

In every age everybody knows that up to his own time progressive improvement has been taking place, nobody seems to reckon on any improvement during the next generation. We cannot absolutely prove that those are in error who tell us that society has reached a turning point, that we have seen our best days. But so said all who came before us, and with just as much apparent reason.[7]

Believing that humanity is approaching its demise, or at least that human progress is coming to an end, is a recurring theme throughout history, and this could be to do with our cautious nature. Scanning and filtering the future for threats is an evolutionary mechanism. A survival technique. How else did we stay alive roaming the dangerous savannahs of Africa if it wasn't for our careful analysis of threats? Remembering where that bear's den was, or keeping an eye on the horizon for that approaching sabre-toothed tiger. Searching out, recognising and committing to memory our biggest risks was one attribute that kept us safe, so much so, that, over time, we became increasingly fixated upon the negative in general.

In our modern world, we still retain a hunger to seek out and remember any threatening information. This is now a cemented quirk of our human cognition, a defect in our thinking; psychologists call it *negativity bias*. We pay special attention to the worrying or bad aspects of our existence and grant them with greater importance than any positive information.

Today, this tendency plays out in our everyday life, influencing our reaction to all manner of unthreatening scenarios. For instance, when I'm reading the online comments upon releasing some new music, my brain is frustratingly drawn to those one or two negative comments among the majority positive. Similarly, one singular unpleasant remark from your friend may have a deeper effect on you than twenty of their compliments altogether. This is a bug in our mental hardware, and it can't really be avoided, but once you know about it, you can at least be wary of its occurrence, enabling you to soften its influence.

In 2014, some researchers wanted to assess which type of news stories participants chose to read during an experiment. Upon entering the lab, the unwitting volunteers were told they were taking part in a simple 'study of eye tracking', with no idea that, in actuality, their choice in news articles to browse was being avidly recorded. As it turned out, participants often chose stories with a negative tone over ones that were neutral or positive in content. Even when participants said they wanted more good news, or preferred reading it, the experiment revealed they were subconsciously more interested in bad news: 'Regardless of what participants say, they exhibit a preference for negative news content,'[8] concluded the authors of the study.

We maintain a preference for negative information because our evolutionary programming tells us it may well contain a warning relevant to our survival, something I'm sure you'll agree is always worth heeding! But in reality, it is not always helpful.

The news industry is more than aware of this innate attraction to the negative – I'm sure you've heard the old newspaper business maxim, 'If it bleeds, it leads'. The profession itself is compelled to concentrate its reporting on negative events and worrying possibilities because it knows that *this* is what best captures the public's attention (and therefore sells the most papers/attains the most clicks).

But also, positive news tends to happen slowly, whereas catastrophes are often sudden. Infant mortality has declined fivefold since 1950,[9] an incredible feat, but being steady, incremental progress, it is not deemed newsworthy. There is always an abrupt or shocking event to publicise, which drowns out any gradual good news.

One consequence of this is that people will vastly overestimate the frequency of negative events due to their over-representation in the news. If we can bring a load of examples of something to mind, we presume that thing happens regularly. This is part of what psychologists call the *availability bias*, another bias or bug in our thinking.[10] For example, murder, crime, and natural disasters are all disproportionately reported on the news, so we assume they are more frequent and widespread than they really are. Events are reported on the news purely because they *are* rare, so it's natural to think our lives are in peril when all the gradual improvements and positive aspects of life are pushed to the sidelines by the *one* rare negative event that happens any given day.[11]

In fact, the more exceptional an event is, the more newsworthy it is deemed to be, and this makes us believe exceptional events are widespread, or even simply the norm. After you put this book down, you may well refresh your news feed and read of a terrible act of terrorism, a murder, a natural disaster, there will be something awful happening somewhere in the world that will dominate the headlines. We may as well call the news 'the skews', as this is what it does: it skews our idea of the world, making us think far worse of it than we should.

It is also worth noting that news reporting is actually becoming *more* negative in general, as time goes on. A study that looked at the emotional tone of media articles worldwide, found that it had been steadily decreasing since the 1980s.[12] In his book *Enlightenment Now*, the cognitive psychologist Steven Pinker writes:

> Whether or not the world really is getting worse, the nature of news will interact with the nature of cognition to make us think that it is.[13]

The flaws in our thinking, along with the news industry's habit of exploiting those flaws, is enough to make us certain that society is at a dangerous turning point. Pinker's quote there is taken from a chapter titled 'Progressophobia', which argues that our world has been getting better and will probably get better still, we just don't see it (or we perhaps choose not to see it). In Pinker's view it is not fashionable to be optimistic, you're just dismissed as 'naive' – we ignore trends of vast improvement in child mortality, poverty and disease, and instead are intellectually drawn to prophesying doom.

Our human mind evolved to digest only the events of our locality – the immediate goings on in our family or our tribe – so we're actually quite poor at rationally evaluating the flood of broad and, quite frankly, shit news that we're pummelled with every day. Instead of judging what information is biased and what information is relevant, we simply have a gluttony for any, and all, threatening information; we lap up negative news like a ravenous Labrador, and we miss all the balancing positive news, it doesn't get a look in. Therefore, we end up seeing our general prospects as more unfavourable or ill-fated than they really are; our worldview becomes impaired.

So perhaps our fear about the future is actually no more justified than at any other time throughout human history? Perhaps we've simply been too focused on the negative?

'Yeah, come on Rou!' I hear you say, 'Stop being so lugubrious! We read your excessively bleak introduction, you didn't mention that in 2016 Obama banned all oil and gas drilling in the Arctic,[14] or that 2017 was actually the first year to have no commercial passenger jet plane crashes at all![15] Where's your balance Rou?'

OK, first of all, double points for using the word 'lugubrious'. Secondly, yes, like anyone, I too have of course been hostage to the mental bugs of negativity bias and availability bias over the past few years. But, I am afraid, dear reader, that after weighing up the evidence and being wary of those tendencies, I do not believe that my anxiety (or my lugubriousness) is unjustified.

It is, of course, very important to keep our human biases in mind as a way to sanity-check our own existential anxiety, but, sadly, post-check, I still find myself far from calm and confident. I wanted to cover the so called 'rational optimism' argument though, as we must understand the biases at play here, and we must consider all perspectives.

To Panic, Or Not To Panic

With all things considered, in 2021, I do not believe a distressed outlook is proof of our continued habit to focus on the negative, I think it is now quite justified. In fact, if you are not distressed, I believe you are simply not paying attention. And *this* is why I wrote a whole album about 'possibility'. To discuss humanity's increasing capabilities, and to discuss how these immense powers may now jeopardise our future survival.

So having looked at the reasons why we should always be cautious when predicting the future, and our tendency to exaggerate the negative, let me now address why I felt compelled to embed existential anxiety into *Nothing Is True & Everything Is Possible*. And let me start by revisiting our old friend, the historian, Mr Macaulay. (I know, he was actually 'Lord Macaulay' but I refuse to call anyone a Lord ... that is, unless they're a Sith Lord, of course.)

Macaulay continued his reflection on our misjudged existential anxiety thusly:

> On what principle is it that with nothing but improvement behind us, we are to expect nothing but deterioration before us?[16]

On the face of it, this seems a convincing sentiment, doesn't it? We live in a safer, less impoverished, more connected, and more technologically proficient world. With this long road of improvement behind us, why would we now expect a dangerous sharp turn?

Well, the thing is, there are now simply *key*, game-changing differences between our modern problems today, and those at any other time in the past.

There were no effects of catastrophic climate change in Macaulay's time. There were no nuclear weapons. No capacity for biological warfare or engineered pandemics. There were simply no broad existential threats at all other than a freak asteroid impact or super-volcano eruption. In short, they only had natural phenomena (or non-anthropogenic) threats to worry about, man-made (or anthropogenic) threats had not yet been invented.

So where Macaulay was probably *right* back in the 19th century, we cannot now mimic his optimistic sentiments. Read his quote again but with a keen eye on his attitude towards risk. It can seem a little overconfident or blasé, no?

Let's try turning his compelling phrase around ...

On what principle is it that with no deterioration behind us, we are to expect nothing but improvement before us?

Well, it's on the principle of faith isn't it? Macaulay is basically saying 'Stuff's been fine so far, so chill out bro, it'll probably continue'. Things have been improving since the onset of time, so there's no need to panic or probe. This stance is a variation on Bert Lance's famous axiom: 'If it ain't broke, don't fix it'.

The essence of this position is *wait for malfunction before taking action*. And that, my friends, is the philosophy of apathy.

Our circumstances are so that we do not have the freedom to sit back complacently and simply *expect* improvement just because general improvement over time is what we've experienced so far. In **Modern Living**, I address this point with the line:

> You're the picture of composure
> You're tossing a coin, getting heads twice, and then expecting it thrice.

To believe that things will continue improving indefinitely, just because they always have, shows a strikingly *bold* attitude to risk. I wonder if the dinosaurs had that carefree attitude 700 million years ago just before their dominion on the planet came to a sudden end? Just because, broadly, things have got better for humanity does not mean our asteroid (in physical or metaphorical form) isn't going to hit in the near future.

But semantics and attitudes to risk aside, let's now look at why our time really *is* drastically different from *any* other time in human history.

The Perils Of Modernity

There have lived around 10,000 generations of *Homo sapiens*, each one taking a pigeon step forward in the grand advance of humanity. From fire to art, from clothing to architecture – great innovations became communicable through speech and writing, enabling a general trend of intellectual and technological progress to be passed down and built upon over generations. But these innovations pale into insignificance when compared to the advancements of the last 200 years. We have seen an incredible acceleration of technological progress that has paved the way for immense improvement to human welfare. But – and this is a big 'but' – these innovations have also placed us at a frighteningly unique point in history.

The top boy on existential threats is the philosopher Toby Ord from the Future of Humanity Institute at Oxford University:

> We live during the most important era of human history. In the 20th century, we developed the means to destroy ourselves – without developing the moral framework to ensure we won't.[17]

Here in the 21st century we are now an anomaly in the human story. We have endowed ourselves with godlike powers, powers that include the capacity for our own complete, and utter, extermination.

In 2008 the Global Catastrophic Survey put the estimated probability of human extinction before 2100 at 19%.[18] But if you split up the risks into the categories of non-anthropogenic and anthropogenic you can see how our ingenuity is dramatically increasing our risk of extinction. Toby Ord puts the chance of extinction from *natural* events this century at 1 in 10,000. *But,* he puts the anthropogenic risk at 1 in 6! That is a colossal difference in degree of threat.

Other estimates are even more alarming. During the summer of 2020, two theoretical physicists who specialise in complex systems science, looked at catastrophic risk with a focus on deforestation. The results of their broad study showed that *if* we do not change course, we have a 10% probability, (in the most optimistic of their models) to survive the coming decades without a catastrophic civilisational collapse.[19] There have been clear warnings about these growing risks since the 1980s. The legendary astronomer and science populariser Carl Sagan provided an estimate of a whopping 60% chance of extinction over the next hundred years.[20]

It is perhaps becoming clear now that I am not singing about the apocalypse because it's 'cool' or because its 'an aesthetic'. Overly dramatic, theatrical or fictional lyrics are a tradition in the alternative world from the birth of metal onwards, and I'm all for theatrics don't get me wrong, but what I'm singing about is very real. This information needs to be spread far and wide if we are to survive this *pivotal* point in our development as a species.

And it *is* a pivotal point: how we act in the coming decades and centuries will basically decide whether our species has a long and prosperous future, possibly even outliving the Earth (which has about another billion years to go in its lifespan) or whether we fail forever.

Human Possibility: The Far Future

Mammalian species typically survive for around 1 million years. Our ancestor, Homo erectus survived for almost 2 million years.

If Homo sapiens were to survive for a similar amount of time, then our species has, so far, only lived 15% of its lifespan. It is safe to say we are in our adolescence. But as I mentioned, the Earth will remain habitable for roughly a billion years. At that point the sun's rising luminosity – as it ages into a *red giant* – will fry our planet's surface, boiling the oceans and eventually destroying all life on Earth. There's no real irrefutable reason to think that Homo sapiens (or, more likely, the descendants of Homo sapiens) could not survive until this point, and even past this point, *outliving* the Earth, going on to terraform Mars and colonise the Milky Way. In fact, it's not utterly mad to think that we could even alter the Earth's orbit, moving it away from the sun's increasing influence and therefore saving all life on the planet. (Sci-fi has already envisioned this, it is the context for Liu Cixin's novel *The Wandering Earth*.)

A billion years is enough time for a trillion human lives.

If this book represented the potential for this increased lifespan of humanity, in 2021, we have just read the 'A' of the title of this book, on page 1. We have read 0.03%.[21] If we were to destroy ourselves now, the rest of this book would be blank pages, the potentially vast human story would be left unwritten. What a tragic waste of discovery, companionship, creativity, artistry, beauty and life.

We may well be right at the start of the human story. If we were to destroy ourselves now, it would be a case of cot death.

This is a moment that *every* intelligent and technologically proficient life form in the universe will reach (or has reached). It is the point where a species invents the means for its own destruction, be that through industry or weaponry. At this particular stage, the question becomes: will it overcome its intra-species division, power struggles, and hostility, and learn to employ its technologies peacefully and wisely? Or … will it destroy itself?

This is what I refer to as **The Great Unknown**. (Toby Ord calls it 'The Precipice' in his book of the same name.)

Carl Sagan was one of the first to speculate about this pivotal point that all technical civilisations will reach:

> The temptation is to deduce that there are at most only a few advanced
> extra-terrestrial civilizations – either because we are one of the first
> technical civilizations to have emerged, or because it is the fate of all such
> civilizations to destroy themselves before they are much further along.[22]

If this outlook is true, it of course means that we shall *never* come into contact
with extra-terrestrials, and well, that's just unbearably sad, isn't it? But, if it *is*
possible for a species to evolve a relative wisdom alongside its technology, then this
elite species *would* survive this pivotal point.

If it *is* possible to achieve this 'maturity', the question then becomes, where are
these elite extra-terrestrial life forms? Why haven't they already made contact
with us struggling humans? Sagan offered a possible answer in a wonderful quip:
'Perhaps there is a waiting time before contact is considered appropriate, so as to
give us a fair opportunity to destroy ourselves first.'

You can just imagine these life forms, sitting back with their feet up, sipping tea
and watching the latest episode of the thrilling reality TV show *Humanity*. And
with all our newly discovered power, it feels like we're fast approaching the season
finale.

Are we currently in a death defying juggling act? And is our cosmic audience – a
universe potentially teeming with extra-terrestrial life – watching, on the edge of
their seats?

(Should they even have buttocks, that is.)

Self-described 'rational optimists' like Steven Pinker and Matt Ridley have
been consistently cheerful about humanity's prospects, always emphasising
our progresses. Their eloquently delivered historical narrative is one I've found
fascinating and encouraging.[23] But with all this groundwork covered, I believe
that their usual optimism is *now* quite misplaced.

Perhaps they, like many of us, are so cautious of falling for the *negativity* and
availability biases we're so weighted towards, that they begin to fall for the
normalcy bias I discussed in this book's introduction – they're rejecting negative
or disastrous possibilities simply because we don't previously have an example
of them, and instead they keep an overconfident faith in the continuation of our

trend of progress ('That *won't* happen to us/that *can't* happen to us'). But simply, the existence of a trend does not assure its continuation, *especially* when we keep *adding* to our capability for existential destruction, changing the parameters of the great human experiment. Trends do not continue if the input or influences change.

A wholly optimistic argument begins to appear tone-deaf to our new and growing technological capacity for self-destruction. But more importantly, it also appears tone-deaf to the broader *systems* of influence:

• The current breakdown in civil public conversation; the acceleration in this breakdown by social media; the increasing political polarisation; the distrust and anger at government, experts, media, institutions, and democracy itself. These all provide a *social atmosphere* for disaster. (I address these in **The Dreamer's Hotel**, Chapter 4.)

• The terrifying problems of climate change, resource depletion, species extinction, antibiotic resistance, rising inequality, social destabilisation, and environmental migration.[24] These provide an *environment* for disaster. (I address these in **Crossing The Rubicon** and **Elegy For Extinction**, Chapters 3 and 5.)

• The threat of nuclear war,[25] and forthcoming leaps in artificial intelligence,[26] nanotechnology, and biotechnology. These all provide an *arsenal* for disaster. (I think these risks are probably rather self-evident and self-explanatory!)

• And all this is taking place within a global economic system that is completely oblivious and detached – it simply continues demanding growth, as if we live on a planet of infinite resource and in an unchanging vacuum where there is one answer to any problem, the free market, and the freedom to consume. This provides a *framework* for disaster. (I address this in **T.I.N.A.**, Chapter 6.)

In the song **Modern Living** I ask:

> How can you never be nervous?
> How can you never consider the risk,
> Consider a hideous end?

We *must* consider the risks that humanity faces. We cannot ignore that, which through human industry and technology, is now possible. This isn't just the elephant in the room, there's a whole menagerie of mayhem going ignored by the majority of us populating this room, and especially by those in power.

But regardless of our willingness or unwillingness to consider our risks, we as yet don't even appear fully equipped, morally or rationally speaking, for this pivotal era in our development. As Toby Ord posits:

> The issue is not so much a surplus of technology as a deficiency of wisdom ... What we need is wisdom to catch up.[27]

Our morality, our rationality, our patience and tolerance of each other, our ability to discern cause from effect, and to understand problems thick with nuance – is it possible for our wisdom to catch up? Is it possible for us to accept the predicament we're in and address our many existential risks with clarity and wisdom? Let's pivot back to Carl Sagan:

> The existence of a single message from space will show that it is possible to live through technological adolescence: the civilization transmitting the message, after all, has survived.[28]

Just *imagine* if we were to receive that confirmation. A message from another life form, giving us faith that a technological species *can* indeed evolve with humility and compassion instead of being on the receiving end of its own capacity for destruction. This is the yearning I sing of in the chorus of **The Great Unknown**:

> If there's anyone out there, just give me a sign!

Often through art, entertainment and religion we find ourselves looking to the heavens in desperation. We look to nature, to gods, to wiser life forms for guidance and liberation, for a saviour and a sign:

> I stare at the skyline, I reach for a lifeline

But for now, at least, it appears that we are on our own. At present there has been no reifying message sent by another life form, so we simply don't know whether any other species has successfully passed this pivotal juncture. To have evidence of this, would certainly give us more belief that we can achieve it ourselves, but for now, the question as to whether *we* will safely navigate this precipice is still an unknown. *The Great Unknown.*

Our Response: Fear And Frustration

The Spark was an album about *personal* anxiety; *Nothing Is True ...* is an album about *existential* anxiety.[29] But of course, the fact that our precarious situation is not being addressed with any real concerted effort *also* fills me with personal anxiety too! The two major emotions I feel are fear and frustration.

The *fear* derives from the knowledge of what is possible when our species is at its most self-serving, ignorant and merciless.

Optimism all but disappears when we realise that our current socioeconomic system is structurally committed to *amplifying* these traits. Capitalism is based on competition and self-interest, it fans the flames of the worst aspects of our human nature, helping increase the crippling inequality and parochial tribalism we see today. It's based on values of exploitation and marginalisation and these values then overpower our capacity for compassion and cooperation (which, as we shall see later, are the two pivotal traits involved in humanity's survival and success).

It is hard to see how humanity will surpass *The Great Unknown* while operating within this current socioeconomic structure, it puts us at a huge disadvantage.

The *frustration* derives from the knowledge of what is possible when our species is at its most ingenuous, creative, and compassionate!

We are capable of great leaps of progress, of rational and sustainable reformation and redesign. So far, I've spent a good while addressing the destructive aspects of our technological innovations, but you only have to spend five minutes researching our ever-increasing medical capability, or the fast rising efficiency and practicality of our renewable energy technologies, to understand that we are absolutely capable of innovating our way out of this mess. We *should* have positive expectations about our capability for progress. But so much of our capability is being held back by a systemic condition that hampers our cooperative and creative ability. Nye Bevan, (the founder of the National Health Service here in Britain, and a key inspiration for our song **Anaesthetist**) once said:

> Discontent arises from a knowledge of the possible, as contrasted with the actual.[30]

For example, we *can* transition quickly from fossil fuels to *100%* clean, renewable energy, *now*. The science is clear.[31] And the financial incentive is starting to become clear. But our socioeconomic system is rigid and cumbersome, and many people in positions of power have vested interests in our archaic infrastructure. There is no inbuilt incentive to change how we source our energy. The incentive is for short-term profit instead of long-term sustainability. Therefore, things stay, largely, as they are.

This type of situation is referred to as a *Tragedy Of The Commons*. Each individual, company, or even nation, is acting in its own self-interest, concentrating on its own short-term profit, and therefore neglects and degrades the collective outcome. The effects or 'costs' of pollution and climate change aren't borne solely by the groups who cause them, so each group continues engaging in their profitable activities to the detriment of all. If they were to change, they would lose their market share, their wealth, their power.

Lack of ability for change is *immensely* frustrating. Especially when surviving (and adapting to) climate change demands quick action.

Frustration at what we are capable of, but held back from, is an emotion that runs through the album (and most of Shikari's material to date), we see it first introduced at the start of the first verse of **The Great Unknown**:

> I've been waiting for the great leap forwards
> I'm so impatient, yeh, I want to cut corners

We'll look at the restraints on progress that our socioeconomic system produces throughout the book, and impatience will be looked at properly in Chapter 6.

I sing of the 'beauty of the twilight glow' in the second verse. This is a view of the capitalist system as its relevance begins to fade. Its inability to acknowledge environmental changes and adapt to the new environment in which it operates, an environment of pandemics, climate change, and resource depletion (and all manner of other crises), shows clearly that it has become incompetent at coping with reality today. It simply must be in its twilight stages as an economic structure.

I compare our desperate position and our resulting frustration with psychiatric illness, which I manifest by introducing one of my favourite painters, the famously afflicted, Vincent van Gogh. He suffered from a tragic case of manic depression.[32] His art, or more specifically, his process of creation, most probably brought him relief from the undoubtedly unbearable pain he suffered. Here, his illness represents our socioeconomic system (and the pain *it* causes), and his process of creativity, the antidote – imagining and engineering new systems and new worlds. For van Gogh, this feeling of frustration at how his affliction held him back is well documented. In one letter he wrote:

> 'If I could have worked without this accursed disease, what things
> I might have done'[33]

We'll look further at how creativity and imagination is restrained by our current state of affairs also in Chapter 6.

With 'a red sky at night' I envisage van Gogh's famous painting, *Starry Night* (1889), with his calming blues changed to red to reflect the dangerous nature of our situation.

I then introduce the 'Shepherd' who roams the hills in the painting. I specifically chose a shepherd, not just because it's a quaint aesthetic, (and they feature too in the famous weather folklore maxim 'a red sky at night') but because even those who tend and lead us are at their wits' end too, completely clueless with how to address the mess we're in. Most prominent politicians, leaders and even activists have no idea how to address the systemic nature of the problems we face. Many of those we look to for answers still place their energy in short-term, 'band-aid'-style responses to our problems. If the general population are indeed sheep, our shepherds are leading us in no helpful direction at all. (You know that classic meme of the guy slapping some duct tape over the hole in a water tank that the water is gushing out of? Yeh, that. We so often only address the effect, and overlook the cause.)

'His beam sweeps like brushstrokes across the sky' is the shepherd (or simply, our leaders') searching for answers. And I use the word 'brushstrokes' not only to build on the imagery of the aforementioned Vincent van Gogh, but also to remind us that it is our creativity and our imagination that must be at the forefront of our focus when it comes to achieving progress. We'll hear a lot more about that in Chapter 6 too, but for now it is clear that we must *paint* a new canvas for the future. We cannot rely on minute incremental changes. We must target the core of our problems – our debilitating system – and we must dream up a new one.

2.2 *Modern Living*

Our Response: A Whole Host Of Other Emotions

The Great Unknown, as a concept, can fuel a lot of existential angst. And in general, people worldwide seem to be getting sadder, angrier and more fearful than ever. All three emotions rose to record levels in 2018, for the second consecutive year, according to a major analysis of global wellbeing.[1] But our emotional reaction to the stress of modern life can also be more nuanced and wide-ranging too. This is what the song **Modern Living** is about – a playful look at the varying ways we respond to the threats we face.

We don't always react with simple fear and anxiety; sometimes (and perhaps more interestingly) we react with fanaticism, avoidance and normalisation, wilful ignorance and distraction, fatigue and denial, fatalism and hedonism. A whole host of peculiar and particular behaviours. In effect, we either fanaticise, or we push our problems away using various techniques, conscious and subconscious. As we look at these responses over the next few pages, ask yourself whether *you've* experienced any of them. I'm quite sure I've experienced every single one at some point over the last few years!

1. Fanaticism

Firstly, when considering frightening future possibilities, it's easy to let despair get the better of you and start predicting the apocalypse every other week – and only half-jokingly! Even just the last few years have contained enough shocks and disconcerting developments for flippant exaggeration to become a common reaction, 'Christ, have you seen what Trump's done now?! Honestly we're so fucked ...'

Treating every negative event with similar disgust, outrage, or fear – however bad it is in actuality – has become a staple in public discourse. As already discussed with media sensationalism, this is probably because – if one isn't being strident, one simply isn't even heard over the mêlée of social commentary and debate. In this way, social media has become a domain where we amplify the extremes: we're simply more likely to engage – retweet, like, or comment – with a statement that is more intense (or at least a statement presented in a more intense way).

With hindsight, I'm sure I have blown some negative events out of proportion, even if that *is* something I've tried to be increasingly aware of doing. Anyone with a public platform and a desire to grow their reach is subconsciously ushered towards exaggeration because the more emotional or intense their comment or judgment is, the more engagement it'll get. It now appears to be a norm of modern communication and often goes unnoticed by the perpetrator as well as their audience. But more about that in Chapter 4.

For our purposes here, just as the word 'awesome' is used to describe something as irrelevant as a new pair of trainers – when it should instead be reserved for something breathtaking or staggeringly extraordinary or beautiful – we inappropriately describe things as 'outrageous' or 'disgraceful' all the time too, catastrophising minor setbacks, which ultimately belittles the genuinely shocking events.

When writing *Nothing Is True ...* I thought it would be good to take a facetious look at our excessive exaggeration and doomsaying, so I wrote a song about a support group for people addicted to thinking about, or predicting, the end of the world – a support group I called 'Apocoholics Anonymous'. A portmanteau of alcoholics and apocalypse felt like a suitably ridiculous response to the ridiculous state of the world.

Apocoholism involves overreacting to negative events, or reacting to every negative event – regardless of severity – with similar intensity. It's probably the best way to quickly heighten one's general anxiety. And I should be clear; I'm taking the piss out of myself just as much as anyone else, here. (It's a very human trait to use humour, and specifically self-deprecating humour, when things seem rather dire or hopeless isn't it? It's like our last line of defence. Or at least a tool that keeps us from going stark raving mad completely.)

> I'd like to welcome all my people here
> But listen, everything you love is about to disappear

I liked the idea of starting the track with a general greeting, but having it immediately followed – with no preamble or small talk – by a direct warning about the apocalypse. From zero to one hundred in seconds! We've joined an apocaholics' support group after all, what use is there for small talk – how Karen's son has chickenpox or how Darren's new car has heated seats – when America has now started building new nuclear missiles as big as bowling lanes!!![2]

This state of constant anguish is easy to slip into but is ultimately no fun for anyone. This is the first of the more subtle and interesting responses to modern living: *fanaticism.*

Our response to adverse events appears to be that we either become captivated – as with fanaticism – or we become reticent and unresponsive as we recoil away from reaction. We can think of the rest of the reactions we'll look at here as psychological protections, or coping mechanisms. These are the differing ways we manage our existential anxiety and control our exasperation over the dismal state we're in. These are the ways we safeguard our sanity.

2. Normalisation

> I feel it coming there's something in the air
> But this is living, oh it's modern living, yeh

To describe something as 'just part of modern living' is in itself a sigh of acquiescence. A kind of tired nonchalance towards the difficulties we face. A defeated acceptance of the situation as 'just the way it is'. We could call this second response *acceptance by normalisation*. I think we all feel this powerlessness at some point. It can feel excruciating when we can't change the wider circumstances in which we live, so we submit, and we say, 'this is just the way of the world'. In effect, this is the broader philosophy behind the word 'meh'.

3. Distraction

A third reaction is the coping mechanism of *distraction*. This can happen subconsciously or consciously. Subconsciously, we may neglect to face our problems and instead favour daily chores or things more immediately pressing. The American psychiatrist Harry S. Sullivan called this 'selective inattention', a 'security operation' that we put in place to stop us achieving a valid interpretation of reality *when* that reality is perceived to be too painful.[3] Generally, selective inattention helps keep you content, it stops the weight of the world from pressing down too hard on you. It protects your wellbeing through denial and diversion.

More than any other period in history, modern living demands blocking things out, looking the other way from inconvenient truths and horrifying future possibilities. Whether it's the homeless person on the street or corruption in politics, we put our blinkers on and stay focused on our own lives. We also achieve distraction consciously; we *choose* to use technologies and trivialities to avoid stressful realities, the classic 'running away from' a problem. We intentionally 'filter' out any aspects of life we simply deem too intense to deal with.

On every face a filter
Masking weakness, masking woe

We do this through social media, games and virtual reality. On social media, we filter out the weak or woeful aspects of our own lives, broadcasting only the best parts. We cheerfully present ourselves as normal, busy, content, or successful,[4] and we (literally) filter our faces with our camera phones, 'improving' our complexions or face shape – or perhaps turning ourselves into a cute cat or pig.

However conscious we are of the ability of technology to shield us from pain and stress, its mechanisms play a huge part in our lives. So huge, in fact, that we all now probably recognise the pressure to veneer, mask, or 'perfect' the photos we post of ourselves online. The dangerous personal impact this new obsession is having is only recently being recognised. Other than the obvious self-esteem issue of not feeling good or attractive enough in our own natural state, it causes what has been termed *snapchat dysmorphia* or *selfie dysmorphia*,[5] where people feel pressured to look like their heavily edited pictures in real life. The pressure can be so extreme that teenagers are undergoing plastic surgery to look like they do in their filtered selfies. Medical reports have suggested that filtered images are 'blurring the line of reality and fantasy' and could be triggering *body dysmorphic disorder* (BDD), a mental health condition where people become fixated on imagined defects in their appearance.[6]

Perhaps this particular distraction technique does divert our attention away from the wider woes of the world, but it only adds to our personal woes and low self-esteem.

The poetry enthusiasts among you may have noticed that the 'on every face a filter' line pays homage to the English Romantic poet William Blake, riffing on the opening stanza of his poem 'London':

I wander thro' each charter'd street,
Near where the charter'd Thames does flow.
And mark in every face I meet
Marks of weakness, marks of woe.[7]

I found it worth commenting upon that, in Blake's time, one could see the pained expressions, one could observe suffering, whereas now we tend to gloss over our lives with these filters. Instead of a visible mark in every face there is the veneer of perfection, or a protective layer of distraction built from playful technology, as we block out the aspects of society (or ourselves) we find too difficult to contemplate.

4. Fatigue

Constant exposure to negative events can produce a fourth reaction: *fatigue*. Apocalypse fatigue is a real thing, the adrenaline and anxiety that keep you up at night after a harrowing 4-hour YouTube marathon on nuclear war and the excruciatingly close calls we've had, will certainly leave you agitated and exhausted.[8]

Fatigue arrives easily when we overexpose ourselves to catastrophic possibilities, and the sensationalism that is abundant in our news media makes this much easier. We all use the term 'clickbait' to refer to articles that, in order to secure clicks in a competitive media marketplace, use headlines that are increasingly reductive, attention-grabbing and overdramatised.[9] One negative effect of this is that people eventually become fed up of being pummelled with exaggerated negative information. The psychologist and economist Per Espen Stokes puts it like this:

> More than 80% of all news and mainstream media play up the issue of doomsday or catastrophe. From psychological research, we know that if you overdo the threat of catastrophe, you make people feel fear or guilt or a combination. But these two emotions are passive. They make people disconnect and avoid the topic rather than engage with it.[10]

Overexposure causes fatigue, and that causes disconnect and avoidance. You may have noticed that, excluding fanaticism, all these reactions actually produce inaction, they cause us to retreat from the problem.

Even fanaticism (however well-meaning its exaggerations) can put others off, especially if talk of catastrophe is repeated enough, without any sign of said catastrophe in reality. It begins to lose its sting and we start to equate the threat-obsessed 'fanatics' with the boy who cried wolf: 'They've been warning of this for decades now, I'll believe it when I see it.' Effectively, we grow tired of being warned and begin to deny the reports, even if they are still largely realistic. In this way, fanaticism can actually breed fatigue and denial. Clearly, the opposite effect from that which the fanatic wishes to inspire.

One example is with the dismissal of climate change. The unrelenting barrage of negative stories; the doomsday predictions of flooding coastlines, forest fires and species extinctions all start to make people glaze over, and the years of reporting it as 'coming', while much of the industrialised world doesn't witness many of its tangible effects, causes people to question its validity.

'Apocalypse fatigue' was one of the proposed causes for the general decline in 'belief' (and concern) in climate change in the US during the late noughties. After the release of Al Gore's famous climate change documentary *An Inconvenient Truth* in 2006, the topic began to receive more attention in the media. We began to see the catastrophic imagery that we're now so used to, everywhere. Unfortunately, rather than galvanising mass public demand for serious action, apocalyptic visions of climate catastrophe led many Americans to instead question the science; in 2009, just a few years later, belief that climate change was actually occurring had fallen to just 56%.[11]

5. Fatalism And Hedonism

The fifth, and final, reaction I will discuss is *fatalism* and *hedonism*. This is an extension to the 'that's just the way it is' normalisation strategy. It's when we decide that we just don't care anymore, 'life is meaningless' and 'come what may'. Or to quote the Bible (Corinthians 15:32) 'let us eat and drink, for tomorrow we die'!

This hedonistic attitude to existential threats was the attitude that most inspired the line:

> We're Apocaholics, drinking gin and tonics
> Lying in the flowers, counting down the hours

I wrote it while quite literally exemplifying it. Bombay Sapphire in one hand, while the other was gliding through scarlet pimpernels and forget-me-nots as I sat drinking in my local park. If my memory serves me correctly, it was just after Trump tweeted boasting about *his* 'nuclear button' being 'much bigger and more powerful' than leader of North Korea Kim Jong-un's.[12]

I think some level of escapism is completely warranted in today's world. Balancing your awareness of future possibilities with your own psychosocial wellbeing is *so* important. If that means having a drink in a field every now and then to get away from it all, yes that may be a privilege, but it is a privilege well worth using, especially if it refuels you for future activism or altruism.

Absolute inaction, though, is something we have to try and avoid altogether, of course. Nature (*and* gin!) won't be available to us if we don't fight for it.

So whether it's inaction brought on by fanaticism, normalisation, distraction, fatigue, or denial, it is inaction itself that is our enemy. Inaction just ensures business as usual, and currently, that would ensure disaster. So how do we avoid withdrawing from the world? How do we avoid feeling defeated? How do we avoid inaction?

The Importance Of Hope

One important answer lies in hope. Hope is a concept somewhat ruined by overuse in Hollywood or politics but it is still a pivotal mindset to discipline oneself towards if one wants to avoid inaction. I mean, in order to *act*, you *have* to have hope. You cannot rationally act if you do not possess the belief that your action will have *some* possible worthwhile effect (even if small, indirect, or delayed).

At this point you may be wondering about the difference between optimism and hope, me having denounced the previous (i.e. the optimism of Lord Macaulay and Steven Pinker), and endorsed the latter.

Hope is an active *desire* for progress. It is contagious. It is motivating. It is the fuel for change.

Optimism, however, contains a degree of *expectation* that things will improve. Voltaire went one further and defined the word 'optimist' as someone who thought the world was, in fact, already perfect, for him, optimism was 'a mania for insisting that all is well when things are going badly.'[13] There is no desire, nor logic within optimism; it is, instead, an anticipation of betterment, or worse, a blind faith that betterment is on the way.

In his book *Hope Without Optimism* the literary theorist Terry Eagleton writes:

> To believe that a situation will turn out well because you are an optimist is as irrational as believing that all will be well because you are an Albanian.[14]

In this way there's something almost maternal about being optimistic, it's a tender assurance that things will get better, even if all around you is clearly crumbling. It is a false comfort. It gives us hasty confidence, and that can be a free pass to passivity. It is the state of mind of a football fan who claims he's *optimistic* about his team winning the league this season, while simply sitting on his couch, cracking open a beer and watching the game with his feet up. If you are optimistic you *anticipate* change rather than actively *seek* it.

Rational optimism specifically, is a faith in progress that, in today's world, borders on an unfaltering dogma. '*Things have gradually got better so they will likely continue to do so*' is a mindset that, as Terry Eagleton writes, has you 'chained to cheerfulness', and therefore lacking the 'strenuous commitment [...] underpinned by reason' that is essential to hope.[15]

Rational optimism turns into *irrational* optimism if it ignores the systemic pressures and trends that are now endangering humanity.

The only way things will continue to 'get better' is if we harness our abilities for analysis, communication, compassion and cooperation. But we should not expect these capacities to blossom and guide humanity when we live within a market-based economic system; a system that, above all, incentivises the maximisation of profits, to the detriment of anything else, and demands a blind allegiance to infinite growth (a concept we'll look at properly in Chapter 6). Neither of these core tenets will deliver a safe and sustainable future. They will impede it, in fact. Indeed, by definition, self-interest actually obstructs compassion and cooperation, the very things that hope and progress are *built* on.

We need vast systemic change to secure the continuation and progress of our species, we therefore *cannot* allow the complacency that rational optimism can spawn. We cannot accept any dogma that tolerates or legitimises inaction. Oddly, it is in this way that the effect of optimism can actually be similar to that of pessimism! The optimistic belief that humanity is probably going to be fine, or that someone (else) will come along and save us, can trigger inaction just as much as believing, pessimistically, that *no one* is going to come along and save us.

In his review of Terry Eagleton's book, the philosopher Slavoj Žižek said: 'In our predicament every direct optimism is by definition a fake – the only bearers of true hope are those who dare to confront the abyss we are approaching.'[16]

Confronting the abyss, looking at our predicament head on, and carefully considering our options, is vital for progress. With hope, we stoke the warm fires of compassion, cooperation, and creativity *ourselves,* and we can then redesign the systems that diminish those constructive human drives, or at least distract us from them. Hope doesn't say that change is inevitable, or even probable, it simply says it is *possible*.

It is with determined, proactive hope that we must face the abyss.

The Importance Of Beauty

Throughout our existence as a band, my lyrics have been centred around our *'common dreads'* (the title of our second album): the threats that we all face. This is a difficult subject to address however you look at it, but especially when, as we've seen, presenting frightening possibilities often leaves us fatigued and distressed. This is frustrating when you create music essentially to inspire, motivate and rouse.

As I was finishing writing this book, a study was published in the *Annals of The American Association of Geographers*, entitled, 'Ruins of the Anthropocene: The Aesthetics of Arctic Climate Change'. This fascinating inquiry looked at what I call the *passivity problem* – how to inspire action rather than withdrawal when addressing the frightening state of the world:

> Depictions of Anthropocene ruins [...] induce feelings of awe, melancholy, and resignation. These reactions might now be more problematic, however, because helplessness and passive voyeurism could inhibit action on climate change.[17]

The author of the paper, Mia Bennett, describes how people exposed to distressing images of the effects of climate change, often do not feel compelled to act, they feel overwhelmed and choose to withdraw.

One of her suggestions to avoid this passive reaction is for us to instead focus on what we *still have* in the world – the prevailing natural beauty worth fighting *for*:

> Rediscovering and representing the beauty that remains on Earth rather than fixating on ecological, geological, and glaciological ruins might encourage an ethics of care and stewardship for what we still have.[18]

Imagine what a pleasant surprise it was, then, to find Enter Shikari in her examples of effective communication on climate change, alongside other pop artists who use *beauty* to stimulate conversation and action. For context on this, let me take you back to the summer of 2019.

The Warming Stripes

2019 was the northern hemisphere's hottest summer on record yet.

Enter Shikari spent it touring throughout the European continent with a backdrop that displayed a climate data visualisation by Ed Hawkins, a climate scientist at the University of Reading. The 'Warming Stripes' plot the average global temperature of each year between 1850 and 2019, with one colour-coded stripe representing each single year. The majority of stripes are blue, until, quite suddenly, they transition to red during the last 50 years or so.

The way this scientific data was displayed was different from any other presentation I had seen before. It looked like a piece of modern art, more akin to the work of Peter Saville than a climate scientist. I saw a real beauty in the visualisation, however tragic the data on display was, and this is why we decided to use it across our whole tour that summer.

Hawkins's climate stripes were a huge success and made the front covers of newspapers and magazines worldwide. In her article, Mia Bennett comments on our use of the stripes at Reading Festival (our last show of the tour) and a general rise in climate consciousness throughout popular music: 'gradually, popular culture is reckoning with climate change, expressing it in visual and acoustic ways accentuating the beautiful.'[19]

Whether focusing on presenting data in beautiful ways, or presenting the natural beauty still worth fighting for, beauty can be a great tool to grab people's attention and to motivate action.

Beauty and hope are two engaging and energising forces (and we'll revisit beauty as a tool when we get to **Elegy for Extinction**), but how exactly do we hold on to them when confronted with all our existential threats?

What do we do with our experience of incurring defeat after defeat, where both social justice movements and calls for serious action on climate change seem to continually fail? (I mean, how many international meetings on climate change have we had now that failed to initiate real change?) What do we do with our exasperation about this situation? How do we keep our proactive yearning for a better world alive?

The Importance Of Perspective

To hold on to hope we must use perspective. The philosopher Noam Chomsky offers some insight here:

> If you look back in history, those movements that succeeded seem like those who have failed or didn't succeed to achieve their goals [...] they left traces and legacies that are bringing us forwards.[20]

Each of us does our little bit to better the world, just as each movement does its little bit. One interesting example is the Occupy movement of 2011/12. I learnt a lot about economic justice and inequality from that movement, and it inspired further learning and activism on my own part (it inspired the song **Gandhi Mate, Gandhi** too). But now it has disappeared into history. Did it have any lasting effect in the world? Or should it be labelled a failure? Noam continues: 'you can say that this movement failed because it did not abolish financial institutions, but that was the very basis for the phenomenon of Bernie Sanders, who was pretty close to taking over one of the two US capitalist parties'.

Failures are often only deemed failures when looked at from a very narrow, short-term perspective. When we zoom out, they appear as stages of great learning, growth and inspiration. Pivotal moments of motivation for the successes to come.

As a side, if you are active in any fight for progress, always try to view your activism from these broader heights. Whether it's environmentalism, or social justice of any kind, try not to think in such a rigid goal-orientated way. It is in that way that fatigue and despair will set in. The stress of caring can be devastatingly draining. So remind yourself that any morsel of progress is a serious achievement when the odds are so stacked against you. You are a link in a multi-generational chain, playing your part, however small or futile it may seem right now.

In the last few centuries, we have seen a dramatic expansion of our collective morality thanks to progressive activism. From women's rights to racial equality, from environmental protection to animal welfare. All of these victories were motivated by the drive for improvement. By imagination, compassion and solidarity.

Progress seems excruciatingly slow at times, and at various points non-existent! But just look back to the 1800s to remind yourself just how far we've come. A broad perspective is imperative to hope, and therefore to further action.

Like playing a video game, the completion of a level or a mission often comes with multiple attempts. Your character dying over and over as you slowly increase your knowledge and ability as a player. To complete such supreme projects as an end to war, poverty and environmental destabilisation, will take a great deal of time. These are vast, difficult levels – really, whole video games in themselves.

We may be crestfallen, yes. We may be feeling powerless and insignificant, but it is imperative to remember that every defeat lays the groundwork for the next endeavour, the next fight for progress. And it is our duty to the future of humanity to continue building upon that groundwork. Just because a result looks difficult or unlikely, doesn't relieve us from the duty of fighting for it. Each pigeon step we take keeps the momentum going in the right direction.

The despairing reactions discussed in **Modern Living** – from avoidance to denial – can all be fought with proactive hope, with beauty, and with perspective. The next track, **Crossing The Rubicon**, is a piece of music built on proactive hope. It is a song about not being broken by failure. It's about not being deterred from taking bold steps for the causes you believe in. It's about perseverance in individual activism and mass civil disobedience even in the face of continuous defeat. It's about an enthused and energetic younger generation storming onto the stage, a bugle-waving climate cavalry, keen to play their part, and consequently emboldening the activists of older generations.

Before we move on though, please understand, I'm not talking about *ignoring* failure and defeat, and warming your heart with empty hopes (as a growing amount of culture and art does nowadays with its platitudinous hope for hope's sake). But, instead, I'm talking about seeing reality in its truest form, and taking whatever steps you can – however small or parochial they may seem – in the right direction. Our action shouldn't depend on knowing how things will play out in the end, or even whether we live to see the fruits of our labour. It is simply an honour to be part of the struggle, part of the transition, to a safer, more stable and sustainable world.

Hope acknowledges the reality of defeat, whilst not being itself destroyed by it. And there are no threats which we cannot surpass, given time and will.

I'll leave you with some more wisdom from Terry Eagleton:

> Catastrophe is not written into the march of history, any more than hope is. However desolate the future may prove, it might always have been different. [...] unless one combats the inevitable, one will never know how inevitable it was in the first place.[21]

3 The Anthropocene

Crossing The Rubicon & Elegy For Extinction

> View the Earth as an inert thing, and what we do is we put a price tag on
> it. We impose a value on it. What we do is we buy it, we sell it, we use it,
> we abuse it, we commoditise it. That's all governed by the law of property.
> However, there is another way of viewing the Earth, and that's about
> viewing the Earth as a living being. [...] it shifts dramatically how we look
> into the long term. Because once we see ourselves as trustees, as guardians,
> we start taking responsibility for future generations.
>
> Polly Higgins (from *Ecocide, The 5th Crime Against Peace*, 2012)

The Rubicon is a river, and the song **Crossing The Rubicon** is a statement of
hope. Proactive hope. It is the awareness of the powerful tide we wade against, but
also the resolute desire to reach the other side.

I wrote this song while on tour in Europe during the winter and spring of 2019.
During this time there was a massive youthful surge of climate change protests
that went under various banners, from Fridays For Future (FFF) to Youth Climate
Strike. Students began striking all over the globe to demand that political leaders
take action to prevent climate change, and for the fossil fuel industry to transition
to renewable energy. I was lucky enough to attend climate strikes in Germany,
the US and Canada, and was taken aback by the intelligence and eloquence of
the young speakers. It was a hugely inspiring experience. I truly wish I could have
bottled that collective energy and determination. I'd take a shot from it every
morning!

On 20 September 2019 we were in Austin, Texas. It was the first day of our
American tour. On that day, 4 million people across 150 countries gathered
worldwide for the global climate strike, likely the largest climate protest in world
history.[1] I went down to the mass gathering in Austin and witnessed the spirit and
focus of the next generation. They were so well armed with facts and so resolute in
their goals.

Grace Meinzer, a 17-year-old high school student, told us, 'I have nightmares about
the environmental repercussions our society will be facing in my generation and
generations to come.' Her clarity and determination was palpable: 'I will no longer
be apathetic as our society refuses to truly act on the climate crisis. I want justice
for those who have been impacted. I will empower myself and others to the science

and data.' I recorded many of the speeches that day on my phone, and hers would go on to become our live intro for the rest of that tour.[2]

After years of involvement in climate activism, and after suffering defeat after defeat, I was definitely beginning to feel fatigued and downhearted, but after that day I felt reinvigorated and energised. I immediately attempted to distil this sense of proactive hope into music. For me, this was as close as I could get to bottling the energy in the air that day.

/ / / / / / / / /

The phrase 'crossing the Rubicon' means to go past a point of no return. It derives from the risky decision Julius Caesar made at the beginning of 49 BCE.

For some time, Caesar's power had been growing at a rate that alarmed the Roman senate. Led by Caesar's biggest rival (and former ally) Pompey the Great, the senate agreed to order Caesar to relinquish his command. Not wanting to forfeit his power to his enemies in Rome, Caesar instead made the decision to bring his army across the Rubicon river. Now that doesn't sound like much of a drastic step, but this river was then a northern boundary of Italy, and by bringing his 13th legion across it, in the direction of Rome, Caesar was actually making a declaration of war. The phrase 'Crossing the Rubicon' has survived over the centuries to refer to any individual or group who commits to a risky or revolutionary, unalterable course of action.

Over the last few hundred years, our carbon-intensive, fossil-fuel-powered lifestyle, along with our short-term profit motive have set us on a very risky course indeed. So far, our global efforts to prevent catastrophic climate change have been, quite frankly, pitiful, even the UN Secretary-General, António Guterres, stated that our efforts have been 'utterly inadequate', continuing: 'The point of no return is no longer over the horizon, it is in sight and hurtling toward us.'[3]

Can we avoid crossing this point of no return? Progressive politics are often thought of as extreme or radical, yet it is surely this current path we are on that is the most extreme? It certainly threatens the most damage and destruction. Can we avoid crossing this Rubicon?

In the absence of major revolutionary action to reduce our emissions, global temperature is on track to rise by an average of 4-5°C, according to the latest estimates.[4] Yet most of us *still* dramatically underestimate what is happening and what is in store, and furthermore, we underestimate just how important *we* are. The human generations alive now *must* act, we are pivotal. To put it simply, we are amongst the last few generations who have an ability to prevent irreparable damage to our planet. We, who are alive *now* have solutions that are *exclusively* available to us. These solutions will disappear, this window for action will close. We *must* take these opportunities now, before amplifying feedback loops really kick in and set us on an unstoppable course of climate catastrophe. We have a massive responsibility. Our activism must be bold and unrelenting.

We must, in fact, cross our own Rubicon. We must use mass peaceful protest, civil disobedience, and direct action like never before. We must reform, redesign, and reimagine like never before. We must all become revolutionaries.

The Lag

So far, since the beginning of the Industrial Revolution in the late 18th century, we've seen global temperatures rise by about 1°C due to the greenhouse gases we have already emitted.[5] But even if those emissions were to come to a complete halt as you read this very sentence, right now, there may still be a further climb of 0.6°C in Earth's surface temperature over the next few decades.[6] This is due to the fact that carbon dioxide – the predominant heat-trapping gas – lingers in the atmosphere for hundreds of years, and Earth's surface temperature does not react instantaneously to the energy imbalance created by rising carbon dioxide levels (mainly due to the ocean's capacity to store heat). So, there may be a time lag between what we do and when we see the effect of what we do.

We may therefore already be looking at a 1.6°C rise *at least*, since the Industrial Revolution.

Now the die is cast my friend

Caesar is said to have uttered this phrase "now the die is cast" ('Alea iacta est' in Latin, if you want to imagine him saying it while brooding upon the riverbank)[7] as his army began to march across the Rubicon river. There was no backtracking, no retreating back across it, the dice had already been thrown.

Waiting until global warming becomes worse to control greenhouse gas emissions is barbarically foolish. If we wait until the impact of global warming has reached an intolerable level, we will not be able to reverse it, or even 'hold the line' at that point; further warming will be set in stone.[8]

This small window of opportunity is exclusively open to us due to *amplifying feedback loops*.[9] The window of opportunity will begin to disappear because, as the earth warms, various systems begin to kick in that *further* boost that warming. The best analogy for this concept – and one I'm very qualified to explain – lies with speaker feedback, that gnarly high-pitched whistle you hear come screeching from a speaker should a microphone's volume be set too high, or that microphone be held too close to a speaker.

When performing, if I move too close to the front-of-house speakers (the venue's main speakers, the ones you, the audience, hear), we will all get blasted with ear-piercing feedback. This happens because, with me approaching the speaker, the microphone begins to pick up the very sounds it just sent to the speaker. The audio output from the speaker is sent back *through* the microphone and out the speaker again. And voilà, we have an amplifying feedback loop, where the signal will reinforce itself, getting louder and louder and ultimately, deafening us all – until the sound engineer turns the microphone off, or I move the microphone away from the speaker, breaking the cycle.

The most obvious climate change-related amplifying feedback loop is the *ice-albedo feedback*. Ice does the helpful job of reflecting a fair amount of the light emanating from the sun straight back out into space. But as we all know, that ice is melting. And the melting is, in fact, accelerating at a record rate.[10] As it melts, it reveals the far less reflective darker surface of the land or ocean beneath it. Less light is therefore reflected back out into space and more energy is absorbed or otherwise available to warm the planet, amplifying the initial warming further. Disturbingly, this warming then begins to trigger other amplifying feedback loops that trigger more warming, and so on. Humanity has pointed its microphone at the speaker, and the shrill feedback is beginning to sound. Where's the bloody sound engineer?!

At the more extreme ends of analysis, some climate scientists have reason to believe that we have already rolled the dice on some of the most catastrophic effects of climate change. 'We've already baked in 20 meters of sea level rise,' says James White, a University of Colorado scientist who has studied ancient climates to gain insights about the future. And as he dryly puts it: 'The coast is toast.'[11]

We must act on the analysis and predictions of climate science *now*, if we are to stop catastrophic climate change. Every day of inaction is another step across the river, another step closer to catastrophe.

I might just pause here to ask you how you're fairing reading this? I would completely understand if at any point, you needed to put this book down and grab a tall glass of gin and sing the 'We're Apocoholics' chorus of **Modern Living** on repeat for a while. Feel free to do so, and don't worry, I'll be here waiting to bombard you with cause for more existential dread upon your return!

Spaceship Earth

What we don't seem to realise is just how deeply our species' behaviour is affecting our planet's natural cycles, our planet's very character. For the majority of human existence, we have been passengers aboard what the economist Barbara Ward called 'Spaceship Earth'.

I first came across this idea of 'Spaceship Earth' from George Orwell:

> The world is a raft sailing through space with, potentially, plenty of provisions for everybody; the idea that we must all cooperate and see to it that everyone does his fair share of the work and gets his fair share of the provisions seems so blatantly obvious that one would say that no one could possibly fail to accept it unless he had some corrupt motive for clinging to the present system.[12]

Our present economic system is oblivious to the limitations of our spaceship and its provisions. It simply encourages more growth. That is to say: more use of those provisions. We can imagine these 'provisions' to be our spaceship's fuel. We only have so much on board but our economic system encourages more and more speed, so we continue blasting through our fuel like your auntie goes through glasses of wine on a Sunday night Netflix binge.

As we burn through our fuel supplies, we are heating up our spaceship. The on-board climate is changing, and that is destroying biodiversity – the variety of life on-board.

We are no longer passengers on this spaceship, we have hijacked it. We are at the wheel. We are hurtling through space, drunk on our own technological power, fixated on growth and consumption.[13] Too indoctrinated by our economic orthodoxies and freedoms to care about the catastrophic damage we're committing.

Our planet no longer just operates according to the laws of nature.

It operates according to the laws of nature + human interference.

World leaders repeatedly meet to set targets to curb our emissions, prevent the further destruction of nature, and halt dangerous biodiversity loss, yet nation states repeatedly fail to meet these targets. A UN report from 2010, *Global Biodiversity Outlook 3*, stumbled upon the core of the problem: 'Actions to promote the conservation and sustainable use of biodiversity receive a tiny fraction of funding compared to activities aimed at promoting infrastructure and industrial developments'.[14]

The latest *Global Biodiversity Outlook* report, number 5, touches on the same conclusions: 'countries have failed, in large part, because they have struggled to address conservation while focusing on their economies'.[15]

This is a recurring conclusion that I will return to throughout this book – our economic rigidity, our allegiance to current infrastructure, and to current economic ideology is the nucleus of our problems today. As the author and filmmaker Peter Joseph notes: 'Yes, everyone feels the long-term incentive to stop destroying the habitat in one sense. They feel that, but the long-term incentive can't compete with the short-term gains required and the competitive nature of the market economy itself.'[16]

Until we target the system – the incentive for short-term profit and economic growth, even in the face of the destruction of our shared habitat – we will fail to meet our targets.

Until our society, at a foundational level, prioritises sustainability over profit, we will continue on our path towards peril.

Delayed Action

In 2018's Intergovernmental Panel on Climate Change (IPCC) report it stated that global emissions of carbon dioxide must peak by 2020 to keep the planet below 1.5°C of warming, an accepted 'safe limit'.[17]

2020 was considered the pivotal year. It was now or never.

Everyone was looking to United Nations Climate Change Conference, COP26: this was to be the big moment. But ... by now we all know very well what happened. That bastard COVID-19 happened. And the conference was postponed to November 2021.[18]

This is obviously a massive set-back, but I should point out that some people do think we can use this situation to our ecological advantage. Governments are set to spend trillions globally over the next few years to help rescue their economies once the pandemic is over. There's a view (however naive) that when the summit is eventually held, it could be an important forum for ensuring that money is spent on sustainable and renewable projects.

Fatih Birol, executive director of the International Energy Agency, said:

> The next 3 years will determine the course of the next 30 years and beyond. If we do not [take action] we will surely see a rebound in emissions. If emissions rebound, it is very difficult to see how they will be brought down in future. This is why we are urging governments to have sustainable recovery packages.[19]

We can only look to 2021 in hope. Determined, proactive hope.

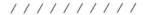

Have you got that gin in hand yet? OK, good. Because I'm thinking that, so far, I haven't been quite clear and vivid enough in my description of our current environmental predicament. Now, I should mention, while it's important to truly grasp the peril we face, don't let this submerge you into darkness and despair. And always keep a close eye on your mental health when looking at our existential threats. My advice would be, upon finishing this next chapter, do something wholesome and fun to rebalance yourself after devouring this hefty three course meal of shite (honey-glazed stool crudités, a coagulated excrement soufflé and a peppercorn shite-roast). After this, perhaps play with your pet, have a jog, watch an episode of *South Park*, bake a cake.

For a description of just how bad things could get, let us turn our focus to **Elegy For Extinction.**

It is a piece of 'programme music'. That is to say, it is a piece that attempts to tell a story through music only, with no lyrical or vocal component. It seems for this album I couldn't even bring myself to sing about climate change anymore, being too angry, hoarse and fatigued from repeatedly addressing the subject previously. On some subconscious level this may well be the reason, but I had also wanted to make a piece of classical programme music for years, and a piece that tells the story of life on our planet as well as the perils of human interference, felt like a suitable, albeit ambitious, topic to try.

This time, instead of letting sadness, frustration and anger once again fuel my climate change-themed song-writing, I opted to be inspired by the beauty still left in the world. The beauty still worth saving.

As we looked at in Chapter 2, focusing on the abundant beauty still here, rather than the beauty we are currently losing, may better trigger a sense of stewardship towards our planet.

I thought for a while about the most beautiful instrument I had at my disposal as a composer. Was it the pristine plucks of a harp? Was it the tender timbre of a lone oboe? Was it a guitar put through 15 reverb pedals? No, I wasn't thinking big enough.

If I was to be telling the story of life on Earth in all it's spellbinding variety, I needed a seriously versatile instrument. I needed ... a full symphonic orchestra. What epitomises and encapsulates beauty more than classical music?

Each instrument you hear in **Elegy For Extinction** represents a species, or perhaps an order of species. First, we have sprightly violins conveying the birth of life. They are gradually joined by little flutters and flurries from other instruments conveying the arrival of multitudes of weird and wonderful creatures. This is the story of the evolution of life on our planet.

As the piece progresses, we enter a section that I hope illustrates the *Cambrian explosion*. I opt for a march tempo and rhythm to depict the *march* of life, the blossoming and branching out of the evolutionary tree.

At 2:22 the opening chorale theme returns, it is bold and celebratory; this announces the birth of humanity. The arrival of a species that is able to contemplate this very story of evolution, and indeed, itself.

But then we all know what comes next.

Welcome to the Anthropocene. The current geological age. In which human activity has begun to dominate and change the planet. And this is happening to the detriment of the other species we share this planet with.

In 2019 I went to the Wildlife Photographer of the Year awards display in London. The photos were everything from exquisite and cute to brutal and harrowing: from groups of fluffy bees sleeping on a stem to macaroni penguins marching up an old volcano crater to their roosting terrace; from the vicious act of hippo infanticide to a polar bear trudging across a now-iceless landscape. It was a phenomenal exhibition showcasing the sheer wonder and diversity of nature. But beneath almost every single photo, no matter its content, was a caption that labelled each species 'endangered', or in some way suffering from human intervention. They were experiencing ecosystem decline due to deforestation and logging. They were experiencing habitat destruction as diverse forests were ripped down for palm oil plantations. They were being hunted for food, fur, or traditional 'medicines'. They were suffering the effects of their food chain disappearing due to climate change. Each compelling picture told the same story. It is now the only story to tell in the natural world, it dwarfs every other.

I had read the headlines from the World Wide Fund for Nature (WWF)'s living planet report from the previous year.[20] It had stunned me to learn that, since 1970, 60% of mammal, bird, fish and reptile populations have been wiped out.

It is this harrowing story of degradation that interrupts the, until then, rather nimble and charming classical piece. At this point, **Elegy For Extinction** begins to relay our future reality should all trends continue. The music becomes more and more discordant, frenzied and cacophonous. We hear the panicked species in the screaming dissonant violins. The menacing blasts on the brass and double basses resemble our terrifying vandalising power. The piece descends into a hellish musical landscape, the one we all see happening right before our eyes.

All melody and harmony begins to die away as instruments go from representing pain, to representing extinction – silence. And it must be said clearly; this widespread extinction directly effects humanity too, of course. We rely on nature and its abundant balancing ecosystems to sustain our very own existence.

Mike Barrett from WWF explains it clearly 'This is far more than just being about losing the wonders of nature, desperately sad though that is. This is actually now jeopardising the future of people. Nature is not a 'nice to have', it is our life-support system.'[21]

Crossing The Rubicon is a track that exudes confidence, it is chipper, positive and motivating, and concentrates on our capacity for progress. **Elegy For Extinction** obviously ends with a finale that is quite the opposite, it ends in colossal disaster. It serves as a warning: This could very well be the future we have in store. No, let me rephrase that: this *is* the future we have in store, if we do not force radical systemic change. There is so much beauty to save, replenish, and then sustain. It is not too late.

The Point Of No Return

Is this at all hyperbole? Am I falling for the sensationalism of the media? Am I exaggerating due to fanaticism, or out of a desperate attempt to be heard, as previously discussed?

No, I'm afraid the science is quite clear. There is now a growing threat of abrupt and irreversible changes to our climate, as we approach a 'global cascade' of tipping points.[22] That is to say, we are beginning to make such drastic changes to our planet's systems that we may not even be able to reverse them. This is *not* an example of our standard *negativity* or *availability bias*.

Tipping points are fascinating: if our individual climate systems exceed a specific level of change, even for a brief period of time, the original state of the system *can* be restored. But more persistent forcing can push the system to the 'point of no return', where, afterwards, even a substantial reduction of the forcing – bringing it back to below the tipping point – will be ineffective in halting the climate shift. Change becomes irreversible. So just as a 200-year-old tree in a forest can remain standing after 50 strikes from a sharp axe, and all the life it provides for in its branches, in its bark, in its leaves, can continue unfazed, when that 51st axe strike happens, it can suddenly bring the whole tree – with all its provisions for life – crashing down. This is a concept I like to call *Jenga-style climate change*. And it's not a game we should be playing.

Evidence that irreversible changes in Earth's climate systems are under way means we are in a state of planetary emergency. Climate scientists tell us that a cascade of tipping points in environmental systems could amount to a *global tipping point*, where we march past the point of no return. That possibility is 'an existential threat to civilisation,' writes Tim Lenton, Professor of Climate Change and Earth System Science at the UK's University of Exeter.[23]

Such a collapse of Earth's systems could lead to 'hothouse Earth' conditions[24] with sea levels rising 20 to 30 feet,[25] the complete loss of the world's coral reefs (as I touched on back in 2006, in our first song inspired by climate change, **Mothership**),[26] and with large parts of the planet becoming uninhabitable.

As Lenton makes clear, a global emergency response is required: 'It's a nasty shock that tipping points we thought might happen well into the future are already underway [...] The stability and resilience of our planet is in peril'.[27]

Faced with this information you may find yourself overwhelmed and wanting to go back to bed to simmer in a state of misery. You now understand the context for the first verse in **Crossing The Rubicon**:

Fill me out a prescription
For this existential dread
I woke up into a nightmare
And I'm hoping that you'll take me back to bed

Staying Positive ...

It is easy to slip into a dismally bleak view of life when we contemplate the position we are now in. The stakes are rising with every day of inaction and with every day of business as usual. As humans we have an immense capacity for invention and meaningful change, but this usually only gets exercised when it becomes absolutely necessary. We often try every other daft idea first, and extend the use of those daft ideas irrationally, but we usually get to the progressive answer eventually. This process is best described (though perhaps unwittingly, as we'll discuss) by the great writer Samuel Beckett. It is him who I'm referring to in the lyric:

> I think Beckett said it best –
> Try again, fail again, fail better

The full Beckett quote I'm alluding to:

> Ever tried. Ever failed. No matter. Try again. Fail again. Fail better.

This wonderfully succinct, tweetable portrayal of the ability of failure to eventually bring about progress, is the perfect lens with which to address our defeats and reignite hope.

I want to dig into this quote a little more though, as it brings up some important questions. Have you ever seen a rather saccharine or faux motivational quote against a serene backdrop, online? Surely you have. Theses memes and desktop backgrounds are how many Millennials and Generation Zs discover great titans of literature. It's how I first came across this Beckett quote, in fact. It was written in a slender, pleasing, italic font, placed over a beautiful photo of a rugged coastline, fit with frothy waves crashing up against the ragged rocks.

And this is where it gets interesting. By employing this quote from Beckett in a motivating context, the internet community (and the entrepreneurial community who also use it in this way) have actually misinterpreted it completely.

If you're familiar with Beckett's work, your intrigue, or even suspicion, may have already been pricked by the fact that this inspiring and positive quote was accredited to an author who is famous for dark, brooding, pessimistic, or intense pieces of work. (In one piece of life advice, Beckett declared 'Despair young and never look back.'[28])

My first experience of Beckett was through studying his play *Waiting For Godot* in secondary school. It's an incredibly odd piece of theatre, seemingly open to hordes of interpretations, and a far cry from the upbeat nature of the 'fail better' quote. How could this gloomy author have written such a contrasting phrase? Perhaps we should look at this quote in its original context:

> Ever tried. Ever failed. No matter. Try again. Fail again. Better again. Or better worse. Fail worse again. Still worse again. Till sick for good. Throw up for good. Go for good. Where neither for good. Good and all.

Not so easy to interpret, is it? Not so easy to see any inspirational intention... or any intention for that matter! It has a curiously terse and obscure meter and syntax. The quote comes from Beckett's penultimate piece of prose writing, his 1983 novella, *Worstward Ho*.[29]

The title is a parody of Charles Kingsley's *Westward Ho!*, an historic phrase associated with expansion, discovery and optimism. Beckett's contrasting title reminds us that we are not all journeying 'westward' to new lands and possibilities, but ultimately *worst*ward, towards the grave. A bleak view of the world overall, but perhaps a worthy warning against the inevitable folly of becoming complacent with the status quo.

The journalist Mark O'Connell describes the ironic twisting and meme-ification of the 'fail better' quote:

> The entrepreneurial fashion for failure with which this polished shard fits so snugly, is not really concerned, as Beckett was, with failure per se – with the necessary defeat of every human endeavor, of all efforts at communication, and of language itself – but with failure as an essential stage in the individual's progress toward lucrative self-fulfillment.[30]

Beckett had no intention of setting failure in a positive light, as the meme does, or of making failure out to be a useful tool that brings eventual progress. He was interested in failure itself. Exploring failure as this seemingly continuous, unending, and unavoidable reality. Failure forever. Failure ad nauseam.

For me, this immediately begs the question, is context always pivotal? Should we be allowed to cherry-pick authors' words and contort them to fit our need for positivity? Should an author's intent always be shackled to their words? If a quote inspires people, isn't that simply a good thing in and of itself? Where do you stand on this, dear reader?

And while you're contemplating that, perhaps also ask yourself, are we as a species doomed to failure? Is hope dead? Is Beckett's bleak and seemingly defeatist view more realistic?

It strikes me that this motivational meme, this quote that inspires so many, may well be a fabrication. It may well be a complete repackaging of a man's interest in the sombre and forlorn. *But* – it is also a universal truth. Defeats and failures *do* offer the insights that illuminate paths forward.

In the context of human progress, the fact you are alive now reading this, means there has not been an ultimate defeat. History is paved with great slabs of heavy defeat, yes. But each slab is something to stand upon, something to build upon, something to step forward from. We must not 'despair young and never look back' because despair is a self-fulfilling prophecy. Instead, we should frame defeat as a foundation for future progress. And as I addressed through the thoughts of Noam Chomsky at the end of Chapter 2, it is through the experience of previous movements, leaders, and pioneers, that our current movements learn and grow. With this train of thought I often find myself revisiting that famous quote by Isaac Newton:

If I have seen further it is by standing on the shoulders of giants.[31]

Isaac was praising those who had come before him. Those who had opened up whole new fields of scientific endeavour – new areas to examine, new ways to further the knowledge of humanity – which he then took even further. It was through the struggles and efforts of his predecessors that enabled his incredible insight. And just like with scientific progress, moral progress builds on the work – and often the *failures* – of those who came before. It is this idea of multigenerational progress. Standing on the shoulders of those who came before in order to see the next step, the next advance, the next discovery. Newton understood the causal nature of everything. And his intellectual humility, (like with all the greats, from Socrates onwards) enabled him to apply this understanding to his own achievements too.

Just as we misunderstand the self-made man – no one is self-made, that is always a dismissal of causality, of influence, of privilege, of opportunity, of luck – we also misunderstand scientific or moral progress. It comes slowly, through infinite chains of cause and effect, influence and effort. Any success and any development is a result of communal human endeavour.

4   Human Nature, Social Structure, Communication And Mass Media

The Dreamer's Hotel &
Waltzing Off The Face Of The Earth

War is what happens when language fails.

Margaret Atwood (from *The Robber Bride*, 1993)

When Language Fails

With regard to humanity's survival, the only thing that prevents complete failure is *conversation*.

That's it. That's all that stands in the way of complete societal breakdown; humans talking to each other.

Does that fill you with confidence, right now? It certainly doesn't do much for me.

Communication or violence. These are the options humans have at their disposal.

As *you* are reading this book, it's probably safe to assume that you *don't* regard violence as a moral or prudent means to achieve your ends. So, conversation is indeed all we have.

True communication is becoming increasingly difficult in a modern world rife with incivility, lack of trust, anger, outrage, polarisation, bad faith and dehumanisation. With these general conditions how can we expect to respectfully and successfully communicate with each other? Engaging in conversation in the public eye is now akin to walking a tightrope. Any slip can have us misunderstood and misconstrued, and then maligned and mauled by the tigers in the press pit below. The tension mounts even further when we try to converse with someone with a different worldview to our own. Civil political conversation in these instances now seems like a rare event, even a peculiarity! More often, we typically witness people disparagingly labelling and berating each other, with no pause for thought, and no serious attempt to understand each other.

Civility. Not exactly a cool word is it?

It sounds like a word that belongs in a period drama. A dull and antiquated form of good manners, but, honestly, it's more than that.

Civility is treating others as human beings. Taking them seriously. Not speaking over them. Not demeaning or insulting them. It's treating people with respect, and without prejudice.[1] In this day and age, civility can be thought of as a skill to master. A swimming stroke, becoming harder and harder to learn while adrift in a sea of anger and insults. The ability to hold oneself, and others, with dignity, matters intrinsically, because – no matter how much we may disagree with another person's views – we *share the same planet and we share the same problems.*

If conversation is all we have, then we must provide the best platforms possible to aid respectful and genuine communication.

Unfortunately, though, it seems civility is a skill we're losing. Log onto any of our mass communication platforms (be that Twitter, Facebook or whatever your hatred-spreader of choice is, currently), even for just 30 seconds, and you'll likely be flooded with all manner of heated arguments, and surrounded by frothing, spluttering fury addicts. Hell, in the past year, I've been called everything from 'classic privileged centrist twat' to 'typical leftie whinging snowflake' and I'm the type of person who generally goes out of their way to avoid conflict and has no time for party politics. It's always the same; jump to define the person, then insult them. For some, it's easier to simply presume a person's entire worldview based on one tweet (usually taken out of context) and to immediately insult them for it, than it is to engage in conversation or attempt to calmly debunk the belief they take issue with. (When someone resorts to 'playing the man, rather than the ball', criticising a person rather than the point at hand, it's known as an *ad hominem* argument. Despite its rather historic-sounding name – indeed, first definition of ad hominem can be traced back to Aristotle himself – it remains an extremely popular aspect of discourse on social media here in the 21st century.)

If individuals or political groups are only speaking *at* one another, rather than *to* one another, humanity is instantly in a more temperamental and incendiary position. *Possibility* itself becomes a scary vista of doom and distress because, when we aren't communicating calmly with one another, then – as politicians love to say – 'all options are on the table'. Everything is possible.

In the last few years, our tolerance towards others' errors or misconduct has been plummeting, and our patience towards our political opponents is basically zero. In this chapter, I'll look at the role the internet has played in this increase of incivility, as well as the role of political polarisation. I'll also look at life away from the internet, because – as the psychologist Michael McCullough corroborates –

'experiences of incivility online and in person have increased at about the same rates since January 2016'.[2]

The Social Atmosphere For Disaster

I wanted to write a song that conveyed the hostile 'social atmosphere for disaster' I spoke of in Chapter 2. With the bare, punctuated fury of the lyrics in **The Dreamer's Hotel** I attempt to embody this lack of consideration, patience and courtesy that we now encounter widely. The verses are devoid of all melody and harmony, instead narrated by someone possessed by an uncharitable and spiteful mindset; too outraged to bother pausing for 'context', and too staunch in his belief that 'nuance is a nuisance' to ever question his own views or attitude. The confrontational lyrics are propelled by a driving, uncompromising, almost mindless drum rhythm, which also aims to reflect the current lack of social harmony.

Let's begin by talking about outrage.

Social media has aroused our tribal nature like nothing before it. It has provided a quick and easy outlet for outrage, emboldening some of the worst aspects of our nature. Mass online communication has given us an accessible mechanism to express any outrage that takes our fancy and, consequently, platforms have become melting pots of righteous indignation, breeding grounds for modern day witch-hunts, where cancel culture is exhausting and trials by social media are a daily occurrence.

For *Homo sapiens*, shame has always been an important tool. Throughout human history, it has been employed to teach any narcissistic, immoral, or dangerous tribe member 'a lesson', or to broadcast a wider belief about which behaviours will not be tolerated within the tribe. It's been a way to promote rules and norms, *and* a method to uphold them. By reprimanding deviant behaviour that flaunts social laws or values, public outrage becomes the blunt tool used to uphold and solidify those laws and values.

An important human trait, that will pop up again and again throughout this book, is our innate fear of being thrown out of 'our tribe'. For early *Homo sapiens*, publicly expressing outrage about someone's behaviour – shaming that person – was extremely dangerous for them if it meant they may be shunned by the group. To be banished from the tribe in hunter–gatherer times would mean almost certain death, from starvation or predation. Going solo was not a viable option for survival when sabre-toothed tigers often roamed nearby...

Today, though, the obsession for 'calling people out' has become excessive. So much so, that we appear at war with *human flaws* themselves. It's like we've suddenly decided on a zero-tolerance attitude to bad decisions, chastising any and every wrongdoing with equal venom, as if we expect humans to *always* act thoughtfully.

> Outrage!
> That's it, I'm going on a rampage
> Don't waste my time with any context

Fevered mass outrage tends to ignore the circumstances around the mistake, wrongdoing or offence committed, with many people intent on garnering the maximum amount of public outrage, while possessing the least amount of understanding of the event in question.

Not content with just attacking the person in the here-and-now, the outraged will often scour over the accused's past ('I'm gonna pick all your pockets'), hoping to reveal any former bad views or behaviour, and eager to haul them back into the present, where the outraged can then demand repeated apologies for past crimes.

In its extremity, the uproar can reach such ferocity and garner such public attention, that it ruins the person's *future* too. In extreme cases, the accused finds themselves fired from employment, forced to move to a new area, or forced to *change their name* ('I'm gonna ruin all your prospects').[3]

With all the public attention that outrage receives, the outraged gain a heightened sense of importance, convincing themselves that in simply being offended, they have the higher moral ground. The outraged become encouraged by feelings of vindication, fuelled by the size and passion of their mob. Their increased confidence further encourages them into believing their judgement to be just and final – 'I am the judge and I'm the jury'.

Ironically, this particularly unrestrained brand of outrage culture rarely achieves its desired social function of suppressing future deviant behaviour. Shaming works, when it is moderate and proportionate, but when outrage is echoed online by multiple users ... dozens of users ... hordes of users ... the reaction can begin to appear over the top. To bemused onlookers, it can come across as bullying. This then inspires sympathy and support for the accused, who is now considered a victim, and then the function of the outrage fails to achieve its desired effect of behaviour regulation.[4]

As we will discover; outrage is often stoked unfairly. It can be performative, or tribally triggered, and therefore does little in terms of outcome than just further divide our society. Among all the constant clamour and hostility, the public square begins to feel burdensome and exhausting:

> I'll work you up into a frenzy
> But God this baggage is heavy

We now have a toxic environment caused by knee-jerk responses. There is outrage towards *any* perceived mistake or wrongdoing and there is hostile intolerance towards *any* views considered inappropriate. This continues the rise in incivility and political polarisation. It's becoming increasingly difficult to communicate within this social condition. And remember: if communication fails, violence is all that remains.

The current social atmosphere is just as concerning and dangerous as the more irrefutable threats posed by nuclear weapons or climate change.

This may all sound a bit hyperbolic, but, right now, our online communication structures and our wider socioeconomic system is helping facilitate miscommunication, misunderstanding, division and hostility. Communication *is* failing.

How? And why? That's what we'll look into over the coming pages.

Trump, The Source Of Incivility?

Many people think this degradation of our social fabric is a recent development, mainly due to our polarised political atmosphere and specifically the divisive effect of Trump's presidency. Trump's unmistakable narcissistic behaviour – behaviour that epitomises incivility – has made some believe that he was the source of all this, and that things would return to normal now his term has ended. This is, sadly, not the case (I will get to that, shortly), though it *is* easy to see how people come to this conclusion, considering his behaviour.

One point about Trump, which I don't believe is acknowledged enough, is that, psychologically speaking, he was the first president to not step into the role of president. What I mean by that, is that he rarely addressed his 'fellow Americans', he instead always spoke as though he was only addressing his supporters, while berating anyone else that got under his *very* thin skin. He was the first sitting president to effectively continue campaigning for his re-election while in office, once again putting his personal gain over the welfare of the population he presided over. His demeanour was that of dedication to *polarisation*, rather than dedication to the United States. The disgraceful end to his presidency – his incitement of the storming of the Capitol, as part of a violent, but ultimately foiled, coup – was all foreshadowed by years of prodding, goading and emboldening his supporters, as well as courting white supremacists and far-right thugs.

I'm afraid to say, though; while his behaviour divided the United States, and increased hostility at every moment during his presidency, there is actually a far longer historical trend at play here, one that began long before Trump started setting a heinous example for pettiness, bitterness and spite.

The Recent History Of Social Hostility

For decades there has been a measured decline in social engagement, social connectedness and social trust. We interact less and less with people outside of our close social circles, and we are more wary of those who we consider outsiders.[5]

In the years following the Second World War, allied citizens were more cooperative and trusting because they'd experienced a broad tribal nature that helped them shape an ongoing group identity. This identity brought with it a sense of belonging, as well as a willingness to compromise (it's well established, of course, that a common enemy brings people together). But, as time went on, and as those generations began to grow old and retire, our societies began to lose that shared sense of goodwill and unity.

Here's the psychologist Michael McCullough:

> Research shows that generalised trust has been falling in the US since the 1960s, the percentage of people who believe their neighbours are honest and moral has been halved since the 1950s.[6]

Or in the words of our song **The King**:

> I'll die by my own sword, thanks
> I trust no one, as I prowl under the amber street lamps

Today, we are governed by people generally born, or coming of age, in the 1960s, '70s, and '80s; an era during which the political culture war between the left and the right began intensifying. On one side, there were those of a more lenient, peaceful and progressive social attitude. On the other; those with a more traditional and conservative outlook. This political tribalism and general societal divide was perhaps best exemplified by, in the USA, the Vietnam War and, in the UK, the ideological (and at times literal) battle between the miners (or the working class in general) and Margaret Thatcher's Conservative government.

The social atmosphere of those days has a direct impact on us today. If a child grows up around domestic violence, they stand a greater chance of becoming an adult who has normalised violence and, therefore, someone who could develop similar violent tendencies themselves. The generations in positions of power *now* grew up in societies marked by internal division – making them more acclimatised and habituated to division itself. For those generations, hostility has been a normalised and expected aspect of civil life, enabling its continuation and, eventually, today, its acceleration.

As our societies have become increasingly divided and hostile, an immediate serious casualty presents itself: social trust. In 2016 – the same year that Oxford Dictionaries declared 'post-truth' to be their International Word of the Year – the World Values Survey asked the question:

> Generally speaking, would you say that most people can be trusted, or that you need to be very careful in dealing with people?

In nearly every country (yes, including the richest – so one assumes the most 'civilised' and safe – France, Germany, Great Britain, and the United States etc.), the majority of people thought that most other people cannot be trusted.[7] It is perhaps not surprising that social trust has been gradually falling when we've had decades of increasing political polarisation and a more unscrupulous attitude to truth, but I think the true cause lies deeper still than that. It lies at the root, our economic system.

Economic Motivation For Self-Interest

Since the 1970s, our economic narrative has increasingly revolved around market freedom and self-maximisation. This narrative often goes unnamed due to its complete and utter universality. A factor which aids its power in that it is hard to pin down and criticise that which has no name. This ideology does have a name though, *Neoliberalism*. Over these decades we have found ourselves treating the short-term profit motive as an indisputable, 'sacred' liberty, more important than any other. We have created a culture of such rampant individualism and corporatism, that we have convinced ourselves that our true nature is one of nothing but self-advancement and self-gratification.

We see ourselves as *Homo economicus* (or 'economic man'); a species with the distinguishing feature of being governed by narrow self-interest, hellbent on nothing other than maximising our own personal wealth.

By living in this ultra-competitive system, which focuses us exclusively on the selfish side of our nature, we have been effectively embracing, practising and *growing* that side of our nature. It's understandable, then, how we've gradually come to believe everyone is out for their own benefit at all times, as that's simply what we experience! This environment has consequently made us less trusting, more guarded, and generally more suspicious of others.

The historian Rutger Bregman, in his book *Humankind* (the best collection of evidence to contest the prevailing view that we are all naturally and purely self-interested) writes: 'If we believe most people can't be trusted, that's how we'll treat each other, to everyone's detriment.'[8]

A socioeconomic environment built on self-interest doesn't only create mistrust, it also clears the way for incivility to spread through the public domain: when we do not trust each other, we are much less likely to show compassion or goodwill in how we interpret or portray each other. This helps stoke the hostility we see throughout society today.

If you're self-interested and ruthless in this competitive society, you'll find it easier to reach the top. Those men who *do* reach the top (and *yes*, it usually *is* men) then assume that this is their personality or natural state. Furthermore, they go on to mistakenly deduce that this ruthless self-interest is the natural state of human beings altogether. They sadly pay little attention to the possibility that this state was instead absorbed through their repeated experience, cemented by the pressures and incentives which guided their career advancement.

In this way, our socioeconomic system becomes a self-fulfilling prophecy: 'Look how ruthless we humans are! How competitive! How selfish! We really are a self-absorbed species!' When in actuality, this is not a *complete* representation of human nature at all (that would be wildly reductive, ignoring our broad knowledge of human behavioural biology and anthropology), it is instead a representation of our nature *within* a space that *incentivises* self-interest.

We reflect the values our society emits.

We, The Chameleon

In reality, we are like the chameleon, adapting our colours to our surroundings in order to survive. If the world around us is premised on the blood red of self-interest (as opposed to the lush green of altruism, community, and cooperation) then humanity – a complex, yet incredibly adaptable, rainbow-coloured species – will begin to grow redder and redder and redder.

Children who have compassionate parents tend to be sympathetic to others as early as age 3, whereas children with uncompassionate and abusive parents tend to struggle with empathy.[9] As parents, if we teach and embody compassion, we naturally raise more compassionate children. The same can be said of a society.

An acquisitive, self-centred focus and an altruistic, cooperative focus are *both* in our nature as human beings. As parents, we can refine and enrich either attribute in our children. Equally, we can also refine and enrich either attribute in our population as a whole, by how we structure civilisation.

Studies indicate that the brain structures involved in positive emotions such as compassion are more 'plastic'. Which is to say, they're more influenced by changes to one's environment and experiences. So compassion is a trait that can be developed or neglected according to the appropriate circumstances.[10]

The capacity for compassion and cooperation is within us all. But whether we cultivate this capacity is not only up to us as individuals, but also the economic system we choose to implement.

Getting 'Back To Normal'

'Too many fundamental parameters of social life have changed. The effects of these changes were apparent by 2014, and these changes themselves facilitated the election of Donald Trump', wrote the social psychologist Jonathan Haidt.[11]

We're not going to go 'back to normal' now we're rid of Trump, because he *isn't* an anomaly. Nor an abnormality. Certainly not just a 'bad apple'. He is what this mindset, this worldview, this economic system predicated on self-interest inevitably produces; someone who is uncivil and ruthless, with their mind set on self-advancement at all times, whatever the cost.

The general prognosis from psychiatry appears to be that he has narcissistic personality disorder, defined as an exaggerated sense of self-importance, a need for admiration and a lack of empathy for other people.

This purely self-interested psychopathology is a hallmark of our time, a signature of the values our economic environment stimulates. To reiterate, Trump is not an abnormality, he is the very epitome of our times. He is the pus-encrusted haemorrhoid *upon* the dirty arse of neoliberalism. (And getting rid of one haemorrhoid doesn't miraculously clean the arse.)

We cannot be blamed for thinking that humans must be, on the face of it, selfish and nasty, especially when we see these people holding the highest offices. But these are just the people who followed the rules of the game best (certainly not to be confused with being the best of us!). With Boris Johnson and other current world leaders also setting a bad example in terms of their rabid commitment to self-advancement,[12] we see clearly that this is the behaviour that our system not only incentivises, but also rewards.

Acts Of Charity Are Suspicious

Self-interest doesn't just pervade the top levels of society – among the most powerful and morally corrupted – it is also oddly evident within the best attributes of society too; our acts of charity. If our belief is that humans generally act out of self-interest, how do you think we begin to judge and perceive acts of charity?

Well, we become sceptical of them. We start believing that any charitable act must be performative, and deep down, actually inspired by ulterior, selfish motives.

One study in the *Journal of Experimental Social Psychology* concluded that we 'decide that seemingly selfless behaviours must be selfish after all'.[13] Even when we're shown evidence for someone's good and honest intentions, we assume the person has a hidden agenda: 'Oh they're just doing it for the publicity...' etc.

This shows our belief in humans as *Homo economicus* is now so deep, and so entrenched, that we discard evidence even if it reveals altruistic intentions. We're staunchly blinkered. Dedicated to the economic orthodoxy of self-interest.

An Evolutionary Lens

People tend to think of evolution as a strictly dog-eat-dog struggle for survival.

But, according to the great biologists, from Charles Darwin to E. O. Wilson, and much of modern evolutionary science, too, it is *cooperation* that has, in fact, been the most important force in humanity's evolutionary success. Our ability to work peacefully and compassionately with each other is one of the main reasons our species has survived, and continues to flourish.[14]

'Because of our very vulnerable offspring, the fundamental task for human survival and gene replication is to take care of others,' says the psychologist Dacher Keltner. 'Human beings have survived as a species because we have evolved the capacities to care for those in need and to cooperate. As Darwin long ago surmised, sympathy is our strongest instinct.'[15]

As I said in the introductory essay to **The Spark** in *Dear Future Historians*:

> Vulnerability is the default state of our species. Whether you feel a testosterone-fuelled, defensive pang reading this sentence or not, it is simply true. We are fragile creatures. While giraffes are up and running within an hour of being born; while baby sea turtles hatch on the sand and miraculously make their way on their own to the ocean; while most reptiles abandon their eggs before they've even hatched; humans can't even sit unaided for the first six months of their lives.[16]

Due to the relatively slow development of our brains, we need to be cared for in order to survive (it's worth it, of course, because our brain is slowly but surely developing the ability to manage complex reasoning and social interaction, etc., the things that elevate us as a species). But that means we're completely reliant upon our parents, caregivers, and wider community during our upbringing. We literally rely on the compassion of others; it is an integral part of our make-up.

'Survival of the kindest' or 'survival of the friendliest' would be two phrases that describe our evolutionary story (and Darwin's sympathy hypothesis) much better than the now infamous 'survival of the fittest'. Frustratingly, though, this is the phrase Darwin is shackled to. Just as Darth Vader never said 'Luke, I am your father' and Gandhi never uttered the words 'be the change you wish to see in the world', Darwin never coined the phrase 'survival of the fittest'. (Herbert Spencer and the 'Social Darwinists', who twisted Darwin's work to try and justify their belief in the superiority of different classes and races, did.)

Darwin was actually quite clear about the weakness of the 'survival of the fittest' argument. Writing in his seminal book *The Descent of Man*, he said:

> Those communities which include the greatest number of the most

sympathetic members, would flourish best, and rear the greatest number of offspring.[17]

What Darwin called 'sympathy' would be termed empathy, altruism or compassion today.[18]

There is now a mounting heap of research in the behavioural sciences, breaking down the idea that people are mostly selfish.[19] The most illuminating research suggests our immediate impulse is actually to be cooperative and compassionate.

One study gifted participants with some money, but gave them the option to give a portion of it to a stranger. They found that 'forcing subjects to decide quickly increases contributions, whereas instructing them to reflect and forcing them to decide slowly decreases contributions'.[20] It appears our instinctive impulse is for compassion. But, give us a moment to think, and we remind ourselves of our experiences living in an economic system of self-interest. Our learnt behaviour kicks in, and we pull back on the reins of kindness.

For years, Felix Warneken has studied the early drive in infants to help others. To even think of a baby helping someone seems nonsensical doesn't it? Babies are just selfish, right? They want food and toys. They have to be encouraged to share and taught how to be kind. This is the view Warneken came up against, when suggesting the thesis to his PhD advisors:

> I was asking my advisors 'What do you think, would a toddler be clever enough to figure out that someone needs help? [...] Would they be willing to help?' These more senior psychologists said, 'Oh no, if you dropped something in front of a toddler, they'd want to keep it.' What did I know, I was just a PhD student.[21]

But he was determined to find out empirically, and not just rely on 'common sense'. We should all be glad he did, as his experiments (available to watch back[22]) show the cutest little toddlers being the purest wee things possible! His studies revealed that even children as young as 14-18 months are willing to help others by picking things up they had dropped, or by opening cupboards and fetching objects from within boxes that others did not know how to open.

These acts may not seem like much, but they prove, in Warneken's words; 'these altruistic tendencies come quite naturally to them'.[23]

Between this, and similar experiments showing us that altruism is evident even in chimpanzees, we can safely assume that altruism has probably been there since the common ancestor of humans and chimps roamed the Earth. It is deeply seated within us.

We're wired to be cooperative and trusting, because it has been in our best interest if we want to survive, but, today, it's almost as if our socioeconomic system's espousal of self-interest and competitiveness is shrouding and overpowering our better impulses. Here's Keltner again:

> We see that compassion is deeply rooted in our brains, our bodies, and in the most basic ways we communicate. Of course, simply realising this is not enough; we must also make room for our compassionate impulses to flourish.[24]

To help our compassionate impulses flourish, we need to redesign our socioeconomic system so that it *encourages*, rather than actively *discourages*, compassion. This clear distinction between our current self-interested mindset, and a much-needed more compassionate one, is so important to our current predicament. As Rutger Bregman says:

> If we want to tackle the greatest challenges of our times – from the climate crisis to our growing distrust of one another – then I think the place we need to start is our view of human nature.[25]

Checking Into The Dreamer's Hotel

The Dreamer's Hotel is a place where we can escape hostility and recalibrate our view of human nature. It is a place where we can work together to find the solutions to our ills. To stay there is to think, to imagine, to dream, and to reignite one's compassionate impulses.

Isn't it surprising that our compassionate impulse still survives *at all*, within a system that contains no incentive for it? The fact that we generously give our time and money to help others – or even, in more extreme circumstances, risk our lives in moments of heroism – is testament to our ability and desire to help those who need it. Compassion doesn't require an incentive.

The social psychologist Daniel Batson has spent years researching the motivations behind altruistic behaviour. In one study he invited participants to watch a contestant undertake a memory task. When the contestant failed, they were administered electric shocks. The participants watching were then told that the contestant had actually experienced a shock trauma as a child and were asked whether they would take shocks on behalf of the contestant. The participants who felt compassionate towards the contestant, volunteered to take several shocks for them, even when they were not incentivised to and were completely free to walk away from the experiment.[26]

Our compassion is so in-built that it ignores painful consequences. It survives the most intense demotivation and propaganda, and even blossoms when we find ourselves, or even others, in life-threatening danger. One of the best examples I found of this was from Pearl and Samuel Oliner's analysis of the heroic and selfless Germans, Italians, Polish etc., who, throughout the Second World War, rescued and harboured Jews during the Nazi occupation, despite being fully aware of the potential punishments if they were caught. In this landmark study, the Oliners found that one of the strongest predictors of this inspiring behaviour was the individual's memory of growing up in a family which prioritised compassion and altruism.[27]

I want to live in a world full of those fucking legends. I want to live in a world that prioritises compassion and altruism. A world full to the brim with brave, kind and virtuous people. At the moment, though, unfortunately, not everyone grows up in a family that prioritises compassion and altruism. And, even if someone does, the 'real world' of dog-eat-dog capitalism will do its best to gnaw and bite those instincts out of them.

We must write compassion into the code of our social software, so to speak. The system must let it flow – it must *encourage it,* even – rather than ignore or obstruct it as it does now. I can only imagine what a magnificently different world would flourish under those conditions.

Our society is becoming more hostile as we approach **The Great Unknown**. **The Dreamer's Hotel** is where we need to go to reevaluate this dangerous path we are on.

As we've gathered, one of the main reasons why we find ourselves not trusting each other is that we live in a system which increasingly breeds and blooms distrust, and this rising sense of distrust is helping to form our increasingly hostile public square. Let's now look at this rise in hostility specifically, and its root causes.

Moral Outrage And Tribal Anger

Anger is one of the most complex and powerful emotions. It's instantly motivating (e.g. when 'seeing red'), it's abundant (experienced almost every day in our personal relationships, in the workplace, in our cars and, of course, in our political lives), and it's unruly (requiring close management and moderation in order to be helpful and not destructive).

It is as poisonous as it is prevalent. As acidic as it is addictive.

Anger appears to be everywhere, and I think we can mainly put that down to our old friend; social media. Here in the modern age, most of us carry a convenient pocket device that allows us 24/7 access to other people's anger, as well as the opportunity to vent any spare anger of our own. With every refresh of our feeds, we are pummelled with new examples of injustice and grievance. So much so, in fact, that many of us become quite devoted to outrage, be that the activist in hope of provoking moral progress, or the troll dreaming only of antagonisation to fill their empty soul.

There are two main forms of anger increasingly visible throughout society: *moral outrage* and *tribal anger*.[28]

Moral outrage is the emotion we feel from a perceived injustice; it's what we feel upon seeing yet another video of a police officer killing an unarmed black man. It's what we feel upon contemplating that just 26 people own as much wealth as the poorest half of the world's population (4 billion people).[29] It's what we feel when a driver suddenly cuts us up on the motorway.

Then, we have the more vacuous, tribal anger; this is everything from football hooliganism to political tribalism. It differs from moral anger, in that it's not triggered by an affront to our virtues or core beliefs, but, instead, by our blind allegiance to a group.

It is understandable that moral outrage feels like it's on the rise. There is *so much* to be justifiably furious about, and outrage often serves the purpose of highlighting mistreatment or unethical behaviour, which can encourage solidarity or action for change. Moral outrage can also be useful because it is *contagious.* It can spread like wildfire, which is why it's very easy for outrage to go viral on social media. Which, in turn, can be great for moments that warrant mass offence to achieve progress, be that through law, or through a cultural or behavioural change.

Tribal anger is certainly on the rise too, though. The increasing political polarisation of our societies provides us with the best current example of it.

Tribalism Is Innate And Arbitrary

A propensity towards tribalism lies within all of us. As humans, we are quick to form groups. Be that gangs, tribes, cliques, bowling teams or book clubs. We are then quick to discriminate in favour of whichever group we belong to. In social psychology this phenomenon is called *in-group favouritism* and experiments have revealed just how swiftly and decisively this can occur.

In research by psychologist Henri Tajfel, secondary school students were shown a series of paintings by two abstract painters. They were then split into groups by their preference of painter (though this was done individually, so no student was aware of any other participants' group membership). The students were then each given the chance to determine the payment each student would get for their participation in the study. Oddly, they preferred to maximise the gains of their fellow group members, assigning less money to members of the other group.[30] Yes, it seems a simple contemporary art preference is all that is required for us to 'discriminate' against other people! We can think of the art preference as the flag, it becomes a symbol of our tribe, a reason for our tribal instincts to kick in.

Tajfel then went on to show that our readiness to discriminate is even more absurd than that. We do not even require a symbol. Even in studies where people were divided into groups based on the most random or trivial of processes (such as a simple toss of a coin), participants *still* discriminated against those assigned to the other group.[31] The researchers observed that participants 'liked the members of their own group better and they rated the members of their in-group as more likely to have pleasant personalities'.[32] And it's not just a simple case of preferential treatment to those in your in-group, as the legendary biologist E.O. Wilson explains: 'They judged their "opponents" to be less likeable, less fair, less trustworthy, less competent.'[33]

We are so quick to emotionally commit to our in-group because, as we looked at earlier, we gain a sense of security from being part of a tribe. We have a 'baked in' fear for our survival if we find ourselves ostracised and alone, so our in-group becomes considerably more important to us. Even in non-threatening situations like psychological studies, a million miles away from the dangerous savannahs our species evolved in. One of the reasons we're then so quick to judge our group as *better*, is due to *social identity theory*; a desire to improve our own self-esteem. In order to feel better about *ourselves*, we imagine the group we are part of to be superior, even when there is no actual evidence for superiority.

It comes as no surprise, then, that tribal anger and a pious judgment of others is on the rise right now, when our self-esteem is being attacked from every viable angle.

We have record levels of inequality. Neoliberalism has wrecked public services and social security. Corporate monopolies have ruined smaller businesses and their communities. Wages have stagnated and job insecurity has dramatically increased. 'Luxuries' such as higher education, or owning one's own property, have become increasingly unobtainable for most. Is it any wonder that, in these times of increasing vulnerability, with our self-esteem in shreds, we look to groups for belonging? It's entirely understandable that we would look for a sense of safety and normality, for community support, and to feel an accepted part of something bigger than ourselves. We are looking for a sense of worth. A sense of safety. We cling to the groups we *do* have (or the groups we are perhaps a natural part of due to race, culture or religion), and we view those groups as superior, essentially, to subconsciously make ourselves feel better! This also begins to explain why we are so quick to attack anything that threatens our group's integrity. It is everything to us, whether we know it or not.

Many people's lives have become so entrenched in tribalism that, in some abstract way, they confuse their ideology with their identity. Their beliefs (perhaps so muddled up in identity politics) are such a part of their essential nature that any criticism of those beliefs begins to feel, to them, like an affront to their very being or essence. To criticise their political leanings, or the ideological groups they subscribe to, becomes as incendiary as insulting their own face, which, naturally, can have an adverse effect upon one's ability to reply rationally and calmly ...

All Groups Are Feeling Threatened

And *here* is where it gets really interesting.

Recently, we've seen that *all* major political or cultural groups are beginning to feel specifically targeted or threatened. Amy Chua, in her book *Political Tribes*, writes:

> When groups feel mistreated and disrespected, they close ranks and become more insular, more defensive, more punitive, more us-versus-them. In America today, every group feels this way to some extent. Whites and blacks, Latinos and Asians, men and women, Christians, Jews and Muslims, straight people and gay people, liberals and conservatives – all feel their groups are being attacked, bullied, persecuted, discriminated against.[34]

One group's cry of mistreatment is often ignored or criticised by other groups, as they feel it diminishes their *own* feelings of persecution. It is in this way that even justified moral outrage can warp, and turn into the more primitive and blinkered tribal anger. In feeling that our own misfortune is relegated by another's, solidarity fails and, instead, further division solidifies.

It's clear why many groups feel discriminated against. Structural racism and religious intolerance are still rife throughout society, but it's important to understand why even those who are widely considered to be the *most privileged* in society are feeling victimised, too. A Harvard study from back in 2011 showed that more than half of white Americans believe that 'whites have replaced blacks as the primary victims of discrimination'.[35]

If that sounds as laughable to you as it did to me when I first read it, this quote, from public speaker and poet Theo E. J. Wilson, may go some way to explaining it:

> What else led to the momentum of the alt-right? The left wing's wholesale demonisation of everything white and male. If you are a pale-skinned-penis-haver, you are in league with Satan! [...] would you believe that some people find it offensive?[36]

In today's hostile political environment where we generalise, often without thought or apology, it is no wonder that people feel victimised. Interestingly, as a black male, Wilson found himself empathising with the demonisation of 'whiteness':

> One thing kept screaming at me to the subtext of these arguments. That was: 'Why should I be hated for who I cannot help but be?' Now, as a black man in America, that resonated with me. I've spent so much time defending myself against attempts to demonise me and make me apologise for who I am, trying to portray me as something that I am not, some kind of thug or gangster, menace to society.[37]

The reality is, all people want to feel comfortable, dignified and worthy in who they are. A 'clean' and upstanding perception of ourselves is pivotal for our ego, and our mental stability. Part of how this is achieved is through celebrating cultures, encouraging the acknowledgement and reverence of our differing cultural groups. But, with 'the white male' being culpable for so much of our recent historical ills, and then also culpable for attempting to downplay them and whitewash history, it has left some white males feeling ashamed and melancholic in who they are.

Here's Amy Chua again:

For decades now, non-whites in the United States have been encouraged to indulge their tribal instincts in just this way, but, at least publicly, American whites have not. On the contrary, if anything, they have been told that their white identity is something no one should take pride in.[38]

Which goes at least *some* way to explaining the growing numbers of nationalist or white supremacist groups in the US. If humans do not feel respected, they will search for ways to gain the respect they feel they deserve; and one of the easiest ways to do that, is through threat of violence. When feeling shamed or disrespected, asserting your dominance through intimidation or hostility is a way of regaining your sense of self-worth, however pathetic, crass and harmful that is, ultimately.[39]

So, what we have, at the moment, is a society divided into groups. Each group is becoming increasingly tribal and mistrusting of the other. Every group feels victimised. Every group brashly confronts the other. Every group stubbornly ignores counter-arguments or evidence.

Even the discussion around COVID-19 has become hyper-politicised, with people taking up 'team'-like positions that they will defend to the death (and even beyond the grave! One former Republican presidential candidate tweeted of COVID-19 not being as deadly as claimed … *after* his own death from COVID-19!)[40]

For the first time in the US, the majority of both Democrats and Republicans now don't just have an 'unfavourable' view of the other side, but a 'very unfavourable' one.[41] The animosity, according to Pew Research Center, is so severe that almost half of both Republicans and Democrats claim that the other party's policies actually 'threaten the nation'.[42] I should clarify, these results were from 2016. It can only have gotten worse since then.

Disgust

For more and more people, one's opponents aren't just wrong, they are *dangerously wrong*; a danger to society, in fact. And, furthermore, they're contemptible and disgusting. This is where it becomes seriously worrying. Anger, as an emotion, builds quickly, but it also dissipates just as fast. We see red and we calm down. Contempt and disgust, however … these are incredibly strong and rigid emotions.

Relationship psychologist John Gottman found, over the course of his research, that if a couple display anger towards one another, that doesn't necessarily predict anything in terms of the relationship's long-term outlook. But, if either of them shows *contempt* for the other? Well, that's the single greatest predictor of divorce: 'In whatever form, contempt is poisonous to a relationship because it conveys disgust and superiority.'[43]

If both individuals or, for our purposes here, both *groups*, are contemptuous, it means they cannot stand the sight of each other, and cannot communicate. They *refuse* to communicate. This (as is now slowly being realised) is a key ingredient for the breakdown of democracy. If people won't communicate how can there be compromise, cooperation and order?

Contempt is especially dangerous. It is a key ingredient when it comes to encouraging humans to commit atrocities.

When we are disgusted with a person, or group of people, we dehumanise them. Framing them as repulsive and morally deformed. Unchangeable and unworthy of our empathy. And, if we cannot empathise with people, history shows us all too well how we can be persuaded, with relative ease, to act with prejudice and violence.

It has most often been expertly carved political propaganda (as was the case with the Third Reich) that has talked people into dehumanising their fellow humans, but now, thanks to rising inequality, mistrust and hostility, the public is jumping to meet the challenge eagerly, with no need for much convincing. Some politicians are still goading us along, intent on provoking our disgust responses, and using them for political ends. But, today, they are assisted by social media users, all eager to help intensify the division.

An open letter by the United Nations on human rights and the global increase in hate speech said:

> We are gravely concerned that leaders, senior government officials, politicians and other prominent figures spread fear among the public against migrants or those seen as 'the others', for their own political gain. The demonization of entire groups of people as dangerous or inferior is not new to human history; it has led to catastrophic tragedies in the past.[44]

Usually, we only feel contempt or disgust for violent extremists or terrorists, yet now these intense emotions grow for migrants, refugees, and people who could be living next-door to us. There may only be thin physical walls between us and our neighbours, but informationally and morally, we may be in completely different universes.

Influenced by political party affiliation and media choices, one neighbour thinks his neighbour is a selfish, ignorant, gun-wielding racist, and the other thinks his neighbour is a monument-destroying, free speech-erasing, 'libtard'.

With a lack of trust in others and with a rise in division and disgust, democracy itself is now under immense strain. It's impossible to work together and reach pragmatic solutions with people you utterly despise. A lack of ability to compromise means you get exactly the situation that the founding fathers feared – that which James Madison wrote about.[45] This is when people care more about defeating the other side than they do about the common good.

It's important to focus on Generation Z here, for they have truly grown up inside the outrage machine that is social media. As a consequence, they may well be ill-equipped for the serious outpouring of empathy which we so desperately require to lift us out of this mess. The younger generations are growing up with very few good examples of compromise and civility to be instructed and inspired by. They may well be growing up deficient in these skills, and therefore inexperienced in the basic components of democracy.

/ / / / / / / / / /

Instead of embracing a massive extension of our social circles online, we seem to be reverting to tribalism and conflict, and belief in the potential of the internet to bring humanity together in a glorious collaborating network now begins to seem naive.[46]

Gaia Vince (2018)

Social Media

Back in the 19th century, the old-timey people thought the future would bring spectacular improvements in transport. They imagined gleaming city-scapes, linked by monorail, skylines teeming with flying dymaxion cars. But while a Porsche Roadster may indeed appear futuristic and far beyond the comprehension of your average 19th-century horse-and-cart-riding citizen, it was actually a swift and immense development in communication that took the lead instead.

Computing power has improved exponentially (doubling in power every 2 years), and has dramatically transformed how we communicate with one another. Social media has made possible forms of mass communication that were previously unimaginable, and, today, almost all of us use it with zeal. But, unfortunately, no one foresaw the massive negative effects it would also unleash.

With each new technological advancement, there arises a dozen new problems. It is only now becoming clear that we have all been the unwitting subjects of a mass psychological experiment. With disturbing results.

2008 saw Facebook hit the milestone of 100 million users. In 2009 the Like button was invented, in part by Justin Rosenstein:

> When we were making the Like button, our entire motivation was 'can we spread positivity and love in the world?' The idea that fast forward to today and teens would be getting depressed when they don't have enough likes, or it could be leading to political polarisation, was nowhere on our radar.[47]

From 2009 onwards, face-to-face interaction began to surrender to online interaction as our main form of day-to-day communication, and the nature of human connectivity began to change radically.

Email,
   Facebook,
      MySpace,
         Instagram,
            Twitter,
               Snapchat ...
                   Connect with your friends!
             Share photos!
        Join groups!
      ... Lose your social awkwardness
   and your social awareness...
Likes
never-ending notifications
The freedom of anonymity!
Trolls
Hurling insults with no repercussions

OUTRAGE!
Free speech! Free speech! Free speech!
amplified peer pressure
the burning need for validation

OUTRAGE!
Echo chambers

filter bubbles
the amplification of the extremes

OUTRAGE!
Hate speech
cancel culture / call-out culture
virtue signalling

OUTRAGE!
Tribalism
motivated reasoning
attention-whores
WILL EXAGGERATE FOR RETWEETS
Hyper-hyper-hyper-hyperbole

OUTRAGE!
Confirmation bias
Clickbait
contrarianism
nihilism
dehumanisation ...

When I wrote the song **Undercover Agents**, back in 2015, I was aware of social media's ability to ramp up our anxieties and destroy our self-esteem, and that it encouraged us to project false, veneered versions of ourselves out into the world. **Undercover Agents** addressed the unanticipated effects that the online experience was having on our mental health.

Take My Country Back, another Enter Shikari song from the same period, touched upon how social media plunges us into *echo chambers* or *filter bubbles* which entrench our views by repeatedly exposing us to things we agree with, without also presenting the pesky inconvenience of relevant counter arguments or other perspectives. But now, in 2021 we can see the truth; social media is far, far worse than all of that.

At the moment, it is hard to perceive social media as anything other than an unshakable gravitational force, existing solely to bring out the worst in people; a black hole that sucks us in, transforming us into unfriendly, uncharitable, antagonistic arseholes, as it warps our ability to rationally view the world and communicate calmly. Social media has become an intensely draining, and extremely disturbing, place to spend time.

Incivility and hostility now define our online experience.

Tribalism is rife. All information has been weaponised.

Echo Chambers

On social media today, no matter where you sit politically, you are drip-fed events and examples that only serve to reinforce your own views. Your sources of information are cherry-picked; you only follow and interact with people and organisations that match your own political leanings and values, and feedback loops in online algorithms recommend you news articles and videos that further narrow down the content you're exposed to.[48] Therefore, a great deal of your online experience is just you receiving confirmation that you are correct in your beliefs. As a result, your beliefs begin to harden. To ossify. You become overconfident in your opinions. You become less willing (or less able) to converse with anyone with differing political views.

The Illusion Of Confidence

At its most intellectually debilitating, an echo chamber increases your emotional attachment to your beliefs, whilst discouraging contemplation about them.

Upon being asked for a detailed explanation of an opinion you hold, you may actually find yourself struggling immensely! This is simply because you are rarely encouraged to *think* about your opinions in any detail. When pushed, many of us don't really know why we have some of the strident opinions we hold. The systems engineer Barbara Oakley calls this an 'illusion of confidence'.[49]

In this way, social media is conservative by definition. It reinforces *your* status quo and rarely prompts you to challenge or test your ideas. Personal progression is not cultivated and wisdom as a whole is obstructed.

Each of us is barraged by tweets, voxpops and Tik Toks. Surface level information. We're constantly distracted by the next notification that pops up. Delving beneath the surface and taking the time to think about a concept *properly* becomes something that all modernity appears united against you achieving.

Even upon researching concepts for this book, I've found myself constantly pulled by the temptation to open my social media feeds. It's hard to resist the dopamine surge that comes from checking these platforms. But it is not there where I will find substance, depth or detail. Only a continuous flow of reinforcing content. And this, of course, is why it is so alluring! Seeing agreement, validation and confirmation that you're right is satisfying. Seeing those who disagree with you criticised, 'owned' and 'dragged' is also satisfying.

Now compare those quick doses of pleasure with taking the time to explore a concept from different angles, challenging yourself and achieving a greater depth of understanding about something – that is difficult, arduous, testing. No wonder our default is to stay endlessly scrolling through our social media feeds. It feels informative and beneficial to us but these perceived rewards are short-lived and debilitating.

There was a time, of course, not too long ago, when social media was heralded as the means to bring the world together. Looking back now, that view appears naive and quaint. If anything, social media is now seriously pushing us apart. It has ushered us into pockets of like-mindedness, agreement and compatibility, where our opinions and beliefs become rigid and ingrained, while our patience for contrasting opinions and beliefs, plummets.

Other than increased incivility, tribalism and hostility, filter bubbles have also triggered social and intellectual stagnation, due to the simple fact that no one is ever encouraged to question their own views, or understand other perspectives. The philosopher John Stuart Mill once explained that, 'The greatest orator, save one, of antiquity, has left it on record that he always studied his adversary's case with as great, if not with still greater, intensity than even his own.'[50] Mill believed that unless we experience and analyse the views of those we disagree with, we will never really know what they're right or wrong about.

I have been criticised, in the recent past, for following people on Twitter who hold unsavoury views, or dangerous ideologies; but I believe that knowing the arguments of those you disagree with (even intensely) is pivotal to being able to thoroughly condemn them. Here's John Stuart Mill again: 'He who knows only his own side of the case, knows little of that.'[51]

For all we know, our opponents could be right on some subjects. They may be in possession of fresh evidence, or offer a new argument which we've never thought to consider. Perhaps, though, and more importantly; even if they *aren't* right, there may still be sprinklings of insight among their falsehoods, which could guide our minds in new directions, or help us better understand our own views.

Unfortunately, most people are content with the constant flow of pleasing confirmation bias they receive in their echo chambers. We bask in our own narrow bands of light, blissfully unaware of the reality-warping nature of our insulation.

Amplifying The Extremes

Filter bubbles aren't just unhelpful because they reinforce your own views. They also amplify the most extreme aspects of your opponent's views. This is pivotal to understanding how outrage and tribalism spread online. Within your echo chamber, the news you see will undoubtedly show you the worst or most outrageous aspects of the other side, simply because the more outrageous an opinion or event is, the more traction it garners online. Consequently, the most fervent and crazy voices, from either side of the political spectrum, are amplified to the other, creating a public square where, overall, it is the most outrageous aspects of society that are on display.

Throughout 2020, many conservatives, (or those on the right) only had videos appear on their timeline that showed Black Lives Matter (BLM) or Antifa rioting, looting, and violently attacking the police or counter protestors; liberals (or those on the left) only saw videos that showed police brutality and murder, far right militia group activity, or conservative thugs attacking peaceful protestors.

You could be forgiven for believing that BLM were simply violent rioters, if your online echo chamber leant towards the far right, because that's all you would witness. Just as you could be forgiven for thinking that 'all cops are bastards' (often 'ACAB', for short) if your echo chamber was a far left one. Neither views are a truthful representation of reality, but they can *appear* to be, if your media is appropriately and consistently filtered.

Back in Chapter 2, we looked at how the news magnifies rare or extreme events. Social media does the same, but worse – it neatly selects evidence of the rare or extreme events that *you* specifically need to see in order to bolster your hostile view of the other side. Your filter bubble is customised and attuned to *your* political preferences, it feeds your disparaging view of your opponents, regardless of the broader context or actual truth.

Misrepresentation of others and amplification of the extremes is something we see time and time again. Take the example of the coverage of protest marches; Speaking generally, a very small percentage of protest march attendees will be there with the intention of causing a little trouble. They do not represent the peaceful intentions of the majority, but, typically, it will be this violent or destructive minority that will make the evening news.

Similarly, the people who you disagree with politically are mostly *not* like the *extreme* version that you see derided on your timelines.

Bile-filled tweets from the most angry. Videos of the most abhorrent members of the other side. These rightfully cause an intense emotional reaction in us, but they are very rarely the full picture. They are usually a minority that will be amplified, pushing us further apart, while justifying more and more outrage, as each side becomes increasingly sickened by the other.

Amplifying Fake News

To make matters worse, it isn't *just* the extremes getting amplified. The media/ social media also have the propensity for signal-boosting what can only be described as *damn right lies*.

The problem of 'fake news' is well documented but, still, not enough is being done to stop its staggering and harmful effects. At the most tabloid, opinion-based, or simply obnoxious ends of the news media, some anchors are now openly getting away with presenting partisan commentary as actual fact. For their defence, the anchors' lawyers are claiming that the public, in fact, *know* that what they're watching is bullshit, that it's simply 'entertainment', relieving the news channels of their only responsibility; telling the truth. (They had *one* job!)

In one recent example, a US District judge ruled that a Fox News anchor was not 'stating actual facts', and was instead engaging in 'exaggeration' and 'non-literal commentary'.[52] The judge ruled that the public was aware of this because the 'reputation' and 'general tenor' of the show gave it an entertaining context the viewer understood. It is this style of media – exaggerated and bombastic – that most stokes outrage in its viewers; who are then most likely to head to their social media accounts and share the outrageous 'news' they just heard.

Once on social media, its then that the problem of fake news *really* gets out of hand. Let's take Twitter as an example: research shows that truthful news takes *six times* as long as fake news to spread across the platform, mostly due to the fact that falsehoods are 70% more likely to be retweeted than truths![53]

We live in a divided society, where we *all* feel a heightened tribal instinct. Our anger incentivises us to post disparaging articles about the other side, without taking a moment to check their validity. Social psychologist Peter Ditto summarises the research in this area: 'a person is quick to share a political article on social media if it supports their beliefs, but is more likely to fact-check the story if it doesn't'.[54]

We jump to believe, and promote, inflammatory, polarised, or even provably fake news articles, *if* they support our views, and with each retweet we harden our group's beliefs, deepening our contempt for the other side. Civility. Patience. Understanding. Even the truth itself. They are all fighting a losing battle against falsehood, now that falsehood has been turbo-charged by social media.

Cancelled By Your Own Side

In the event that you manage to break out of your perspective-diminishing echo chamber and *dare* to question your *own* group – even just one aspect of your otherwise shared beliefs – you'll most likely receive a torrent of anger in return (oddly, yet inevitably, with a similar fervour to the anger you both previously enjoyed directing at the other side together). Any calm and measured criticism of your own side's exaggerations, false generalisations, or sharing of fake news, is often seen as a complete betrayal and causes a sort of 'micro-cancelling', where you're immediately disowned; becoming, from your own side's point of view, just as bad as your shared political enemies.

Today, we are so inebriated by our tribalism, that any straying from the party line is seen as blasphemy. It's all emotional identification and blind loyalty. Even displaying a smidgeon of civility and compassion towards the other side – instead of the mandated fury and ridicule – as you try to understand their views and pick apart their hypocrisies or faults can get you disowned by your own side.

Ultimately, this only serves as proof that this heightened tribalism is wrong and will only exacerbate our problems. We must feel free to converse with the 'other side', just as we must feel free to calmly criticise our 'own side', when necessary. Truth itself relies on this, as does the healing of our hostile and divided society. Depolarisation can only occur when people have the courage to reach across to other tribes, or to speak out against their own, when necessary.

A Hasty Generalisation

During the BLM protests of summer 2020, I had the audacity to suggest that perhaps ACAB was an immature, and unhelpfully hostile, generalisation. This did not go down well with some Twitter users who considered me to be their 'ally'. On another occasion, I was lambasted for retweeting a video in which some police were giving support to BLM protestors, and even marching alongside them. To some, posting this sort of material was akin to treason. It was as if I were helping the 'racist cops' by posting *their* propaganda.

It is, of course, how you *contextualise* the posting of a video that makes it propaganda or not. I didn't claim that a *majority* of cops were acting with friendliness and solidarity, just as I did not claim that a majority of cops were involved in the kind of police brutality seen in other videos from the protests.

The judging or stigmatising of a whole group, based on the actions of a small portion of that group, is a common *informal fallacy* (in this case probably somewhere between an 'overwhelming exception' and a 'hasty generalisation' – look it up, informal fallacies are fun!). It is the same faulty logic that leads the thoughtless *Daily-Mail*-comments-section-dweller to believe all Muslims to be suicide bombers, for example. At the heart of it, it's simply ignorant of the size and scope of the category in question. It ignores all of the broader issues and nuances. It is the formation of a rule based on the actions of a minority.

The Problems Of Modern Policing

One of the core issues with modern policing, is that it is a job which often sees the deployment of people who are woefully under-trained for such a position of power. Police forces suffer from a lack of specialisation (the same cop who's sent to answer a call of sexual assault, should not be the same cop sent to address a mental health breakdown or psychiatric episode), a lack of tactical awareness (instead of focusing on community policing, they favour sweeping hard-line approaches), insufficient training (specifically; de-escalation training, and instruction in emotional awareness – in order to prevent momentary megalomaniacal acts of violence), along with insufficient psychological education (which they need, not only in order to understand their own biases, but to also better understand the impulses of the varied personalities they will encounter in the line of duty).

Now, on top of all that inexperience and under-education, some cops *do* actually harbour racist views as well! Some cops *are* actually white supremacists, some *are* actually neo-Nazis.[55] Some get kicks out of the power they wield, as well as the violence that they experience, or even incite. These people should, obviously, have no place whatsoever in law enforcement.

The wider reality is, though, that *most* police officers, I expect, are just trying to keep the public safe, and retain public order.

They simply need to be given better training and support.

(Still not convinced? Ask yourself this question: are the cops that turn up when you're being burgled, bastards? Is the cop that arrests a serial rapist, a bastard?

Perhaps it's more likely that police officers are just like the rest of us; fallible human beings. Except they're trying to do an immensely difficult job, while sometimes deficient in the vast forms of training needed.)

We *could* now, of course, go on to look at arguments around the deeper philosophy and purpose of policing within our current socioeconomic system altogether. We could discuss how the police are essentially security for the propertied class, arresting 'petty' criminals while simultaneously letting white-collar criminals go, scot-free, pockets bulging with tax-payers money. But that's probably a whole other book.

Polarisation Is Good For Business

With our eagerness to generalise, chastise and demonise, our society is now becoming increasingly polarised. Spurred on by the emboldening nature of our individual echo chambers, we drift further and further apart.

Can we look to social media companies for help in holding back the tide of tribalism and hatred? Well, the elephant in the room, when it comes to looking at social media platforms' obstacles to addressing polarisation, is that polarisation itself is actually *good for business*. Any attempt to depolarise society, and extinguish rampant tribalism, finds itself absolutely at odds with social media's entire business model.

Social media platforms are monetised through advertising, therefore they want their users to spend as much time as possible on their platforms in order for them to place more adverts in front of those users. The more users that are seeing adverts, the more advertisers consider the platform to be worth of advertising on. More users attract more advertisers, and the platform's advertising revenue increases. More advertising revenue results in more profit.

So, as a business, a social media platform wants to increase its user count, but it *also* wants to increase the amount of *time* users spend on the platform. Because, put simply: the more time you're spending on the platform, the more adverts you're seeing.

What brings people online more than anything else?

And what keeps people online more than anything else?

'Outrage!'

Polarised, extremity-focused, sensationalised content – or often simply *fake news* content – is the type that most easily captures, enraptures, and enrages us. Any content that provokes our outrage and tribal instincts will grab our attention the quickest, and retain our attention the longest.

As we've looked at previously; anger is a powerful motivator. So, when we are provoked by outraging events online, it compels us to *stay* online, ardently sharing and commenting away, drawing more people to the platform as we spread our ire far and wide. It is a self-supporting model of interaction:

Polarisation ensures more engagement on a platform.

More engagement on a platform means more eyes on adverts.

And that means more advertising money rolling in.

Any purely business-minded social media owner is certainly not incentivised to address polarisation.

Here's the ex-Google engineer Guillaume Chaslot:

> The media has this exact same problem, where their business model by and large is that they're selling our attention to advertisers and the internet is a new, even more efficient way to do that [...] From the point of view of watch-time, this polarisation is extremely efficient at keeping people online.[56]

In attempting to quell outrage and tribalism, we are not only up against our own instincts, but also, once again, we find ourselves up against the narrow short-term profit motive; the economic system itself. Ah, a familiar embrace. The amount of times I have ended up here, after looking for the root cause of a problem, almost makes it cosy.

The Influence Of Civility/The Influence Of Incivility

It is incredibly difficult to act with patience and rationality on social networking sites (SNS) when the alternating current of anger shoots back and forth all around us. The only way to reach a more civil public square is to attempt – whenever we can – to break this circuit. If we refuse to react with hostility towards others, or refuse to share that exaggerated, or false, article, we can begin to stop the sequential flow of anger and polarisation. (Think of it like your old Christmas fairy lights. One bulb blows, and the entire string dies.)

Research finds that it is possible to turn the tide on incivility by *refusing* to react rudely and angrily ourselves. In effect, civility can inspire *further* civility. And the more that incivility then becomes atypical, the more that civility takes over as the norm.

A study by economists and political scientists on the behaviour of users on SNS concluded that 'when the initial share of the population of polite users reaches a critical level, civility becomes generalized'.[57]

But of course, it also works the other way around:

> Interaction on SNS leads individuals to condition their behavior on the behavior of other users, in a strategic manner. For example, users may react to a hostile online environment where incivility is prevalent by in turn behaving rudely, or by abandoning the social network.[58]

This takes us back to the 'human beings are like chameleons' school of thought. *We adapt to the environment we experience.* With a hostile social media platform, we learn strategies to deal with it; either mirroring the environment, by simply jumping on in and getting involved, or taking a contrasting form of action, such as fleeing the toxic space altogether.

As social media platforms become places of increased harassment, hate speech, outrageous claims, and generally aggressive and disrespectful behaviour towards others, if you're not the sort of person who gleefully embraces heated debate, where insults wantonly fly, you may well opt to leave the platform altogether. Many who are more introverted in their nature, or not good with conflict, or harsh criticism, *or* who are just simply sick of the toxic atmosphere overall, will chose the self-protective behaviour of avoidance. If things continue the way they are, we can perhaps imagine a mass exodus, where many walk away from the platforms, perhaps flipping them off in slow motion as they do so, like Bruce Willis strutting away from a burning building.

Perhaps a loss of users is what it will take for SNS to pay attention?

The Avoidance Of Outrage And The Death Of Discussion

One sad, subtler, result of a hostile public forum is that we consequently only feel comfortable attacking ideas we *disagree* with, rather than discussing ideas that we *agree* with. The latter becomes too dangerous because, from a social standing mindset, it's much safer to criticise ideas than to advocate them; shooting a target is a far lower-risk activity than exposing your own target for others to aim at.

Much like the avid music fan keenly searching for new, undiscovered bands, some people are now *so* outrage-focused that they'll be out there hunting for the next big thing that gets their veins bulging and mouths frothing. In not wanting to deal with these outrage-zombies, the more reserved, or simply more sane, people – if they have not left SNS altogether – will at least refrain from touching upon any sensitive subjects. The risk of making even a small mistake can result in being catapulted into the wider public consciousness, to be discussed, derided, and mauled by the zombie hordes.

Tristan Harris, a computer scientist, and founder of the Center For Humane Technology, said:

> We evolved to care about whether other people in our tribe think well of us or not, because it matters. But were we evolved to be aware of what 10,000 people think of us? We were not evolved to have social approval being dosed to us every five minutes, that was not at all what we were built to experience.[59]

Our minds aren't calibrated to deal with thousands of negative opinions about us, our mental health certainly won't survive that unscathed. So it stands to reason that any of us would do all we can to avert this, either through avoidance, or by retaliating with hostility.

If the mean average of hostile actors continues to increase, public discussion and public opinion will suffer as a whole. We will see a withdrawal, of not only sane individuals, but also sane ideas. At some point, the only people left on social media may be the extremists. Caps lock on indefinitely. Scolding each other's extreme views. Until the end of time.

King Arthur was said to be a great warrior, who defended Britain from its enemies, both human and supernatural. It amused me to envisage passing him a smartphone, pointing him towards Twitter, and watching him attempt to use all his skill and valour battling the internet's seemingly endless armies of outrage-zombies; an entirely different beast from that which he's used to!

I am King Arthur in Camelot
Connected to the hotspot
For 8 days on the trot
Fighting the trolls and the bots

Core Problems:
Non-Face-To-Face Communication

With face-to-face communication, we use facial expressions, eye contact, tone of voice, gesturing and a myriad of other nonverbal behaviours that make it easier to correctly perceive the feelings and intentions of the person we're communicating with. With non-face-to-face, we lose *all* of that (and, no, emojis don't sufficiently make up for it). Without these clues our empathy cannot do its job.

Being deprived of *voice* is especially affecting. Research shows that when a person hears someone speak on an issue that they care about, they find it more rational, refined, warm, sophisticated, and persuasive than when reading a transcript or written piece by the same speaker.

In one study, psychologists performed a series of experiments that looked into the humanising effect of hearing someone *speak* on an issue, as opposed to *reading* their words. For example, in one experiment, they chose three particularly polarising topics of discussion for a group of communicators to speak and write about: abortion, the US war in Afghanistan, and music preference for country vs. rap music. They then had another group, 'evaluators', who listened to or read the communicators points of view on the polarising issues. The evaluators were consistently more likely to dehumanise the communicator when *reading* their opinions, as opposed to hearing them speak. Especially if they disagreed with them. The study concluded that the tendency for people to criticise and belittle people they disagree with may be 'tempered by giving them, quite literally, a voice'.[60]

Further research has shown that when evaluators disagreed with the communicator, they 'judged communicators who expressed an opposing opinion via video or audio as more humanlike – that is, more sophisticated and warm – than those who described their opposing opinions in text form'.[61]

This may seem quite obvious, but, nowadays, when the bulk of our communication (especially with strangers and those with opposing views) is by text, this really is rather chilling.

Without audio or video our normal sense of social awkwardness and empathy is blinded, allowing us to readily act meaner should we want to, and, boy, do we ever!

Our normal social awareness becomes blinded when we cannot see or hear the other person, too, meaning we easily misconstrue and misunderstand them. We jump to interpret other's words negatively, and then react defensively. We hide our upset or hurt, which has the effect of removing the last remnant of any humanity to the conversation. We then miss the emotional impact that *our* meanness may have on *others*. Discourtesy and hostility become effortless and more likely, when we cannot see the emotional effect they have.[62] On social media, spite effortlessly encourages spite.

Core Problems: Anonymity And Non-Anonymity

The problems with social media anonymity are obvious: anonymous users are inclined to scream their heads off, incite hate, or launch personal attacks with, literally, zero personal consequences. But, with non-anonymous users, we actually see the opposite problem; an increased sense of being visible and feeling under the spotlight. This can have the effect of pressurising us into instantly announcing our righteous anger, about whichever thing our online peers are currently enraged by. We want to remain 'seen' and popular within our in-group.

This has been dubbed *performative anger* or, even, *virtue signalling*.

I often feel the compulsion to immediately denounce almost every bad thing that happens in the world, not just to use my platform for 'good' (i.e. raising awareness of important issues), but for fear of not being seen as morally consistent and dependable by my peers, friends, or followers.

This pressure is much more likely to birth mistakes, as we rush to outpour our anger without sufficient time to consider the details or broader perspectives. On social media there is no 6-month court case – the jury of Twitter casts its decision within minutes.

Outrage becomes continuous, as each of us feels the pressure to rush to comment on every new event in the world, which just helps to over-amplify the availability of negative information, reinforcing *the availability bias* as well as strengthening our group biases and echo chambers.

Core Problems: The Incentive To Exaggerate

The social pressure to rush to broadcast our outrage encourages us towards exaggeration, be it knowingly or otherwise. The more extreme a post or statement, the more likely it is to get social recognition, and the more likely you are to get more limelight and followers.

Research into how we communicate on social media has consistently found that emotion heightens the spread or reach of content, with one study published by the National Academy of Sciences concluding: 'the presence of moral-emotional language in political messages substantially increases their diffusion within (and less so between) ideological group boundaries'.[63] To put that more simply; the more emotional or extreme your statement, the more traction it will garner, though, most likely, only really within your own filter bubble (further amplifying the disconnect between groups).

Personally, I've found this to be true in my own social media posts. Even to the extreme that simply including the word 'fucking', as an angry adverb within a politically critical tweet, will earn me more interaction and retweets than my more cool-headed and measured critiques.

Most friends, followers, or peers don't assiduously analyse what you say for bias or overstatement. Instead, they feel the surge of outrage upon reading your message and simply hit like/share/comment to support it. (Again, they may also rush to do this in order to signal *their* virtues, presenting themselves as in agreement with the tribe.) The incentive, then, for a public figure especially, is to attach themselves to cases of moral outrage and comment with fiery emotion in order to gain 'moral points' and further their reach. Ultimately, this will increase their notoriety, regardless of the veracity of the story they're sharing, or interacting with.

In these circumstances, we're actually disincentivised from getting our story straight, or from looking in more detail at the facts. Context, nuance, and complication are worthless currency in the economy of social media status. They rarely bring you substantial social recognition. It is outrage that sells.

We're acutely aware that the news cycle moves incredibly fast, these days. We're bombarded with fresh, newsworthy events 24 hours a day. As a society, we forget or discard stories swiftly, or are, at least, distracted by the next outrageous, attention-grabbing story. Therefore, there is a very real pressure to make the ultimate impact and strike hard while the iron is hot. We are lured into exaggeration, in order to have the maximum effect in the insufficient sliver of limelight each issue receives.

So, not only do we have an instinctual drive towards tribalism and outrage, and not only does the social media business model *profit* off of that drive, but we, as individuals, are also incentivised and pressured towards dramatisation and falsehood, in order to gain social recognition. Which, in turn, only propels tribalism and outrage further. What a disorientating and daunting state of affairs.

There is certainly a lot to be addressed, when it comes to social media in the future.

Overuse And Ostracision

With outrage now so prevalent, it almost feels like it has become our default mode of social interaction. Unsurprisingly, there is a serious problem in this.

Moral outrage is becoming *so* ubiquitous, and relentless, that it is demeaning its own righteous potency. That is to say; moral outrage is becoming devalued through overuse. By saturating our social media, it's losing its power to affect.

Where a truly outrageous event *should* provoke moral outcry and action, it often provokes nothing more than a fatigued sigh, as we expect it to be just 'another tempest in a teapot'.

After so stridently broadcasting anger at the smallest of misdemeanours or disagreements, we put a limit on the effect our anger can have when we need it most. In those moments, of genuine outrage at deliberate prejudice, corruption, immorality, or violence, we only have the same tool to employ that was just used against someone who simply made a risqué joke, or genuinely mistook someone's pronoun.

This behaviour – holding the whole of society up to incredibly high and rigid standards, and then punishing, with shame and ostracism, those who do not reach them – is what many refer to as *wokeism*. It has had the unfortunate effect of causing us to assume each consecutive outcry to be just another exaggerated or unfair accusation, along with pushing people further away from corrective behaviour. In the same way that incarcerating someone for a small drug-use misdemeanour can have the detrimental effect of transforming them into a hardened criminal, ostracising someone for some small mistake, making them feel no longer accepted or welcome on 'your side', can encourage them to alter their perspective dramatically, too. Even to the extent of pushing them into your political opponents' arms.

As an obvious example (and I use the terms 'the left' and 'the right' here, which is obviously reductive); you can be sure as hell that when the left cancels someone for some ill-considered joke or minor wrongdoing, the right will swoop in offering them sympathy and friendly banter about their new shared adversaries, welcoming them into a new social group to feel connected to and respected by. This person could actually have politics that are, in general, aligned to yours, so perceived as 'good', but they'd feel a subconscious allure to 'the dark side' because, as humans, we view ostracism as being a direct threat to our wellbeing.

For progressives – those who I presume want to see progress – by administering this hard-line, pious, moral purity, you lose potential brothers and sisters in your fight. If your group treats humans as unchanging and rigid, and unable to learn or improve, jumping on and shaming every mistake, your group is not only wrong; you will lose.

To judge people as only as good as their worst moment is as harmful as it is thoughtless.

If you want your side to win, you must offer compassion, forgiveness, and education when there are mistakes. Not ridicule, shame and ostracism. You need to make it out like yours is the better house party to be at. Everyone wants to be at a house party, so make yours the most welcoming, accepting, safe and fun! Rejection only encourages people to check out the competing party next door.

Factionalism

If we're not piously banishing people from our own group, then we're busy splintering ourselves off into narrower and narrower sub-groups.

In the same way that music has divided down into more and more descriptive sub-genres these days, each one more complicated and historically convoluted than the last, social media is splitting us into sub-tribes, each one more convoluted and hard-line in its beliefs and exclusivity. This makes it harder and harder even for people who are, otherwise, in general ideological agreement, to concur on basic principles and events.

This penchant for purity and factionalism is another problem that appears to afflict the left more than it does the right, and is part of the reason for the conservative neoliberal consensus which has dominated the political middle ground, driving the economic status quo, for decades. (One of my favourite Monty Python sketches brilliantly satirises the left's long-term tendency to splinter into warring factions; the People's Front Of Judea and their hatred for the Judean People's Front, in their timeless masterpiece *Life of Brian* will, seemingly, always be relevant!)

Forgiveness is important. Alliances with people you may disagree with on some subjects, but align with generally, are pivotal.

We can't see someone's singular bad act as their whole entity, and then consequently banish them for it. It's immature, and detrimental to progress. In cutting off your own potential numbers, you are just sabotaging the better future you are trying to achieve for yourself.

In fact, it's worse than that; you are sabotaging that better future for everybody.

Waltzing Off The Face Of The Earth

Right. Now that we've grasped the extent to which social media is fucking things up for us, let's get back to the music!

I wanted to describe, via music, just how precarious truth has begun to feel in this age of mass anger and mass deceit, so I set out to write a piece that personifies the, seemingly uninterrupted, downward spiral that society appears to be in.

As I began writing this album, I couldn't seem to rid my mind of an image: a thousand couples, pristine in ball gowns and tuxedos, waltzing, slowly and nonchalantly, off the face of the Earth. And not as in rising from the lower echelons of Earth towards some heavenly plane, but drifting off into the cold, dark, vacuum of space. In my mind some of the dancers appear unaware of their situation – too involved in their own dance – and some are fully aware but appear apathetic, having simply resigned themselves to their fate. This echoes two of the reactions to the state of the world discussed in Chapter 2: distraction and fatalism.

A waltz felt like the perfect rhythm to employ. It can be unhurried, almost lumbering, yet still have an alluring and dutiful momentum. For most of us, the main genres we are brought up listening to are pop, rock, hip hop and dance music, all of which overwhelmingly use a time signature of 4/4 (i.e. they have 4 beats to a bar). To have 3 beats instead of 4, as a waltz does, immediately drops us into a different rhythmic territory, as it falls outside of our overly familiar musical experience. We might feel slightly uneasy and almost suspicious towards the music, and this is bolstered further by the playful, cartoon-like brass and arpeggiating, atmospheric circus Wurlitzers, all playing harmonic sequences which seem to spiral endlessly downwards. I hope the descending root notes instil a sense of flippancy, as well as the more obvious disheartened and depressed emotions.

As I discussed in Chapter 2, we can react to the current calamitous state of affairs in a variety of different ways, but I'm sure at some point over the last few years (if not the last few weeks!) you've found yourself utterly stupefied. As 'normal' people, we're often just spectators gawping with disbelief at the state of the world, and grappling with our overwhelming feeling of powerlessness.

The intense and relentless nature of our hostile post-truth society sometimes just makes us sigh or groan, and we just sit shaking our heads with almost no emotional reaction at all. We simply do not know how to react, anymore. I decided that *vacant disbelief,* a refusal to digest reality or know how to react to it, would be the main emotional tone for this track. When writing the descending bassline and performing the vocals, I imagined someone fatigued by the state of the world, sitting still, with their face blank and eyes glazed over.

We repeatedly witness one example after another of mistruth, corruption or injustice committed by those in positions of power. And we should not be surprised by this when we're only changing the players in the game and never the game itself. We all have, within us, the ability to lie, to be corrupt, and to act unjustly, and we certainly *will* do if our systems coax us towards those vices, by glorifying and rewarding self-interest and self-advancement. I thought this continuity of corruption was best exemplified by that defining moment in George Orwell's *Animal Farm* (from which I paraphrase in the lyrics):

> The creatures outside looked from pig to man, and from man to pig, and from pig to man again; but already it was impossible to say which was which.[64]

Society's downward spiral is visible and quantifiable. We can see that the root causes lie in the systems we employ. Yet the system is still so supported, sturdy, and rooted. I thought that having the track in waltz-time, 3/4, felt quite apt, being that a 3-sided structure is the strongest and hardest to topple. The waltz's inflexible and relentless rhythm helps to symbolise why we are failing to achieve meaningful progress in our current efforts. We are not targeting the root systemic causes, so any attempt at progress inevitably fails, and the 3-sided structure stands, untroubled.

3/4 time is so merciless, and has such mesmerising momentum, that once you're hearing it, it is simply hard to imagine anything else. This is exactly the stasis we are in, with regards to needing broad system change, while being unable to imagine or initiate such a thing ever happening. This, along with the line 'Our future's been denied', subtly introduces the topics of frustration and social rigidity which we will explore together, soon, in Chapter 6.

/ / / / / / / / / /

> Regardless what you feel
> This song isn't real

I begin the piece with a disorientating opening announcement, immediately challenging the listener's sense of reality.

The confusion and absurdity that stems from the singer – surely the main authority on the song itself – asserting that the song he is singing does not, in fact, exist, felt suitably Orwellian and timely. Four seconds in, and you're being gaslighted by the song itself! Something we've grown used to from many of our backtracking and truth-twisting corporate and political leaders.

I should point out that even though I label modernity 'the era of post-truth', I realise that, to some extent, this isn't a new phenomenon at all. The use of rhetoric, oratory, and a little persuasive framing (... or just downright lies) to achieve political ends, is as old as time itself. Indeed we could ask, if *this* is the era of post-truth, when exactly was the era of truth? We only have to look through the history of war propaganda to be bludgeoned with falsehood. And if we go back further, even the Bible and other historic religious scriptures are 'fake news' (also proving that fake news can last for thousands of years ...).

The important, and troubling, difference today is that the mistruths are far more available, believable, and disguised, than ever before (not to mention more dangerous too). So, instead of having **Waltzing Off The Face Of The Earth** concentrate solely on the customary lies of politicians, I reflect the pervasive nature of post-truth by listing off falsehoods from wherever they have occurred.

Online, you can find 'evidence', confirmation, and community support for any whack-job conspiracy theory, dangerous ideology, or immoral view you can think of. One quick Google search, or one long YouTube binge, can convince you of almost anything – from the comical, such as flat Earth theory ('the Earth isn't sphere'), to the poisonous, such as climate change denial ('climate change is fake'). Since the album's release, we've seen that online conspiracy communities can now inspire serious, real world, violence, too; the insurrection and the storming of the Capitol in Washington DC, at the beginning of 2021, was inspired by many 'closed' conspiracy-riddled social networking sites, as well as the now infamous, and batshit crazy, far-right conspiracy theory, QAnon.

The internet search engine is the biggest confirmation bias tool there has ever been. Looking for evidence of something you think may be true? Chances are you will find some site or network that 'confirms' it. Looking for evidence to disprove something you *don't* think is true? Chances are you can find that, too. And all regardless of the validity of the belief about which you're enquiring. It doesn't take much to lose your faith in mainstream media nowadays, people on all sides do so all the time, and once you start looking for other sources of news, and *believing* that any source can be 'legitimate', a whole world of falsehood opens up in front of you. There's all sorts of conspiracy theories, and communities with dangerous beliefs to welcome you with open arms. There's a whole buffet of bullshit to believe.

And as discussed, if people feel ostracised from a community, they will look for acceptance elsewhere. This happens with conspiracy theorists, too. People who are dismissed or ridiculed for their conspiratorial leanings, may simply harden their beliefs and look for acceptance elsewhere. For example, the computer scientist Shruti Phadke has studied Reddit users and their likelihood of joining conspiracy theory groups. She found that banning people from subreddits (user-created communities on the website) or 'downvoting' people's inaccurate posts, pushed them away from these open political discussion groups and into more conspiracy theory-based discussion groups, where they then found acceptance. 'It's as if they're being shunned by other communities, getting ostracised and then they go into these conspiracy communities and find a home for their thoughts.'[65]

In this way, social media seems to make it easier for false or dangerous views to be consolidated. In providing a home for the believers, it incubates their beliefs.

Our social media platforms are also guilty of reinforcing harmful social aspirations and cultural norms. Just like in the real world, financial success and fame are presented as the most worthwhile and virtuous things to crave and work for online, with likes, followers and limelight, all ostensibly offering a route to happiness. Many social media users feel an unmatched delight when their follower numbers or likes rise, a delight that quickly becomes an obsession, and an obsession that ultimately leaves them deflated and dejected as the increase inevitably plateaus. I've felt this, and I'm fairly sure anyone who has experienced public limelight has as well. Fame is *not* a route to happiness. And neither is wealth (which we'll look at in Chapter 5). Yet the cultural norm persists:

> You must dream of being rich and famous
> Only then will life be painless

Ask a child today 'what do you want to be when you grow up?' and the answer you'll hear from some will be 'famous', bypassing the normal youthful wishes of becoming a superhero, firefighter or astronaut, to instead wish for a nebulous objective they regard as some sort of ultimate triumph. I look forward to the day when the desire to be famous is thoroughly debunked and derided, when it's recognised as simply a morally indiscriminate, and mostly unhelpful side-effect, of doing something of note.

While my evidence for kids wanting to be famous is purely anecdotal, there *have* actually been surveys of children which reveal their early thirst for accumulating wealth: 'One in five children aged up to 10 years old say they "just want to be rich" when asked what they would like to be when they grow up.'[66] Social media and the internet search engine provide a nurturing and supporting platform for countless detrimental and mind-numbing social norms, just as they do for fake news and fake values.

100 Years Of Post-Truth 1: Muddying The Waters

We've seen how fake news moves faster than truth on social media.

And we've seen how messages that include extremities and expletives move faster than calm, measured criticism.

But another aspect of the quick spread of lies – and something that the corporate world knows, only too well – is that truth also moves slower (sometimes grinding to a complete halt) when conflicting information is presented alongside it, regardless of the information's authenticity.

If there is disagreement on a subject, or, at least, if we *perceive* there to be disagreement, then we have to stop, study and analyse the evidence *ourselves* in order to get to the truth. Most people don't have time for that, so they default to whatever their tribe's position is on the matter. Facts are then framed as emotional choices, rather than provable absolutes. This is how you muddy the waters. Confusing the public and manufacturing distrust prevents truth its safe passage.

Throughout the 1950s, the tobacco industry spent immense amounts of money pioneering this strategy. They emphasised uncertainty, doubt, and expert disagreement, in order to prevent the scientific *fact* – that smoking cigarettes are incredibly harmful to one's health – from becoming widely accepted among the general public.

Now, of course, this was the tobacco industry simply protecting its profits. Once again, if we take the systems perspective, it was the profit-incentive that pushed them into lying and scamming the public. They were just playing the game.

The strategy itself is exceptionally easy to implement. Worryingly so, considering the vast effect it can have on public awareness and acceptance. If you're able to fire out as much hot air as possible into a discussion, you will create hesitancy. You do not need to present solid, contradicting evidence or water-tight arguments (or even *half-decent* ones!), you just have to make enough noise to disorientate people, derail the discussion, and cause a small minority of people to question the science. Basically; if nobody really knows the truth, people can believe whatever they want, and companies, governments, or individuals can carry on profiting, thanks to the uncertainty they've created.

When you're at the forefront of a very wealthy industry, you can keep this schtick up for a long time.

In 1964, the US Surgeon General released an independent advisory committee report, that had considered more than 7,000 published papers; they concluded that cigarettes were indeed causing a lung cancer epidemic that was impossible to ignore. The science was clear, and this had a profound effect on the public, prompting many smokers to quit. But the tobacco companies held their ground. They went on denying that cigarettes cause cancer, and continued muddying the waters for, astoundingly, another 35 years![67] Huge amounts of money was put into the spread of disinformation. Disinformation they *knew* was killing people.

For years, we have seen the same strategy implemented to ramp up support for climate change denial.

Since 1997, the Koch Brothers alone have spent $145 billion attacking climate change science and policy solutions.[68] On top of that, the world's five largest oil and gas companies (BP, Shell, ExxonMobil, Chevron & Total) spend approximately $200 million, *every year,* on lobbying designed to control, delay, or block climate change policies.[69] Most recently, as global accords such as the 2015 Paris Climate Agreement have been put in place (which you would think would make these industries finally play ball), we've actually seen them up their efforts, and spend over $1 billion over a 3 year period.[70]

Just to exemplify the depth of the sickness: fossil fuel industries have also been found to have taken out patents on electric cars and solar technology, purely to suppress the development of those technologies.[71]

Peculiarly, climate change denial and scepticism are mainly found in the English-speaking world. But, actually, maybe this isn't so peculiar after all. There has been massive amounts of money spent on denial propagandising by English-speaking companies, publishing disinformation in English-speaking media outlets.[72]

It's also no coincidence that it is these parts of the world that we find the most dedication to self-interest and short-term profit. 'It's the countries where neoliberalism is most hegemonic [...] that have bred the most active denial campaigns,' says the sociologist Riley Dunlap, who studies the climate denial movement.[73] It's clear that, as we saw with the tobacco industry's efforts, the short-term profit motive (a motive native to the western, or English-speaking world) is the root cause of *this* reprehensible behaviour too.

Wherever the profit-motive is most sacred, you will find the most science denial.

These next two phrases aren't particularly revelatory:

- Money is power.
- Smoking kills.

They are both self-evident. But the thing is, they really don't go far enough.

Smoking kills. Yes. But try this for size: the self-interested, short-term profit incentive also kills.

It was the motivation of our socioeconomic system, the free market, that pushed the tobacco industry towards unethical behaviour, in order to protect their business. Smoking continues to be one of the most preventable causes of death in the world today.[74]

It was the motivation of our socioeconomic system that pushed the fossil fuel industry towards unethical behaviour in order to protect itself. We are probably not too far away from seeing climate change join smoking, in becoming one of the most preventable causes of death in the world.[75]

These are just two examples of an economically motivated assault on truth. They have both had massive consequences for human health on a global scale. But, of course, it's not just the corporate world using 'muddying the waters' as a go-to tactic. The same strategy we see in the corporate world is used in the political domain too; create noise, even nonsensical noise, that sow seeds of doubt in just enough people, and you will prevent (or at least delay) progress.

Politicians are at it on a daily basis; simply refuting facts, while providing no compelling argument against the fact in question. And now that the news cycle moves so quickly, they don't even have to deal with the circumstances of their lying or manufactured doubts. Something else will soon come along, to take the spotlight away from their spin or lies.

Truth has never been a clean and free-flowing stream. Muddying the waters has been a tactic used often. Thanks to our socioeconomic system (with a lot of assistance from the internet, and the polarisation it fuels), its waters are becoming ever murkier, and much harder to clean.

Truth In The Future

As if matters couldn't get any worse, ascertaining truth in the future looks like it'll be even *more* difficult. We are now extremely close to the point where we can no longer trust video as evidence.

Waltzing Off The Face Of The Earth's line 'you can't trust your own eyes' is not hyperbolic or metaphorical. It is quite literal.

A recent example of the progress in AI-based video technology shows a fake video of President Nixon reading his 'failure speech' for the moon landing (that of course, thankfully, never had to be read).[76] It may look a little ropey right now to us, but it's honestly not all that far away from being believable is it? Remember, this level of technical mastery will probably appear comically amateur in a few years time, given the speed of progress in these technologies (just as *The Matrix* or the early *Star Wars* films are mocked now for their rudimentary visual effects).

We can only live in hope that an equally impressive technology progresses with the same speed, one capable of identifying between natural and doctored footage.

/ / / / / / / / /

In a society where no real systemic changes are being made, we will continue on our downward spiral. The remainder of **Waltzing Off The Face Of The Earth** focuses on what felt like key moments of intellectual and social decline during the year I was writing the track, and the years preceding.

Examples Of The Downward Spiral: Guns

I started writing the lyrics of **Waltzing Off The Face Of The Earth** in the
summer of 2019, not long after two shootings had taken place at Walmart stores
in the space of one week (two employees shot dead in Southaven, Mississippi and
the famous El Paso, Texas shooting by a white nationalist domestic terrorist).[77] The
fact that shootings are now so prevalent that they happen in supermarkets resulted
in a *Wall Street Journal* article leading with the headline, 'Walmart Workers' New
Security Threat Is Active Shooters, Not Shoplifters'.[78]

> There's been a shooting at a Walmart
> So put guns on every shopping cart

Shootings just keep on happening, and little to nothing gets done in way of
prevention. A common suggestion, that comes from a blinkered individualist
perspective, is that we should all just 'tool up'; acquiring guns to secure our own
personal safety. Not a surprising conclusion to come to, for some, in an era of
systematised self-interest; and when there is intensive lobbying and propagandising
to 'help' you reach that conclusion (the National Rifle Association spent a record
$9.6 million over 2017–18 to further its aims of installing gun-friendly politicians,
passing gun-friendly laws, and keeping Americans armed).[79]

This insistence, that more firearms are the answer to the problem of gun violence,
seems to be one of the most glaring confirmations of society's downward spiral. A
firearm may give *you* more protection as an individual, but simply as a matter of
probability, the more individuals with firearms within a society, the more unsafe
that society will be. Gun ownership worsens the very problem it professes to solve.
You may as well be suggesting more chocolate gateaux to combat obesity.

Examples Of The Downward Spiral: Refugees

> There's dead kids on the beach

In 2015, a three-year-old Syrian boy made global headlines, after a photo emerged
of his drowned body washed up on a beach. It was an image that spread far and
wide, and triggered what, at the time, felt like a real moment of shared reflection
and coming change. Where there *was* immediate and genuine moral outrage about
the little boy's fate at the time, the news cycle quickly moved on and the usual
suspects turned against refugees once more.

Throughout the whole time we were writing this album, refugees were making perilous journeys across the Mediterranean Sea. Week after week, we saw the photos: desperate people packed into dinghies, fleeing war, human rights violations, and the effects of climate change. Yet, here in Europe, our welcome continues to be ambivalent, at best.[80] We continue to turn a blind eye to violence against refugees, on land and at sea,[81] and ignore the horrific nature of refugee camps, where children even as young as 10 are attempting suicide.[82]

Examples Of The Downward Spiral: Religious Intolerance

In 2019, parents began protesting outside of primary schools in Birmingham, concerned about the introduction of a new, compulsory relationships education programme. The programme introduces children to the concept of different types of families, including same-sex couples. Some parents, mistakenly, believed the programmes were actually 'promoting' LGBT+ ways of life, which was against their faith, and threatened to pull their children out of the school, while calling for teachers to be sacked.

> Bigoted parents decide what teachers teach

The only mention of 'LGBT' on the government website for the programme is as follows:

> Families of many forms provide a nurturing environment for children. (Families can include for example, single parent families, LGBT parents, families headed by grandparents, adoptive parents, foster parents and carers amongst other structures.)[83]

This simple fact about a reality of human life, and the relationships all children will come to recognise, was unfortunately deemed too much for some local dogmatists. This frustrated me greatly at the time, and only served to highlight how much work there is still to be done, to quell the intolerance of archaic religious views. The more young people who grow up knowing there is nothing wrong, uncommon, or remarkable about being LGBT+, the less homophobic bullying we will see in our schools and in our societies. We'll revisit this theme in detail in Chapter 5.

Each Has Their Own Truth

I can't help thinking the answer to a lot of our problems here regarding truth, trust, and tribalism, is that we simply need to disseminate facts with greater ferocity, in order to persuade those with misled beliefs. But tell me, dear reader, how often do the fact-based arguments that you use in debate with your online adversaries or political opponents, actually work? I'd imagine, not a lot. It appears, as humans, we opt to dismiss factual evidence if it doesn't configure with our deeply held political, or spiritual, beliefs. Instead, we search out evidence that verifies our own beliefs. Which is the very essence of confirmation bias.

So, the situation regarding post-truth is actually more severe than we think. Each of us has our own reality, with our own set of facts, and we accept that reality, without question. We save our questions exclusively for the other side, ('How can *they* think that? How can *they* support that party? How can *they* believe that?!') Our filter bubbles continue to provide us with justification for our beliefs, helping us ignore whichever factual information we choose.

Simply shouting truths *louder* is not going to rectify our situation.

So, what then? If we can't even agree on what is actually real, there's no hope of agreeing on what is morally correct or socially judicious.[84] We become deaf to anything that isn't authorised or championed by our own side and, at the same time, ignorant of any wider truths. Our tribalism, (which appears to be our main driver at this point) pushes us towards hate, while blocking and ignoring reasons to show compassion, patience, or civility. Continuous outrage and polarisation appears unstoppable.

> If love is blind
> Then hatred is deaf

What I meant by this phrase is that if true love is supposedly this feeling which blossoms, without regard to what the recipient of our love looks like, then hatred seems to be this feeling that blossoms, without regard to what the recipient of our hatred *says*.

When our group allegiances are so strong and inflexible, we become deaf to facts and dedicated only to tribal anger. Any points of view or facts which are offered by the other side are dismissed and derided, without hesitation. Our hatred cannot be tamed or tempered; it is 'deaf' to outside influence.

The more we continue on this current trajectory, where our systems of communication feed polarisation and hostility, the more rigid our allegiances become, and the more unfriendly our demeanour becomes. Without systemic change our hatred will continue to be 'well fed'.

100 Years Of Post-Truth 2: Our Aversion To Fact

Let's look back at the history of truth. Or, at least, the history of our willingness to refuse to believe what is assuredly true. Scientists began to research this phenomenon as early as in the 1950s, when the theory of cognitive dissonance – the extreme discomfort of simultaneously having two thoughts or views that are in conflict with each other – was first developed by the social psychologist Leon Festinger.

For the purposes of a study, Festinger and his colleagues went to live with a doomsday prophet, Dorothy Martin, in Chicago. Martin had convinced a group of followers that beings called 'the Guardians' were coming to collect them in flying saucers, to save them from a coming flood.[85] Like a 1950s Louis Theroux, Festinger and his colleagues gradually earned her trust and were granted permission to observe the group. During cult activities they would analyse how Martin's followers dealt with the continuous disappointment as her predictions repeatedly failed to materialise. The psychologists watched with fascination, as followers continued to believe the predictions, despite the mounting evidence that they were wrong.

'A man with a conviction is a hard man to change', said Festinger in his 1957 book presenting the study:

> Tell him you disagree and he turns away. Show him facts or figures and he questions your sources. Appeal to logic and he fails to see your point [...] Suppose that he is presented with evidence, unequivocal and undeniable evidence, that his belief is wrong: what will happen? The individual will frequently emerge, not only unshaken, but even more convinced of the truth of his beliefs than ever before.[86]

To reduce the discomforting cognitive dissonance of, on the one hand, believing in Dorothy Martin's predictions yet, on the other, repeatedly seeing them proven wrong, her followers curiously refrained from revising their beliefs to match the evidence and, instead, doubled down. Why? Well, having quit their jobs, left their spouses, dropped out of college, and given away money and possessions to prepare for their 'departure', what choice did they have? They were so emotionally invested, and had given up so much, that the disappointing truth had to be ignored. Altering their beliefs at this point wasn't an option, they were committed to maintaining them, so instead, they focused on converting more followers. Why? Because, as Festinger wrote, 'If more and more people can be persuaded that the system of belief is correct, then clearly it must after all be correct.'[87]

Dorothy Martin's followers were using what is known in psychology as *motivated reasoning*. They were *motivated* to believe something. They were motivated by their own dedicated actions, by the amount they'd given up, they were convincing themselves to keep on believing. To walk away after they'd devoted so much time and effort to the group, would mean admitting to have acted incredibly stupidly. An issue, then, of self-esteem, really.

We generally reason our way to conclusions we favour, or are emotionally invested in, so upon confronting something that we do *not want* to believe, we ask ourselves '*must* I believe this?' and search for any shred of evidence that will allow us to disbelieve it. For Martin's followers, there was always another prediction to distract from the previous failed ones.

Similarly, when we *want* to believe something, we ask ourselves '*can* I believe this?' and search for any reasoning that will *allow* us to believe it. If we are motivated to remain true to our beliefs, we will find a way to continue believing – we will seek out agreeable and corroborating information, and learn it more easily, and we will avoid, devalue or argue against any information that contradicts our beliefs.[88]

What motivated Dorothy Martin's followers? Was it just a case of bad decisions and then protecting their self-esteem? What good reasoning is there to motivate *anyone* to *ever* discard truth?

Group loyalty.

Once again, it is this familiar fear of ostracism we've already looked at. We allow ourselves to absorb information that supports our beliefs, and banish information that opposes them, in order to remain true to our group.

Whether people 'believe' in evolution or not has nothing to do with whether they understand the theory of it – if you happen to be in a religious group that believes in young-Earth creationism, saying you 'don't believe in evolution' is just another way of proving your religiosity and, therefore, your group allegiance.[89]

When something is dragged into the political arena, we often prioritise tribal belonging over considerations of truth. For example, a PEW Research Centre study on the politics of climate change showed that a high level of science knowledge didn't make Republicans any more likely to say they believed in climate change.[90] Their 'scepticism' remained strong even in the face of a good factual grasp of climate science. Whether they believe the science or not, they publicly choose to express a position that is against it, in order to protect their group identity.

What should be an issue of physics becomes an issue of petty tribal identity.

Similarly, presenting anti-vax parents with hard, scientific evidence which proves vaccines do not cause autism, does nothing to persuade the parents to vaccinate their children.[91] Group allegiance overrides.

We can even go back to the infamous presidential inauguration crowd size debate, mentioned in Chapter 1. A study found that even when shown the clear, visible evidence, Trump supporters *still* disagreed that his inauguration crowd was smaller.[92]

Dismissing any clear evidence that conflicts with our position, is described as *expressive responding*. This is essentially where we view factual questions, not as questions to be answered truthfully but, instead, as questions to be answered in the way that expresses your team 'colours'.

This isn't a consequence of people lacking intelligence, or of an inability to comprehend evidence, it's down to the simple fact that we value the comfort and safety of a social group remarkably highly. *So* highly, in fact, that truth becomes subordinate to group values and beliefs.

> Trump supporters, therefore, would misidentify the inaugural photos not because they actually believe that the larger crowd is Trump's, but because that response is the sort of thing a Trump supporter ought to give.[93]

We stick to our guns, and stick it to truth.

This is especially the case when the truth in question doesn't really effect us; as the anthropologist and psychologist Pascal Boyer explains: 'Having social support, from an evolutionary standpoint, is far more important than knowing the truth about some facts that do not directly impinge on your life.'[94]

Returning to the example of climate change denial among Republicans: if you take an ordinary member of the public, their individual actions appear to have no tangible effect on climate change, at least not to them anyway, so acting as if climate change isn't real, or as if it is inflated, has no adverse effect on their life. Therefore, they can deny climate change and not see any personal repercussions. It is, ostensibly, a 'safe' belief to hold. Now, the opposite option – agreeing with the scientific consensus – will put them at odds with their own social group and will see them shunned, ostracised, or otherwise disadvantaged – a direct negative outcome.

Which brings us to an interesting conclusion: in a way, these people are acting quite logically. Albeit selfishly.

/ / / / / / / / / /

Isn't it interesting how our socioeconomic system downplays how intrinsically communal we are? How we *thirst* for social support, and will believe anything in order to keep it? Capitalism focuses us on self-interest, and, in doing so, it ignores and rejects our integral need for community and compassion. The fear of being kicked out of our communities is *so* incredibly powerful, it effects our actual ability to accept truth. Yet this drive for social support is thought to be insignificant and uninformative to the way we structure our society.

/ / / / / / / / / /

So, what's the solution here? How do we get people to see truth, and act according to those truths?

It appears to me, that with each case being so deeply detailed and different, we must adjust our persuasion attempts according to what is motivating each person's specific denial.

Instead of pulling our hair out, shouting 'how can you disagree with facts?! You moron!', ridiculing the person and then bombarding them with more factual evidence, in a vain attempt to persuade them of their folly, we need to calmly ask ourselves, 'Why does this person *want* to disagree with the facts?'

We must identify the fears, ideologies, identity needs, and vested interests which stop individuals from accepting clearly provable evidence. If we want to convince an anti-vax parent that vaccines are safe, we first have to find out if they are fearful of medical intervention and possible side-effects, or if they are a big-pharma conspiracy theorist, or if, deep down, they are just scared of being ousted from their social support group. We must be civil, ask questions, and listen patiently. Which is incredibly difficult, when someone holds a view that you consider worthy of contempt, of course, but it is essential, if we are going to be able to persuade them of their fault.

Remember, treating someone with a compete lack of respect and civility is the very thing that will harden someone's beliefs further. The social psychologist Troy Campbell says:

> One of the most important ways to inoculate people from false information is to befriend them [...] There's a time for the middle finger, and a time to put it away.[95]

Checking Into The Dreamer's Hotel 2

It is clear that we need a more compassionate discourse, and a more compassionate society. This is the what **The Dreamer's Hotel** was built to encourage. When creating the concept though, I didn't imagine it as a newly built, shiny, modern complex. No, I imagined it would be a rather deserted, perhaps even dilapidated, old building, suffering from years of neglect, with very few guests left occupying its shabby rooms. There are very few people left in society who have managed not to get sucked into constant tribal outrage, very few left actually embodying compassion.

Five stars but all rooms are vacant

Everyone seems too busy defending their 'honour' in online duels to have the time to 'check-in'. And that's the truth; modern living leaves us with little time to find perspective and civility, and little time to grow our capacity for compassion. In the spare time we do have, tired and overworked, the allure of a heated debate and the 'release' of insulting someone we disagree with often overpowers a more patient, and compassionate, social contribution.

I wrote the song about my personal experience of living both inside and outside of the hotel. I try, of course, to consistently exemplify the positive qualities symbolised by **The Dreamer's Hotel** but, same as anyone, I can easily be dragged back outside to revel in the more uncivil or primitive behaviours. The appeal of petty point-scoring, of stubborn incivility, of demonising others – especially when acts of selfishness, corruption, and greed are so common – these emotions and actions can be irresistible. Righteous rage can be seductive. Hurling insults can be very tempting ...

These unhelpful behaviours are habitual too, and even if we manage to break out of a bad habit, we're hard pressed not to slip back into it, especially if the habit occurs all around us. It's extremely difficult for a drug addict to even start the journey to sobriety, until they remove themselves from the environment and social circles that perpetuate their addiction. It is the same with our own hostility.

Mindfulness/Practising Compassion

For me, this is where mindfulness comes in. Mindfulness is a tool I find especially helpful for regulating and mastering my own reactions and behaviour. To be mindful and present, in the conversations you are having, enables you to keep an eye on your demeanour and on any corrupting, hostile emotions. Which is another reason why the hotel metaphor felt so appropriate; the term 'checking-in' is also used within the mindfulness literature to describe paying attention to, and analysing, what is happening in the present moment. To 'check-in' with yourself is to become aware of the here and now – your thoughts, sensations and emotions – enabling you to avoid being directed by compulsive waves of emotion. When checking-in regularly, you begin to notice any subtler changes in yourself, and any broader trends of emotion. Being mindful then becomes like living with more detail, awareness, and therefore with a greater sense of control and equanimity. I have made an introductory podcast to mindfulness meditation should anyone be looking to start.[96]

If we live each day on autopilot, caught up with what angers or disgusts us, without curious analysis, and without pause for thought, we become increasingly accustomed to the overwhelming presence of hostility, to the point that it becomes normalised and acceptable to us. Without compassion, mindfulness, and perspective, we're all, basically, slowly becoming intolerable. While simultaneously perceiving *others* to be the increasingly intolerable ones!

Just as we have difficulty noticing the signs of ageing on our faces, because we see ourselves in the mirror every morning, it's hard for us to gauge the speed with which our society is changing and the magnitude with which it is souring. When we're living it every day, we're distracted by the onslaught of fleeting intricacies, and fail to see the larger trends of change.

Checking into **The Dreamer's Hotel** offers respite from the onslaught beyond its walls. Respite from the division and hostility. Relating this back to the music; the harmonic nature of the chorus – in stark contrast to the barren mindless fury of the verses – creates a space that encourages reflection, perspective and a compassionate analysis. It is a place where we take a time-out from the hostility outside (epitomised by the verses) and pause to see the bigger picture. It is a place where those who dream of a better world can practice listening, practice patience, practice empathy – and ultimately, practice building that better world!

The Dalai Lama was asked what to do when someone approaches you with hostility. His answer was:

> Practise warm-heartedness.[97]

Note the word 'practise'.

The direction here is just as important as the action he is directing you to. He is directing you to *repeatedly* employ warm-heartedness, even if it fails (… and believe me, it *will* fail!). In those moments where it has no effect on the hostility you encounter, it may, of course, seem like a complete waste of time, but practising warm-heartedness is *very* worthwhile for three reasons.

Firstly, it means there's a chance you'll be proficient at warm-heartedness come the time you encounter someone who *can* be brought down from their tower of fury and persuaded to engage in dignified civil discussion. Secondly, practising warm-heartedness also means it will, over time, come to you more naturally, although not without considerable effort, of course (remember; you're going up against a lifetime of learnt mistrust and bad faith, and where much of your human communication has been besieged by incivility, blind group allegiance, and anger). Thirdly, practising warm-heartedness will help *spread* compassion, it has a wonderfully contagious effect (as we'll look at shortly).

The Burden Of Knowledge

A fair and logical response to my suggestion of restraint and compassion, may be: 'Why do *I* have to make all the effort? If others hold views I consider bad, and are hostile *on top of that*, why must it come down to *me* to try and remove their hostility? Why must *I* have to use considerable effort being the calm one?'.

It is because of the *burden of knowledge*. You are, now, I hope, coming to understand the serious and precarious position we find ourselves in, right now, as a civilisation, and that the normal solutions and short-term fixes are no longer enough. Hopefully you're also coming to understand that courageous compassion is one of the few things that will help haul us out of this mess, (alongside serious systematic change). It is, therefore, up to us to spread this knowledge and perspective.

If we can understand the root causes of people's ill-held beliefs, and understand our human vulnerability, as well as our need for group protection, then we can genuinely approach each individual with compassion. If we grasp that broader web of influence we can then employ compassion with less and less effort. It becomes the logical reaction. Eventually, even the instinctual reaction. If we understand the underpinnings of someone's behaviour, the causality, we do not see an angry person, we see a closed book ready to be opened, however difficult it may be to read. We see a case to be cracked.

Compassion Is Contagious

When we behave in a compassionate manner, our bodies produce oxytocin – often dubbed the 'love hormone' – its effects are most obviously felt during hugs, massages, breastfeeding, and sex. Its warming sensation is an evolutionary reward mechanism, in place to encourage us to act with further compassion. Here's psychologist Dacher Keltner:

> We have found that when people perform behaviours associated with compassionate love – warm smiles, friendly hand gestures, affirmative forward leans – their bodies produce more oxytocin. This suggests compassion may be self-perpetuating: Being compassionate causes a chemical reaction in the body that motivates us to be even more compassionate.[98]

This is a pivotal point to remember; compassion grows stronger with *practice*. The Dalai Lama is right.

Kindness Of Interpretation

At the moment, one of the most lacking forms of compassion is *kindness of interpretation*. Put simply, this is how calmly and logically you interpret what people say and how people act. Sadly, it seems the norm is to jump to quick – and often unfair – conclusions regarding the behaviour or words of those we do not see eye-to-eye with.[99]

It struck me the other day, that a lot of this penchant for fury online may actually correspond with some of the problems that *Cognitive Behavioural Therapy* (CBT) is designed to deal with in our personal lives. CBT is a well-documented and helpful form of psychotherapy, in which regular negative thoughts are challenged, in order to alter unwanted behavioural patterns, or to treat mood disorders such as anxiety and depression. I've been using it myself, on and off, for several years now to help with my social anxiety, and the similarities struck me while recently completing an exercise.

When we make it our routine to ignore the context around other people's statements, or to take their words in bad faith (i.e. always assuming the absolute *worst* in what others say), we may be performing what, in CBT, is referred to as 'mind reading'.

This is a mental error often experienced with anxiety and depression. We experience an event, and then interpret it in a destructive, or excessively negative, light. The same occurs with our hostility towards others. If we have earmarked someone as an opponent or enemy, and assume we know their intentions, values, and motives, we often then incorrectly frame what they say. We shuffle through various evaluations of what we're seeing, determined to find the worst possible intention.

So, with CBT, an example would be: If someone you know walks by you in a hurry, and doesn't return a smile when they see you, you may believe that you did something wrong and they now clearly hate you. This is referred to as 'catastrophising'. When you are in the grip of the mind reading error, it does not occur to you to interpret this experience in a more charitable way. The other person may be stressed and running late to get somewhere. They may be listening to something on their phone and be completely distracted. They may have just received bad news, and can't bear to have any social interaction at that moment. Their behaviour may be influenced by any number of circumstances, yet you pick the most negative explanation, and assume their intentions. This struck me as similar to the way in which we stigmatise another person's political or social views, before understanding their intention or reasoning. Once again, unfortunately, we live by the maxim: 'don't waste my time with any context'. Our first (usually uncharitable) assumption sticks, and it is case closed.

We need to employ more charity in how we judge statements we disagree with, more compassion in how we interpret the words of people we dislike. We need to take things – if not in *good* faith, then at least in neutral faith – rather than instinctually assuming the worst in everything our opponents, or even strangers, do, or say.

Importance Of Curiosity

One of the best ways to stop yourself indulging in the aforementioned behaviour, and instead engage in successful, calm conversations – however difficult the subject matter – is to frame such conversations as fact-finding missions. To ask yourself, 'how has this person come to this conclusion?'.

We should be aiming to follow in the footsteps of the great philosopher Baruch Spinoza:

> I have striven not to laugh at human actions, not to weep at them, nor to hate them, but to understand them.[100]

Approaching any dialogue with curiosity is favourable, for two reasons. Firstly;

if you are committed to curiosity, the other person will feel listened to, which is important because when people don't feel listened to, or respected, they can become angry. We must give people dignity, and we can do this by, at the very least, listening to them. The social scientist Arthur C. Brooks says:

> The opposite of dignity is despair. And when there is despair, people lash out. Dignity is like air. [...] We can all restore someone's dignity – listen empathically to people you disagree with.[101]

Secondly; approaching a dialogue with curiosity is motivation for you to actually understand the other person's views. Which is pivotal in itself, but will also lessen your anger or hatred for the people with whom you disagree. If you discover what influenced and formed someone's beliefs, if you walk the same path that led them to their current actions, you are then free to blame the root causes, rather than the person. You can, of course, still believe their views to be stupid or abhorrent, but you are free from knee-jerk and all-encompassing fury.[102]

Different narratives, told by a variety of media channels and tribal groups, result in you living in an entirely different universe from your opponent. Remember; each online antagonist you argue with, and each political tribe that holds the other in contempt, has likely received a whole lifetime of experiences that differ from yours, birthing, and then moulding, their beliefs and indignation.

Which is why it is important to, as best you can, separate the belief, from the human. Target the ideas, not the person. Play the ball, not the man. It's difficult, of course, as it's far easier to condemn people than it is to condemn ideas. It takes no time at all to criticise – or simply insult – someone you disagree with. Whereas understanding the root causes of their beliefs, and targeting the systems that perpetuate them, is much more time-consuming. No wonder we just call each other a 'prick' and move on.

It is worth remembering, when coming up against an individual whose beliefs you dislike or even detest, that if you were to trade places with that person (i.e. if you had their genes, their parents, their upbringing, and their entire life experience), you too would hold *every* view that they hold. You would, of course, *be* them. The person you disagree with did not choose their genes. Just as they did not choose their parents, their upbringing or their culture.

People deserve compassion and civility – even those with views we consider to be anathema – because we are all victims of circumstance. Therefore, compassion is a wise default.

'You're Either Good Or You Are Evil'

Unfortunately, our *actual* default is the exact opposite of compassion. Each of us has a deep-seated tendency to categorise others as either 'good' or 'evil', and then sear them, like cattle, with the indelible mark of a hot branding iron. This black-and-white, all-or-nothing labelling, gives us an excuse to withhold our compassion. It sort of 'relieves' us of the need to act compassionately, believing, as we do, that it is unwarranted; evil people simply do not deserve it.

This reductive, binary tendency has been studied and categorised in psychoanalytic theory as *splitting*. It is considered a defence mechanism, one which helps us deal with the frustrations and disappointments we experience as children.

We were all, at some point, let down and hurt by the very people we looked to for comfort and safety. These frustrations felt so unbearable at the time, we subconsciously protected ourselves by categorising people into one of two polar opposite positions. Everyone that frustrated us was evil, everyone who pleased us became perfect.

The psychoanalyst Melanie Klein argued that this was because as children, we struggle to integrate the two primary drives, love and hate: 'the earliest experiences of the infant are split between wholly good ones with "good" objects and wholly bad experiences with "bad" objects.'[103]

As we get older, we gradually, and painfully, begin to understand that, in reality, people are complex and cannot be split into these oversimplified ranks. We then begin to depolarise the two love and hate drives. A parent can be absent in some ways, yet gracious in others; someone can criticise us, without being evil or stupid; and we ourselves can have multiple genuine weaknesses, or faults, and yet still be a decent human being.

Accepting this more complicated reality is a struggle, though, and, as Klein says of our two primary drives, 'being able to balance [them] out [...] are tasks that continue into early childhood and indeed are never completely finished'.[104] Which is why we still obsess over good and evil as fixed binary categories, even though the truth is that none of us are these fixed Hollywood caricatures – the hero and the villain.

No one is entirely good. We all believe in, or have at some point believed in, bad ideas, false ideas, dangerous ideas. We all have made mistakes and made bad decisions, and will continue to occasionally do so! I should think it impossible for someone to be permanently and wholly evil. As is often mentioned, even Hitler was a vegetarian, and sympathetic to the suffering of animals!

These terms simply aren't helpful. They're just judgments. Describing someone as 'evil' is helpful only to the point of it being a warning of any immediate danger. Otherwise, it tells us nothing about *why* this 'evil' person acts the way they do. It implies a natural, inexplicable, depraved instinct for wrongdoing and immorality, which only serves to stunt enquiry. It hinders us in finding out how to address the aberrant behaviour, and, therefore, understanding how to *prevent* people behaving like that, in future. In this way, it is a direct obstacle to progress. Why? Because it terminates our curiosity. The French philosopher known as Alain said 'never say that men are wicked; don't ever say that's their nature. Look for the pin.'[105]

To be human is simply to be an accumulation of everything you've experienced, alongside the limitations of your genetic composition. We're a coalescence of it all.

Narcissism

Take a guess at which trait decreases your ability to see humans as complex beings, and increases your likelihood of reductively classifying them as 'good' or 'evil'.

If you said 'narcissism', then you guessed correctly (or maybe you just read the header of this section).

The more self-interested we are, the more we cast our friends and foes as strictly and wholly 'good' and 'evil'. Splitting is a narcissistic defence mechanism.

Now, what does our socioeconomic system incentivise in us?

Narcissistic tendencies. Or, simply, as we've discussed, self-interest.

Our system motivates, and actually *rewards*, narcissism. We become more likely to define others as either 'good' or 'evil', society becomes more divided and hostile, and that further justifies and reinforces our self-interested tendencies.

My routing here is slightly reductive, yes, but there are clearly some paths that systemic pressures go some way towards clearing, and other paths that systemic pressures leave to become overgrown and difficult to navigate. The path towards narcissism is clear, but the path that leads towards compassion and understanding? Well, you will need a sizeable machete to chop down the obstacles.

Narcissim And Wealth

Over the course of a host of studies, social psychologist Paul Piff found that as people grow wealthier, they are more likely to feel entitled and to exploit others, as well as more likely to cheat, and *less* likely to give to charity.[106]

One study found that the richer participants were more likely to consider 'stealing or benefiting from things to which they were not entitled' than those from a less affluent background. In another study (almost too cartoon-like in its comically evil nature to believe), participants primed to *feel* rich helped themselves to more sweets – which they were told were meant as treats for children in a study in the next room – than those who were primed to feel disadvantaged. Piff also discovered that wealthier people were also more likely to agree with statements such as 'I honestly feel I'm just more deserving than other people'.

It appears that the more wealth we claim, the less compassionate we become, and this strengthens our ability to *justify* our accumulation of wealth. It even allows us to justify inequality more broadly.

This feeling of increased entitlement and superiority is central to narcissism, and once again, is systemically incentivised.

It is not the rich who are 'the problem', per se. Going around proclaiming 'eat the rich' isn't really targeting the root cause, and your tirade shall simply be never-ending. The rich and narcissistic have simply been following the rules of the game, goaded into socially destructive forms of behaviour, through being repeatedly rewarded for their self-interest. As Piff says: 'We're not suggesting rich people are bad at all, but rather that psychological effects of wealth have these natural effects.'[107]

Evil, narcissism, immorality; they are all learnt, incentivised, motivated. The way to destroy them is through curiosity, compassion, and most importantly, structural change.

Checking Into The Dreamer's Hotel 3

As mentioned earlier; **The Dreamer's Hotel** is a place of empathy, civility and compassion. These can sound like old, utopian, hippy ideals; the softest, or even most feeble of human behaviours. Many, including myself, commonly ignore calls for more kindness and respect in the world, negating their worth as too nebulous, soppy, overly simplified, or naive.

Compassion has been treated with derision in the past, too; the philosopher Immanuel Kant, for example, notoriously campaigned against being 'infected' by another's pain, and claimed that actions motivated by compassion have no worth:

> Such benevolence is called soft-heartedness and should not occur at all among human beings.[108]

Don't be fooled, though. Here, Kant was wrong. Warm-heartedness is not *soft*-heartedness; to offer warmth, you must have fire.

In truth; warm-heartedness is an incredibly difficult trait to embody, in a world so hellbent on the opposite. Especially in a world where everyone is out to catch everyone else out. To expose and pounce upon every mistake. To belittle or demean every conviction. Compassion and civility require courage, and serious levels of self-control. Warm-heartedness is a character trait that should, in fact, be lionised as the height of nobility and bravery. Chances are, if you display it, you will have to deal with incivility and insults with next-level, Gandhian strength, restraint and patience.

To Believe People Can Change Is A Revolutionary Act

As we've explored, it's clear that civility can become generalised over time (next-level Gandhian strength, restraint, and patience *can* pay off!), but, in order to start that friendly feedback loop, we need to have faith in people's ability to change.

It's often easy to forget – especially online where we all seem so rigid and stand-offish – the fact that people *can* actually change their beliefs and *can* edit their ideas and outlooks. We act as if everyone is an obstinate character, with their mindset and convictions set in stone. We are, of course, all playing the cards we've been dealt, yes, but we are still a dramatically adaptable and inquisitive creature, one that is ever-developing and capable of serious redemption and reorientation.

I want to highlight some examples where even those who seemed fully entrenched in hate were able to change for the better, through kindness, gentle persuasion and respectful discussion. As Martin Luther King Jr. correctly pointed out back in 1957:

> Darkness cannot drive out darkness: only light can do that. Hate cannot drive out hate: only love can do that.[109]

Megan Phelps-Roper was a member of the Westboro Baptist Church, infamous for its anti-Semitic and anti-LGBT+ rhetoric, and for its cruel picketing of funerals for military personnel, AIDS victims, and even children murdered in mass-shootings. From the age of five, Megan was present at those picket lines with the rest of her family, holding placards reading 'Gays are Worthy of Death', 'God Hates Fags', or many other of the church's hateful declarations, which she was too young to comprehend.

In 2012, twenty years later, Megan left the church, citing the gentle criticism and compassionate discourse of Twitter users for befriending her, gradually opening her eyes, and encouraging introspection and perspective.

She was patiently led out of a lifetime of indoctrination, persuaded to walk away from a tight and loving family unit – the *only* support group she had – through civility and compassion:

> It took time, but eventually these conversations planted seeds of doubt in me. My friends on Twitter took the time to understand Westboro's doctrines, and in doing so, they were able to find inconsistencies I'd missed my entire life. [...] My friends on Twitter didn't abandon their beliefs or their principles – only their scorn. They channeled their infinitely justifiable offense and came to me with pointed questions tempered with kindness and humor. They approached me as a human being, and that was more transformative than two full decades of outrage, disdain and violence.[110]

Another fascinating example of persuasion through friendship comes from the story of musician and activist Daryl Davis. Daryl has a rather odd hobby: he befriends white supremacists. An odd hobby for anyone, sure, but especially for an African American! In doing so, Davis has collected over 200 Ku Klux Klan robes from men who have quit the Klan and denounced their previously deeply held bigoted views thanks to his influence. This takes incredible levels of compassion, patience and bravery, and proves even the most rigid and obnoxious ideologues can be shown the light.[111]

Lastly, let's look at the cases of two founding members of the American non-profit organisation Life After Hate.[112] Angela King became a member of a neo-Nazi group, after they welcomed her aggressive nature (a nature instilled by her parents, who she describes as racist and homophobic). She was befriended by a Jamaican woman while serving time in jail. Over time, this woman was able to change King's mind on white supremacy.

King's Life After Hate partner, Tony McAleer, grew through the ranks of the

White Aryan Resistance, after being influenced by, among other things, the racist elements in the British punk rock scene. He became the spokesman for the neo-Nazi movement in Canada, throughout the 1990s. Following the birth of his child, he began to notice changes in his outlook. Changes which were solidified upon befriending the Jewish speaker, and leadership trainer, Dov Baron. An epiphany for McAleer came when he brought up his white nationalist views to Dov, who replied: 'That's not who you are. That's what you did, but that's not who you are. I see you.'[113] At which point, McAleer broke down into tears.

McAleer suggests that neither he nor others who embrace white supremacy are drawn to the movement by its conspiratorial ideology, that the white race is under threat: 'The ideology is secondary,' he says.[114] Rather, they find acceptance in a group of people like themselves. People angry and hurt by emotional trauma in their life. McAleer speaks of the cold relationship with his father, and beatings by administrators at the Catholic school he attended, as some of the influences that set him down his dark path. Though it may seem a contentious point, it is consistently proven that the people we label as 'evil' are those whose lives have been *most devoid* of compassion. Often they have suffered serious emotional and physical neglect or abuse in order to be able to commit such evil acts or hold such evil views. 'It's the need to belong that makes them susceptible to white nationalism. If a child had to believe that the Earth was flat in order to get that attention and acceptance from that community, he'd believe it.'[115]

There it is again, as with Dorothy Martin and her cult followers, people believe whatever is necessary, in order to remain accepted in their support group. For us, as *Homo sapiens*, the striving for belonging is inherent. To be accepted is to be safe.

Wired For Sociality

We will do whatever it takes, and believe whatever it takes, to ensure our safe inclusion in a community. We do this because we are profoundly wired for sociality. On a neurological level, the same parts of the brain that react to physical pain also react to emotional pain – for example when we feel neglected, excluded or shamed.[116]

From day one, human connection is so important. Socially isolated infants, not receiving proper touch and affection, will have impaired cognitive development and their actual physical growth will be stunted.[117]

Furthermore, solitary confinement, perhaps the most extreme form of ostracism

– and a tactic still used widely in prison systems throughout the world – literally causes brain damage. The psychiatrist Stephanie Cacioppo said: "We see solitary confinement as nothing less than a death penalty by social deprivation".[118]

Whether we understand our inherent drive for community and connection or not, we act in all sorts of baffling and extreme ways in order to keep ourselves securely connected.

Our political landscape has mastered mockery, sarcasm, extreme hyperbole, sharp insults, condescending dismissal and mass ridicule as the norm for coping with differences. It will take intentional, sustained effort to counter the deep conditioning of this culture, and we can each do our part.

We must learn to replace our judgment with patience, and our anger with curiosity. That is how we rebuild burnt bridges, and maybe even persuade people to cross back over them.

To check in to **The Dreamer's Hotel** is by no means a form of escapism. You still live and work in the world beyond the hotel walls, you just have a sense of duty to understand the deeper perspectives and their root causes, and possess the will to face them, with courage. A willingness to break the cycle of endless outrage and hostility, and to refuse the allure of continuous contempt is, in itself, a form of activism. To break this cycle is to rehabilitate and revolutionise yourself and then, hopefully, many of those you subsequently encounter. It is revolution, of the self and of society.

Pick Your Targets

But, hey, don't be fooled by all this serenity! I probably seem like I'm verging on stoicism or Buddhism here, what with the dedication to restraint and composure I'm preaching. It can take phenomenal levels of Zen to show patience and compassion to those with whom you vehemently disagree, and I am very aware that many people simply *are* intolerable and unchangeable. Many will never mirror your good will, nor friendliness.

To this, I simply say; pick your targets. Don't waste vital energy on the older, more rigid, more pathetically hive-minded or disastrously stubborn dogmatists. Those with no curiosity, and no ability for self-criticism, cannot be saved. If you found yourself stuck in a lift with Nigel Farage would there be any point in making calm, curious conversation?

Conserve your energy.

This should go without saying, but certainly do not speak to violent extremists or anyone that could ever put you in danger. I'm not telling you to be a brave and selfless, proselytising, kindness warrior, searching out difficult people in an attempt to pacify them. Your part is as simple as not diving into conflict, online *or* offline, when someone criticises you, or your views, and not reacting with hostility in conversation or debate. If we each do our little bit to normalise compassion and civility, we'll be on the right track.

5 Human Complexity

5.1 The King

The Great Orgy Between Archaic And Modern Humans

Like a gang of Liam Gallaghers (except even hairier), *Homo sapiens* swaggered, all newly bipedal and vocal, onto the stage around 200,000 years ago. Over the millennia, we shared this stage with many other hominins,[1] and much like the common perception of rock 'n' roll's sex and drug-fuelled lifestyle, we all occasionally slept with each other too. We coexisted and interbred with Neanderthals and Denisovans, and today we can have up to 4% Neanderthal in our DNA.[2] (Though I should point out that this metaphor doesn't quite work anymore because the common perception of sex, drugs and rock'n'roll is rather out of date now in the 2020s. I find that a biscuit being dunked in tea is about as titillating an insertion as you'll see backstage today.)

The Neanderthals and the Denisovans were the last of the other hominins and our closest evolutionary cousins. They became extinct around 30,000 to 40,000 years ago, leaving the whole stage, and all the hominin humpin' to us Sapiens.

So, why did us *Homo sapiens* outlast the other early humans?

Is it because we were more intelligent? Neanderthals are often regarded as stupid – in fact in 1866, the German biologist Ernst Haeckel proposed they be called *Homo stupidus*[3] (Ernst, you're brutal mate). But with their larger lung capacity, their larger muscles and their larger brain size, they may well have had more stamina, strength, and smarts than us ... so how on Earth did we conquer the planet instead?

Our Superpower

Have you ever been at a natural history museum and felt like the artist impressions or the waxwork replicas of our early human ancestors were a bit ... creepy? You probably thought this because just like all living primates today, they had pigmented eyes. Melanin tinted their outer eyes – or specifically, their sclera – dark brown, making their eyes like mysterious, undefined marbles, and their gaze very difficult to interpret. Like bodyguards or poker players watching us carefully behind dark sunglasses, the direction of their gaze was shielded, and therefore, their intentions hidden.

We are the only species to have universally white sclera, as well as a more prominent iris, making our gaze easily readable, even from a distance. The adaptive advantages that this type of eye provides would have been selected over tens of thousands of years of human evolution. The ability to follow someone's gaze and gain emotional clues from their eye movement increased our ability to communicate, cooperate, and trust one another, and if we could better trust and cooperate with one another, that gave us a better chance of survival.[4]

We also happen to be the only species – that we know of, anyway – that blushes. Blushing is such an odd act, and there's many unanswered questions as to why we do it, but what we can say is that blushing helps reveal our innermost emotions and shows very clearly that we care what others think.

Aside from these physical aides to our intraspecies communications; humans are also the only species to have developed intricate language, enabling cooperation between individuals and groups, and even down through generations, as information was recorded and passed through the ages, via everything from cave paintings, to the written word.

What am I getting at here? Well, it's becoming clear that *Homo sapiens* conquered the planet because we were better able to cooperate with each other, better suited to trust each other, and better adapted to act compassionately with each other. That's likely how we outlasted other hominins. Our superpower is our prosociality.

Chimps Versus Humans

Chimpanzees, our closest living relatives, cooperate with each other somewhat,[5] they are courteous enough to warn each other if there happens to be a dangerous snake approaching and they are kind enough to inform each other where any sweet-ass honey is (the hyphen placement is pivotal to that sentence not being bizarrely vulgar). This, as well as lab studies,[6] show us that some level of altruism is well settled in us. As I touched on in Chapter 4, if humans and chimps show similar behaviour, it is most probable that our common ancestor already possessed these behaviours as well. That is to say; even before chimps and humans evolved, further back in the evolutionary tree, altruism was surfacing.

But these are examples of the kind of cooperation that serves to meet only the immediate needs of one individual. Some studies have shown that chimps are actually no more likely to choose an option that benefits them and another individual, over an option that only benefits themselves, even if the prize is exactly the same in both options.[7] Total douchebaggery right?

Humans, on the other hand, are an anomaly in the animal kingdom. Our prosociality sets us apart, not just from chimpanzees, but all other species. We routinely help others to achieve their goals, even complete strangers, and often with no benefit to ourselves. This altruism towards strangers is extremely rare, evolutionarily, and most probably happens due to uniquely human psychological mechanisms.[8]

By working together in groups – and not just with an immediate short-term goal, such as with animals that hunt in packs, nor only a specific or non-flexible way, as with bees or ants – we are capable of flexible, collective intentionality, and in very large numbers. We don't just communicate with each other, we undertake whole tasks together, and layered tasks together. This enables us to far surpass our abilities as an individual: we build together, we eat together, we plan together, we dance together, we sing together. We share information and work as one in order to meet common objectives, even those far in the future.

For tens of thousands of years, before we developed these traits and abilities, modern humans and other hominins were most probably rather evenly matched. If the gods were fond of a bet, they could have put their money on any hominin species conquering the planet – or none, for that matter, as hominins weren't having any more impact on the Earth than bees, whales or frogs were.

Our Prosocial Social Beginnings

Throughout human evolution, natural selection favoured increased in-group prosociality over aggression.

In English please, Rou?

For early humans, any individual with an aggressive or domineering nature was an issue when your best chance of survival was through cooperating well in a group, so aggressors would be ridiculed, shunned, ostracised, or even murdered, leaving the friendliest humans to raise the most children.[9] It seems in the days before agriculture and 'civilisation', bullies and dictators were actually quite rare, and when they did arise, they were dealt with swiftly! In fact, there is increasing evidence that these types of human behaviour and our modern hierarchical structures have largely appeared more recently.

The anthropologist Mark Dybe:

> There is still this wider perception that hunter–gatherers are more macho or

male-dominated. We'd argue it was only with the emergence of agriculture, when people could start to accumulate resources, that inequality emerged.[10]

In direct contrast to the common prejudiced assumption that hunter–gatherer societies were 'impoverished, backward, uncivilised',[11] early humans actually evolved to become what we could call domesticated apes. Just as dogs are bred for friendliness and intelligence, natural selection, the greatest of all breeders, bred us for our ability to communicate and cooperate. As I mentioned in Chapter 4, it was *survival of the friendliest*.[12] Arguably, we outlasted the other hominins because we excelled at communicating, cooperating, learning and bonding.

Dispersing out of Africa, exploring new lands, settling in new environments all over the globe, and surviving extreme historic climate change took extreme cooperation. Cooperation never previously seen from any other species on Earth.

Connection And Cooperation

On an individual level; if I was to be placed on an island with a chimpanzee, who would fare better? It is not difficult for me to let go of my pride and safely admit that the chimpanzee would! But, as Yuval Noah Harari points out, place 1000 *Homo sapiens* on an island with 1000 chimps, and then the humans will fare better, easily,[13] and for the same simple reason; humans can cooperate. Our biggest strength is our ability to connect, to help each other and work together.

As individuals, early *Homo sapiens* were mediocre. As a collective, they were breath-taking.

Today, we appear to have forgotten this. It is as if we are so ashamed of this superpower that we've disowned it, and instead we centre our societies around individual responsibility. We focus on competition; we pit individuals against individuals, workers against workers, citizens against citizens, schools against schools, companies against companies, and countries against countries.[14]

Hold on a minute, Rou. You're not saying we need to return to our early hunter–gatherer ways, are you? Walking around scantily clad in animal fur, foraging for berries FFS?

No, I'm not. We have come a long way in 40,000 years (although *I* made a lovely blackberry jam with foraged berries in my pants the other day, so maybe I haven't). I'm simply asking that we better recognise that cooperation is a defining aspect of our species, and also, more importantly, one of our greatest strengths.

A focus on ultra-competitiveness has turned us into our own worst enemy. As discussed in Chapter 2, our biggest threat is now ourselves. If we're going to transcend **The Great Unknown** we must refocus and regroup; our prehistoric cooperative traits must be at the centre of our future societies, and not just because cooperation and compassion are natural to us and we excel at them, but also because they are pivotal to our future survival as a species.

Empathy

A key element of the prosociality that evolution has endowed us with is the power to understand and share the feelings of others: empathy. To be able to put yourself in someone else's shoes, see the world from a different point of view, feel the emotions that another feels; empathy is like a form of telepathy, and has been a vital component of our species' success.

I don't want to just leave it at that, though, as there's much more to the concept of empathy than meets the eye. In fact, the more I discovered when researching empathy, the more I realised how crucial it is to understand its nuances. So let's delve a bit deeper.

One crucial way to address our self-interest obsessed modern world is to practise empathy; to exercise one's empathic muscle, to broaden one's perspective. We've talked a lot about this already. Along with civility, it's one of the key skills that **The Dreamer's Hotel** advocates practising.

But conversely, and before we get carried away, empathy, would you believe it, has also been a vital component in our worst mistakes and our darkest moments! See, you really have to be careful with empathy, it's incredibly complex. You have to make sure you're aware of its biases, for it can be a disastrously restrictive moral guide. This idea seemed extremely nonsensical to me at first, considering that empathy, on the face of it, is such a wonderful power for good. But let's have a brief look at its negative effects and what we must do to avoid them. After which, I'll clarify what I'll mean by the word 'empathy' going forward.

The psychologist Simon Baron-Cohen (yes, cousin of the actor and comedian Sacha Baron Cohen) introduces us to *cognitive empathy* – 'also known as theory of mind, which is the ability to imagine another's thoughts'.[15] When this means simply understanding others, it can be (1) enjoyable (like sharing in another's happiness or success) and (2) helpful (cementing friendships or fuelling activism).

But the psychologist Paul Bloom warns us that the type of empathy that means specifically *feeling* what another person is experiencing (i.e. sympathy = feeling *for*, empathy = feeling *with*), can lead to some unnerving outcomes. It can actually restrict your feelings for others by narrowing your focus onto one person or group exclusively.

It's relatively easy to empathise with someone who you consider to be similar to you, or someone who is going through something that you've experienced. But it becomes more difficult the more you perceive a person to be different from you, or who's experiences differ from yours. This presents us with three, quite negative, potential consequences; Firstly, it can result in you showing bias in favour of those who you easily empathise with, and therefore – secondly – neglecting, undervaluing, or disregarding the feelings of those others who you empathise less easily with. Finally, your empathy can then be 'hacked', and you can be persuaded to actually feel intensely negative feelings against those others.

Instead of feeling another's pain, we can begin to feel enjoyment from it. We have all experienced this, I'm sure. The most likely exemplification being with viral outrage culture, when people start to 'pile on'. For example: when someone's widely despised actions elicit such a torrent of hate that they are shamed and otherwise impacted negatively, (e.g. they end up losing their jobs, or have to move away, or change their name), you may then celebrate their misfortune and misery. Cue the memes about drinking 'liberal' or 'conservative' 'tears'. Your empathy for those who call out the bad behaviour causes you to act in a way that completely disregards the feelings of the perpetrator. 'Tribalism reverses empathy', to quote the psychologist Jamil Zaki.[16]

It is easy to stimulate empathy for people who are like you. That's a fire that is easily stoked. But it's also a fire that can then easily be driven dangerously out of control by bigots or xenophobes. Here's Paul Bloom:

> I actually feel a lot less empathy for people who aren't in my culture, who don't share my skin color, who don't share my language. This is a terrible fact of human nature, and it operates at a subconscious level, but we know that it happens.[17]

Bringing Out The Worst In Us

As a result of these potential biases, we leave ourselves open to being goaded by those who know how to exploit them.

When Donald Trump, for example, speaks disparagingly about Mexicans or Muslims, he often talks in terms of the supposed suffering they *cause* him or his supporters:

> In his rallies, he would tell stories of victims of rape and victims of shooting. He would tell stories of people who lost their jobs. And he was appealing to the empathy of supporters, whose concerns extended mostly to their own tribe.[18]

This example from Bloom shows us how our empathy can be *weaponised*, transforming us into more ignorant and insular people. A couple of stories, even if true, should obviously not have the power to taint a whole population. But they can, and they do. We're persuaded away from thinking rationally by the empathic fuelling of strong and absent-minded emotions. This reminds me of the great quote from Aristotle: 'an emotional speaker always makes his audience feel with him, even when there is nothing in his arguments; which is why many speakers try to overwhelm their audience by mere noise'.[19]

This is the prime tactic that divisive politicians use; they speak emotionally so as to *hoard* or *shrink* your empathy. They are making sure you *only* exercise it towards people in *your* group. Then, in failing to empathise with *other* groups, you become ignorant of other perspectives and you can effectively begin to dehumanise those other groups. At this point, you are only one small step away from being able to cultivate hatred towards them.

It is, therefore, no coincidence that the root of the word 'empathy' is the Greek *empatheia*, which other than meaning 'affection' or 'passion', can also mean prejudice, malice and hatred. This is what empathy can produce in us, if we do not keep it in check.

Our empathy can actually result in us ignoring the feelings of others, rather than doing what we expect it to do, which is help us understand the feelings of other humans and seeing life through their eyes.[20] When humans dehumanise fellow humans like this; that is when they commit their worst atrocities. Rutger Bregman explains:

> If anything, empathy makes us less forgiving, because the more we identify with victims, the more we generalise about our enemies. The bright spotlight we shine on our chosen few makes us blind to the perspective of our adversaries.[21]

Oxytocin

The evidence seems compelling even at the biological level. Oxytocin, 'the love hormone' we looked at in Chapter 4, (or 'the moral molecule' as Paul Zak calls it in his book of the same name) has this warming and caring effect to a greater degree, for those *within* one's own group. And sometimes it can even intensify a wariness or dislike of strangers, i.e. those we perceive *outside* of our group.[22] Zak says:

> The Moral Molecule works like a gyroscope, helping us maintain our balance between behavior based on trust, and behavior based on wariness and distrust. In this way oxytocin helps us navigate between the social benefits of openness – which are considerable – and the reasonable caution we need to avoid being taken for a ride.[23]

So it's this idea of balance that becomes pivotal. To go to the extreme of getting rid of empathy would be utterly disastrous; a complete absence of empathy is associated with psychopathy and can be incredibly destructive. Simon Baron-Cohen has argued that 'empathy-erosion' is the root cause of many malicious acts today.[24]

So we must, instead, keep our empathy leashed by rationality, making sure it does not compel us towards misinformed, biased or violent action. We must direct it thoughtfully, with consideration, and always seek to expand it. We must not let our empathy be monopolised by a certain group we are more fond of or familiar with. A recipe for a healthy 'empathy salad', say, would be to serve your empathy with rationality, patience and compassion.

Stress Is Preventing Empathy

It's becoming harder and harder, today, to find that correct balance, and to behave in ways that support openness and friendliness, because in our increasingly hostile society we are spending less and less time in physical scenarios with others, and it's those face-to-face situations that help to spark and solidify trust and affinity *in* others![25] As we'll look at further, shortly, our lives these days are more fractured and solitary. More and more often, our experiences of strangers feature them as 'complete arseholes' online, rather than as the moderate, modest, and tame people who make up the majority in everyday walks of life. As discussed earlier, our society is built upon rampant self-interest, which results in our levels of stress and mistrust rising and rising. Stress is at all-time high levels in our society today, due to inequality and insecurity. And guess what? Unfortunately, stress is one of the prime blockers to a helpful and openness-boosting oxytocin surge.

Modern Examples Of Empathy Gone Awry

No matter your party-political outlook, you've probably had your empathy hijacked at some point:

Britain's exit from the EU, and the propaganda directed at Brussels that preceded it.

Trump's demonisation of Mexicans, and subsequent insistence on building 'the wall'.

The EU's shocking treatment of refugees, which we touched on in the **Waltzing Off The Face Of The Earth** section.

All these are recent examples of how we disparage other nations and other peoples. But, as if that's not enough, we also create division *within* our own nations too; such as with the political polarisation we looked at in Chapter 4.

Useful, measured and rational empathy becomes increasingly hard as we become more divided, and then identify ourselves more and more *by* those divisions. For example; it requires extreme effort to empathise with people of different political persuasions, these days. This is not only because your empathic response is biased, but because – even if you *did* manage to empathise with those others – your empathic response is fighting a losing battle with your moral anger, which is constantly fuelled thanks to your filter bubbles. Your will to empathise with the other will most likely be drowned out by the pressures of your tribal loyalties. This is the real danger our species faces in the digital age; it is a laborious uphill climb to see *any* other perspective, when most of the time we only have our own perspective echoed back to us.

We're actively discouraged from useful empathy. While actively encouraged to dehumanise others.

The good news is this: in understanding these empathy biases, we can overcome them. As Paul Bloom says, 'We're smart enough to realise that empathy can lead us astray. [...] We're smart enough to act so as to override its pernicious effects.'[26]

Again, it's about the importance of patient curiosity. Of acting like investigators when conversing with people whose opinions and beliefs we dislike. This can be incredibly difficult, a test of patience and tolerance, but is pivotal to creating a more civil society and getting to the root causes.

Empathy's Expansion Over Time

Empathy has been a core strength of our species, a precious resource, pivotal to our success so far. Early humans started by showing interest and care only for their own family group or tribe. This then expanded to the village, the region and the nation; and furthermore to other races, to other genders, and even to other sentient beings (through animal welfare and veganism).[28] It's astounding to think how we have expanded our limited interests and empathic responses further and further over time. Over the course of human history, empathy has taken an evolutionary quantum leap. Humanity now, when at its best, values the interests of all beings everywhere.

How was this expansion achieved?

Through a few pivotal human-specific inventions.

Gathering other perspectives first became possible through humans' ability to employ complicated language. The written word then made perspectives documentable, meaning they could spread far and wide throughout a society and be recorded as an historic perspective for future societies. Literature helped us become more adept at projecting ourselves into the lives of other people; those who exist now, those who no longer exist, those who do not exist yet, those who will never exist, and – perhaps most importantly – even those who at one point we wished didn't exist! By reading the stories of other lives we absorb their circumstances, their trials and tribulations—and we better understand the world.

As *the other* has become understandable, we've been able to expand our individual universe and our moral horizons.

The Ancient Greeks – What Would You Do?

Then, around 2,500 years ago, the Ancient Greeks invented theatre and drama. Most important of all, in my mind, they gave us tragedy; a form of drama centred on human suffering (famed proponents of the genre include William Shakespeare, you might have heard of him, and my boy Samuel Beckett, who you remember from Chapter 3).

Tragedies were not just strange and violent, as they sometimes appear on the face of it, but moral challenges that engaged the audience. Not just mindless entertainment for the masses, but food for thought. A performance would drag the audience into different situations, forcing thought and analysis as well as providing new perspectives. By encouraging an empathic response, the audience were able to experience for themselves the strong emotions felt by the characters.

Aristotle suggested that this would emotionally cleanse or heal the audience. He called this *catharsis*. (Aristotle held theatre to be pivotal in Greek life. Unlike old Plato, the bloody proto-fascist, who thought all theatre and poetry was a dangerous lie and would've sent all playwrights into exile! Discussing the detail or relevance of these two views on drama is *far* too big a rabbit hole to digress down for this book. Someone grab me by the scruff of the neck and pull me out, quick!)

In one of the plays from the *Oresteia* trilogy (written by the father of tragedy himself, Aeschylus, in the 5th century BCE) we witness a character poised on the verge of exacting revenge upon a foe. He pauses and asks 'What shall I do?'.[29] This is the *key* question of all Greek tragedy, and it demands a response from the audience. In that moment the audience transport themselves into the character's position, and ask themselves 'what would I do?'. Their imaginations run wild as they use the situation as a moral quiz. The relief and clarity gained from experiencing difficult or violent emotions in the calm environment of the theatre, detached from real consequences, leaves the audience better equipped should those emotions or situations occur in real life, while putting themselves in the position of another broadens their perspective.

First through language, and then through mobility and eventually literacy and the arts, humans beat the typically parochial effects of oxytocin and empathised further and further outward. Our expanding empathy enabled us to work together in bigger and bigger groups, facilitating our 'domestication', our technological advancement and our *civil*-isation.

Revenge In Oresteia

Aeschylus's aforementioned *Oresteia* is a group of plays so full of revenge and murder that it makes Liam Neeson's *Taken* franchise feel like a gentle wee fairy tale. The story centres around a cycle of vendetta, with retributive murder inspiring further retributive murder, and it ultimately came to establish the role of revenge drama in the European tradition and beyond. It perfectly encapsulates the self-reinforcing nature of revenge.

(Just as we've discussed earlier in relation to social media – where online hostility only incentivises users to act with *further* hostility – it's an *amplifying feedback loop*. Revenge itself is an *amplifying feedback loop of retaliation*. Revenge inspires further revenge. This sounds very technical though, so instead I'm going to label it the *bloody death spiral of revenge*. Yes, that's more like it.)

Through the series of plays, the city's elders, who make up the chorus, narrate us. They wisely assert that pain leads to wisdom. But, even by the end of the first play, it appears, in this instance at least, that pain only leads to more pain, thanks to the acts of revenge. Even some of the characters are aware of the *bloody death spiral of revenge* their actions motivate. This leads one character to prophesy: 'there shall come one to avenge us also'.[30] Yet, regardless, revenge remains the principal motivator for almost all of the characters throughout the trilogy.

The characters ignore the risks and simply cannot help themselves, they are gripped by an insatiable drive for vengeance 'this is a strong oath and sworn by the high gods'.[31] In any walk of life, when you believe that you have been in some way wronged, ridiculed, ignored or unfairly treated, the urge to retaliate can completely possess you.

A Deeper Look At Revenge

Watch your back my friend
I'm about to kickstart a cycle
Of never ending revenge
And this time it's primal, it's tribal

With **The King**, I explore how revenge can be one of humanity's most foolish desires, often creating a spiral of endless conflict. The vocal is performed by a protagonist not too dissimilar from the one we met in **The Dreamer's Hotel**. Here, though, I'm not just attempting to convey anger, but anger against the backdrop of their innate frailty. While we often see revenge presented as an ostensibly tough act (e.g. our friend from a few paragraphs ago, Liam Neeson in *Taken*), it is actually something much more emotionally complicated.

Whether we're retaliating to an online insult, or acting to spite or injure another in the real world, revenge is often a compulsion birthed from feelings of shame, or by injury to our pride. These feelings of shame are powerful because, again, we care greatly about what others think (remember; for our human ancestors, to be shunned by their group meant probable death). So, when wronged, we feel instantly compelled to take revenge in order to show we are *not* to be ridiculed or badly treated. We feel that we must prove that we *are* an accepted and respected member of our group/society.

The better, and far simpler, way to fix a dent in our self-esteem would be to strengthen and fortify it by gaining love and respect from others ('I just want to be adored'), as well as working on self-love. But, unfortunately, we seem only capable of regaining our self-esteem by demanding it back from the person who damaged it in the first place, as if only the thief can restore our dignity.

The psychiatrist James Gilligan suggests that plainly, violence is an attempt to replace shame with self-esteem.[32] Asserting yourself as a threat to others is the type of behaviour we see from internet trolls, far-right militia groups and murderers, and could be viewed as them simply crying out 'respect me'. Our individual egos need to feel justified, we need to feel the respect of our peers and if we do not attain these through positive means, or worse, if we feel *dis*respected, we then move to extort respect through violence:

I can't walk away, I can't walk away,
I got all this pride, all this shame, all this anger to obey

Regal Revenge

I used to be the king
But they took everything
They even stole my crown
I'm gonna track you down

I chose a monarchistic theme for **The King** because today's society reveals an obsession with Machiavellian theatrics. The rise and fall of kings and queens, along with the revenge drama central to their blood-sodden stories, is everywhere (the most obvious example of recent times being HBO's *Game of Thrones*).

A key component of these revenge dramas is the tendency for characters to perceive the harm inflicted upon them (or upon those they care about), to be somehow far worse than the harm they inflict upon others. In psychology, this is referred to as the *moralisation gap*. It's exceptionalism, a lack of perspective, a self-supporting bias that helps to reinforce the cyclical nature of revenge. (In *Game of Thrones*, Tyrion Lannister is really the only main character who doesn't typically fall into this biased perception of reality.)

When someone perceives the response of their adversary to be unacceptable, it further prompts them to strike back again, with even more force. We see this impulse in our relationships, we see this in our online debates, we see this in politics. It is a truly pernicious force.

Revenge And Inequality

If we seek to punish those who have treated us unfairly (or, at least, those we *perceive* to have treated us unfairly), it's not surprising to see an increase in hostility. We live in times of increasing vulnerability arising from obscene levels of social inequality so our self-esteem is very fragile. Any perceived attack is met with a full scale attack back. When everyone is feeling unfairly treated, we are, as a society, in the prime state to be seized by the revenge drive. As we discussed in Chapter 4 with the help of Amy Chua, feelings of victimisation are universal, we are all quick to jump to blame, and even quicker to lash out as a result.

Continuing on **The King**'s regal theme: when writing the lyric, I couldn't help but visualise a landscape full of dark, imposing, unwelcoming castles. The inhabitants of each, unwilling to communicate with the other, unable to 'let people in', to forgive or *empathise*, as they become increasingly insular: 'All our drawbridges are up'.

This public mood is easily exploited by the far-right and by populist/nationalist politicians. Public anger (in reality, a by-product of inequality, employment uncertainty and social insecurity) is stoked, and misdirected towards migrants and minorities, rather than those in positions of power, or the socioeconomic system itself.

It's far easier to believe you hate a specific human, or group of humans, than to properly analyse a situation and unearth its root cause. Giving 'enemies' an easily identifiable face and pointing fingers at 'the other' (who are 'coming to steal your job' for instance), scares people. It incites anger in them, and further motivates them to join the populist's cause. This example illustrates how oxytocin can manifest in its cautioning-protecting effect, rather than its loving-compassionate alternative. The 'other' becomes the perfect scapegoat, bearing the brunt of our anger, while protecting the actual perpetrators; those responsible of our unequal and precarious society.

Revenge And Vulnerability

> I used to be a charmer
> But now there's holes in my armour

If we're honest with ourselves, there are 'holes' in all of our 'armour', no? As humans, we are innately vulnerable, it is a defining trait of our species. We've all suffered in some way or another and none of us are as tough, or powerful, or strong, or important, as we think we are or would like to be. This brings us face to face with our own natural frailty and our need for empathy and acceptance. (Again, this was core thesis to our 2017 album, *The Spark*.) When we realise and accept this truth about the human condition we free ourselves from the pressures of 'performing' toughness, we liberate ourselves from the grip of fury, we are free to forgive (should we wish to), and we are able to face forwards. We are able to lower our guard and allow kindness to become our default behaviour, for if my armour is full of holes, and yours is too, we should be considerate and compassionate with each other.

But too often we refuse to accept our own vulnerability, we cover it up with demonstrations of dominance, and our default behaviour is eternally motivated by spite.

Revenge And Masochism

Have you ever looked down at an angry little yapping dog, as it brashly tries to intimidate or dominate, and thought to yourself just how feeble it looks? Maybe you sort of feel sorry for it, or just laugh at it, as it continues to yap away, full or rage, unaware of how pathetic it appears to us. We laugh, because we see its innate frailty, even if the dog can't recognise it in itself.

This is the innate frailty we fail to recognise in ourselves when we puff out our chests and try to 'protect' a strongman image. This behaviour can often end up damaging us as much as any foe:

> I grab my sword and swing
> But I go and pull my hamstring

I loved this image of someone *so* in the grip of uncontrollable anger, that they only end up injuring themselves. Which appeared to me like a grand truth, often in our attempts to hurt others, we only do harm to ourselves.

Relying on anger to restore your honour or self-respect is not only unhealthy for yourself though, it is also unhealthy for society. A vengeful nature is, of course, a sadistic nature. It derives pleasure in harming others. But, if we take a step backwards, and view it from a broader perspective, the revenge drive ultimately becomes socially masochistic, too. When we see red and lust for revenge, we only envisage wounds to our immediate nemesis, unaware that we are almost certainly fuelling a cycle of *unrelenting* payback. We injure not only the target of our vengeance *and* ourselves, but *also* others beyond our initial target, and possibly even generations to come.

Our society is one where division, outrage and lust for revenge are completely normalised, and they are doing immense damage. Vengeance, with no forgiveness or even inquiry, with only a backward-facing deconstructive urge, can hurt wider society just as much as it hurts our target. As Gandhi famously said: 'an eye for an eye makes the whole world blind'.

Backward-Facing Versus Forward-Facing Anger

Backward-facing anger is a purely destructive anger. It longs only for payback; to *take* from the world. Whereas, to respond to any setback, maltreatment, or injustice with forward-facing anger is to be constructive: to concentrate on preventing similar events from occurring again in the future. To *give* to the world. Making it safer, kinder and more sustainable.

If anger is forward-facing it can achieve real progress in society through righteous activism; it spurs us on in the fight to ensure injustices are not repeated, or that immoral and dangerous events or situations do not occur again. It is centred around compassion and creativity.

This has been discussed by philosophers for millennia. You may have already heard some variation of the old Japanese proverb (often mistakenly attributed to Confucius) quoted in the second verse of **The King**:

> If it's revenge you seek,
> Then be sure to dig two graves

On the surface, a wise piece of advice. Affirming that revenge will only bring further revenge against you. But a piece of advice that is ... well ... rather brutally dismissed by our angry protagonist!

> Why? One for my enemy
> And fucking one for you, preferably

He's offended by the pious pomposity of this advice. He sees it as so trite, preposterous and unfulfilling in its lack of retribution, he can't even consider it an option. Instead, he ridicules what he deems to be an insipid suggestion. This habit of ignoring, or, more often (and even worse), actively mocking wisdom from the past partly informs the statement behind the *Nothing Is True ...* album artwork.[33]

Criminality

A good example of *structural* backward-facing anger are our prison systems. *Retributive justice* is a system of criminal justice based on the *punishment* of offenders rather than their *rehabilitation*. Historically, punishment has been the main principle defining the American prison system, and it is *this* system that has made the United States the incarceration capital of the world, with one person imprisoned every 90 seconds.[34] If that isn't shocking enough for you, try this one for size: There is a grand total of 11 million people incarcerated world-wide, and 1 in 5 of those prisoners are incarcerated in the US.[35]

Why are American prisons so damn full? Well that, again, is another book entirely, but as we'll see, research is starting to make something quite clear; retributive justice does *not* rehabilitate human beings, and does *not* help to reintegrate offenders successfully back into society as peaceful and law abiding citizens.[36] This is confirmed by looking at the *recidivism rate* (the amount of criminals who reoffend once released).

According to independent estimates, a whopping 60% of US prisoners are back behind bars within 2 years of release.[37] The US Department of Justice itself released a report in 2018 showing that 83% of state prisoners released in 2005 (across 30 states) were arrested at least once during the following 9 years.[38]

Perhaps this system of retributive justice simply isn't very good then? I mean, this data seems to suggest that if you treat criminals like criminals – punishing them instead of seeking to help them and better them – they will absolutely continue to act like criminals.

How do other countries and prison systems fair against those scarily high numbers? The UK and Australia both have recidivism rates of around 45% (so, just under half of offenders *reoffend* within 2 years of release),[39] and notably their systems are not *quite* as brutal and punishment-focused as the US system, but they are simply not different *enough* to offer any helpful perspective. Interestingly, though, one study from the UK's Ministry of Justice found that prisoners are at higher risk of reoffending than those who served community service sentences. So it seems there are still serious problems in the UK with prison's lack of ability to reform, though the problems are not quite on the same scale as in the US.[40]

To compare this globally prevailing retributive justice system to a truly *different* prison system, we have to look to Norway. Norway holds the lowest recidivism rate in the world. Just 20% of those imprisoned reoffend, once back in society. An article about life in Norway's maximum security Halden Prison reveals an astonishingly different experience to punishment-focused prisons:

> Barefoot murderers, rapists and drug smugglers practise downward-facing dog and the lotus position alongside their prison officers, each participant fully concentrating on the clear instructions from the teacher.[41]

Yes, that's right, they do yoga. In fact, the whole experience at Halden is mind-blowingly different. Halden is situated in the middle of a beautiful forest, there are en suite rooms for inmates, and daily educational and training programmes. The prison officers and inmates do everything from eating dinner together to exercising together. In fact, the officers are thought of more as mentors than guards. It's important to note that, for many of the inmates, this is the first time they have had an empathetic ear or any positive role model in their lives.

Norway's prison system wasn't always so different, though. In the early 1980s, it too resembled the more retributive, punishment-focused US prison system. Halden Prison's governor, Are Hoidal reminisces: 'It was completely hard, [...] It was a masculine, macho culture with a focus on guarding and security. And the recidivism rate was around 60–70%, like in the US.'[42]

But in the early 1990s, the Norwegian Correctional Service had a complete overhaul, focusing more on rehabilitation instead of focusing on what Are Hoidal terms 'revenge'. (There's that word again!)

It is clear that prisons with a focus on 'revenge' are actually harmful to society. They do not correct violent or antisocial behaviour – which *is,* in most cases, correctable, to some degree – they *aggravate* that behaviour. This is yet another example of the way in which backward-facing anger can breed cycles of violence.

What's more, it's taxpayer's money that is used to fund prison facilities. Facilities that, according to the Forum on Global Violence Prevention: 'exacerbate violence in some cases, both within the prison walls and in the broader community'.[43] Pumping our money into prison systems that ultimately do not reform offenders (and occasionally even compound their behaviour), is another act of social masochism; a societal act of self-harm.

Disinterest Is Key

You may be wondering how Aeschylus' long and bloody trilogy, *Oresteia*, finally ends. Do the curtains close upon a limp pile of bodies? Is their society ruined by the drive for vengeance?

Somewhat surprisingly, among all the bloodshed, Aeschylus gives us a relatively 'happy' ending. Out of the many mortals and higher powers all striving to enact justice in the story, the Goddess Athena becomes the only one who ultimately succeeds. She understands that justice defined by revenge will only result in a vicious cycle of continuous retaliation, one that perpetuates cycles of war, be that metaphorical or otherwise. Athena thankfully realised that anger can be backward-facing or forward-facing and implements a new form of fair and civilised justice. (It's OK, dear reader, this isn't a 'spoiler'. Aeschylus gives the reader a clue from the beginning with the chorus' narration; 'Sing sorrow, sorrow: but good win out in the end'[44]).

Good wins out. Athena establishes an Athenian jury, taking the responsibility of verdicts and repercussions out of the hands of the emotionally entangled, and placing them with uninvolved, 'disinterested' members of the public. The realisation that a thirst for bloodshed does *not* help society, nor indeed bring back the losses of the vengeful, helped prevent further bloodshed and misery throughout Athens.

In the ideal, a jury would empathise with all involved. It would attempt to understand the experiences and motivations, as well as the intentions, of the accused. Then, and only then, should they give their verdict. This sense of empathy and perspective in terms of *how* offenders come to offend, as well as understanding how best to *stop* them reoffending again, has been somewhat lost with today's punishment-focused judicial system. It appears that good is still yet to win out in the end.

Beating The Revenge Drive

Through Athena we see the invention of the modern concept of justice, devised to replace the *bloody death spiral of revenge*. There are many others, throughout antiquity, who also offer advice in quelling the revenge drive (Seneca, Marcus Aurelius and the other Stoic philosophers are perhaps some of the best teachers in the field of restraint) and, personally, I think one should lap up as much advice as one can in this domain as it sure is a hard instinct to subdue! I thought, though, I should try to relay the advice of someone who lived more recently, and you don't need a background in classics to be familiar with the name Nelson Mandela.

Institutionalised racism existed in South Africa until 1991. (It's crazy to think how recent that was!) Apartheid began in 1948 as an official system of segregation, and existed in South Africa and South West Africa (now Namibia). The authoritarian political culture ensured that the nation's minority white population dominated politically, socially, and economically.

Nelson Mandela was sentenced to life imprisonment in 1964 for conspiring against the state and fighting against apartheid as a founding member of the armed wing of the African National Congress (ANC). The first 18 years of his sentence were spent at the Robben Island maximum security prison. Upon his release 27 years later, Mandela went on to lead the ANC to victory, in the country's first ever democratic elections. The 1994 election result threatened to tip the country into all-out civil war but Mandela decided to meet his opponents in person, inviting the white Afrikaner leaders to his house for tea.[45] We have to understand how bizarre and brave this was. Nelson Mandela became President at a time when the country was bitterly divided by decades of racism and hostility, and had personally suffered greatly during those years. Yet he met the Afrikaner leaders, learnt their language, studied their history, and slowly earned their trust and respect.

Mandela often said that he knew anger well, and that he had to struggle against the demand for payback in his own personality. He reported that during his 27 years of imprisonment he had to practise a disciplined type of meditation to keep his personality moving forward and avoiding the anger trap.[46]

It is said that the prisoners of Robben Island had a copy of *Meditations* by the Stoic philosopher Marcus Aurelius smuggled in, in order to master the intensely difficult skills of patience, compassion and tolerance. This helped them in understanding and ultimately controlling their urge to retaliate. It is one thing to philosophise over how to fight human urges or act morally. But to find a high profile, successful example of the philosophy enacted in real life gives it real weight and prestige.

Mandela went on to exemplify these virtues throughout the rest of his life, in his fight to unite South Africa and quell the continuation of its horrifically divided history. His experience at the hands of the evils of white supremacy should have given him great motivation to take his revenge, yet he was unshakeably forward-facing in his actions. He wanted only to change society in order for it to leave its violent past behind.

A great example of Mandela's commitment to prioritising healing over revenge occurred in 1995, when he was put under tremendous pressure to decertify the national rugby team. The Springboks, as a team – and the sport in general – had a long connection to racism and Apartheid. Rather than punishing the team and the sport (i.e. fulfilling a vengeful drive), Mandela instead took the fully opposite approach. He actually publicly *backed* them and encouraged black South Africans to join him in his support. The Springboks went on to a Rugby World Cup victory, increasing the sport's popularity within the black South African community and earning him the respect of millions of white South African rugby fans. The white players went on to teach the sport to young black children, and friendships grew, where before there was only ignorance and hatred. On 24 June 1995, Mandela walked out into Johannesburg's stadium, in a Springboks shirt, greeted by chants of 'Nelson! Nelson!' from a crowd that just 5 years earlier would have considered him a terrorist.

His detractors said he was too soft, too willing to see the good in people. His response was profound:

> Your duty is to work with human beings as human beings, not because you think they are angels. Once you know that this man has got this virtue and he has got this weakness you work with them and you accommodate that weakness and you try and help him to overcome that weakness. I don't want to be frightened by the fact that a person has made certain mistakes and he has got human frailties.[47]

Revenge arises from a lack of perspective and serves to only narrow one's perspective further. It is ultimately a futile endeavour. The ability to empathise with people, even those who wrong you, is key to understanding the complexity of human behaviour and forging a kinder, gentler world.

I try to constantly remind myself that, in befriending an enemy, you conquer with greater finality than when fighting them.

5.2 Satellites

The song **Satellites** is an *exercise in empathy.*

> I don't like the limelight
> So we don't hold hands in daylight

Over the course of a conversation with a friend of mine one afternoon, he opened up to me about his anxiety around displays of public affection. As a gay man, he felt he couldn't even bring himself to hold hands when walking with his new partner. As well as being heart-breaking to hear, his honesty made me consider my own 'privilege' and freedom, and made me examine and reimagine a romantic gesture I had taken for granted my whole life.

Social anxiety can make you feel as if there is a blindingly bright and intolerably hot spotlight shining down on you. It makes you sweat. It makes you hyper-aware of everything you do or say. It makes you constantly guess what other people are thinking about you. I've suffered from social anxiety as far back as I can remember. It has been my constant, standard inner experience, to some degree. I understand how it presents itself: the rigidity, the discomfort, the inability to think straight, the rumination, the fear, the frustration.

The majority of my social anxiety triggers are fabricated; worries overblown in my own overactive mind. When it strikes, my perception of reality will be very different to other people's perceptions of reality at the same moment; I could be ruminating about how I look stupid, or that what I just said sounded stupid, or the fact that I haven't contributed enough to a group conversation. I'll be working myself up inside, yet others will have no idea; they won't have even noticed what I was wearing, nor noticed any stupidity in what I just said, and would be nonchalant toward my lack of contribution. Yet I am unaware of *their* reality, still convinced that they are internally criticising or ridiculing me, and so my anxiety continues, even though it is often uncalled for.

Now as palpable and debilitating as this experience can be for me, it is very unlikely that I will *actually* experience a lot of the things I am getting worked up about, or fearing may happen. But, for my friend, walking down the street hand in hand with his new partner, the fear of being insulted, heckled, threatened, or even physically assaulted, can be very real. Even in the modern, progressive UK. In fact, even right here in my own cosmopolitan London, homophobic hate crime is on the rise.[1]

Just a few months after the conversation with my friend, a homophobic attack took place on the N31 night bus, a bus I often get through central London.[2] The photo of the two women's bloodied faces angered and saddened me deeply, and pushed me further to write some music as an exercise in empathy towards the LGBT+ experience.

These incidents are, of course, still rare, but it's important to note that 80% of anti-LGBT+ hate crimes or incidents actually go unreported (with younger LGBT+ people particularly reluctant to go to the police).[3] I think this makes it clear how vital it is for allies to be supportive and visible, in every way we can.

Whether incidents go unreported because of a fear of repercussion, or a sense of restrictive humility (where the victim thinks their incident isn't important enough, i.e. 'Oh I'm sure the police have more important things to be concentrating on'), or just a defeated belief that nothing will come of it, it's clear that much more support and solidarity is needed. We must apply more pressure for public education, and we must do all we can to ensure the safety of LGBT+ people. Our empathy and our action are pivotal.

Striving To Understand

In the summer of 2020, during the height of the Black Lives Matter protests following the shocking murder of George Floyd, there was a meme doing the rounds online. You may even have noticed it yourself, as it was everywhere: 'I understand that I will never understand, but I stand'. Now, it was obviously intended as a message of support, and certainly came from a good place, but I believe the sentiment could also be viewed as an unhelpful position to take when considering adversity experienced by others.

If taken at its most literal, essentially this meme is stating 'I do not experience what you experience, therefore there's no way I could understand what you experience, so I will not bother trying to understand it, but still, I will stand with you in solidarity and fight for justice for you anyway'. Now of course I feel a little hesitant to take apart any attempt at anti-racist solidarity, all is certainly welcome in this day and age, but I want to just take a quick moment to explain why this sentiment specifically is the wrong way to think about solidarity.

Trying to understand the plight of another is paramount to being able to support them in their fight for justice. To state that you will 'never understand' is just ignoring or demeaning your own empathic nature! It's a statement of support with no responsibility to try and comprehend what it is you're actually supporting.

Worse actually, it's a statement to *excuse* yourself from understanding. It's remarkably close to a philosophy of apathy.

As I said at the start of Chapter 4, communication is all we have. Speaking to people and gaining insight into how their lives are different from yours, as well as making the effort to learn their history is pivotal to true solidarity. We must state instead: 'I will *strive* to understand further, but I will stand with you regardless'. This phrase, of course, doesn't have quite the same rallying effect though, and I do not want to blunt any tool that succeeds in galvanising social justice here, but we must understand that stretching your empathic muscle is key to understanding a problem fully and keeping your humanity alive and well.

Public Displays Of Affection

Let's return to **Satellites**, and to being afraid of showing affection in public.

For perspective: there are many places around the world, even today, where members of the *opposite* sex will get in trouble for showing affection in public. What is considered a reasonable public display of affection (PDA) changes by country and by culture. Historically, in China, almost all physical contact between opposite sexes has been viewed as unacceptable, and many regions still hold onto this outdated point of view today.

Interestingly, in India, same-sex physical contact is allowed, but a PDA between opposite sexes still triggers a lot of commotion, and many regions can be incredibly strict. For example, a 16-year-old boy was expelled in 2017 just for hugging a girl who had 'won a prize at an arts competition at the school'.[4]

In the Middle East, the Islamic religious police prohibit any PDA across much of the region, and almost every year we hear about some randy tourists getting jailed in Dubai for kissing in public.

In 'Western' countries, though, a heterosexual PDA is perfectly acceptable and completely normal; a kiss on the lips here, a peck on the cheek there, holding hands and hugging, maybe even a cheeky cupping of a buttock, it's all good! But members of the same sex showing affection? Ignorance and prejudice still cause some people not to accept it.

For LGBT+ people, to show affection in public can be risky, and in some countries, even a death wish. Same-sex sexual activity is still illegal in 70 countries worldwide, and you can actually receive the death penalty in 11 of those.[5] In 2016, 40% of the world's population lived in jurisdictions which criminalised same-sex sexual activity between consenting adults.[6]

But, even in countries without these archaic and barbaric laws, there are still difficulties for LGBT+ people. In 2020 the EU Fundamental Rights Agency released the results of the biggest ever survey of LGBT+ people in Europe. In the research two in five LGBT+ Europeans confirmed that they had been harassed because of their sexuality. Which goes some way to explaining as to why, even in the more liberal and accepting societies, 60% of LGBT+ people fear holding hands in public with their same-sex partner.[7]

The restriction of natural and consensual love is one of the sickest failings of modern 'civilisation'.

Whether through fear and ignorance, or through tradition and doctrine, we've seen the disruption of LGBT+ relationships, and the demonisation and obstruction of their ability to express love, for too long. As a male who has only ever been in relationships with females, I felt it important to explore this subject; to imagine and inquire about the situations I have been privileged to have never experienced.

Satellites

Satellites begins by developing a metaphor I first used in **The Sights** (which opens our 2015 album, *The Spark*), a song about a new beginning, and its chorus, specifically, is about looking for love:

> I'm searching far and wide, to find a planet to orbit
> Far and wide, I wanna scan and explore it

When you're interested, attracted or enraptured by someone, they're often all you can think about. This is because, when we're falling in love, we have heightened activity in the core parts of our brain's reward system. The neurotransmitter, dopamine, starts to flood these key areas of the brain, triggering feelings of pleasure. Nearly all addictive drugs produce this acute increase of dopamine, and in the same areas. If our longing for our new beloved seems analogous to a drug addiction, well, that's basically because it is! It's the same brain circuitry being triggered as when using nicotine, alcohol, cocaine, heroin or when gambling.

To me, the metaphor of being in orbit, oh so willingly, around a new 'planet', felt perfect. The gravitational pull of the person becomes a captivating force. We are, at all points, entranced by them.

Now, imagine being stuck in that orbit and never actually being able to 'land' on your new-found planet (I leave it up to you to decide what 'landing' means to you in this situation, dear reader ...).

The extension to the metaphor came to me in the vision of a meteor burning through the planet's atmosphere; it perfectly conveys the fiery passions at the beginning of a new relationship. Being 'let in' to that person's life for the first time, intellectually and intimately.

The frustration of being unable to show affection (be that by fear of public reaction or by keeping your sexuality a secret), then became the central theme of the track; and satellites, being objects that are in a constant orbit, observing a planet from a distance, yet unable to land on the object they're so fixated upon, felt like the correct cosmic expression for this upsetting situation.

> I wish I was a comet
> Burning up into the night
> I wish I was a comet
> But I'm just a satellite[8]

Anxiety Versus Excitement

With the subject matter being so pensive, I knew the song could easily go down a dark, brooding route, while musically I wanted it to be true to the experience of falling in love. The process of falling in love is obviously a thrilling one, so I wanted to try and convey excitement, purity and hope within the music, and that's when I remembered about the surprisingly close relationship between anxiety and excitement. I had learned about this a few years before, in therapy, and began to employ what I'd learnt, in the crafting of the song.

Anxiety and excitement are both arousal emotions and provoke very similar biological states, what separates them is the associations we make *about* those states. Anxiety focuses on what could go 'wrong'; excitement focuses on what could go 'right', and there has been some interesting observations about how we can exploit their close biological relationship.

Next time you're full of anxiety about something – maybe your heart is pounding like randy teenage lovers in a bedroom, maybe the butterflies are bouncing off your stomach lining like moshers in the pit – perhaps it's right before your big job interview, or right before a public speech – just try telling yourself that these feelings are actually not due to anxiety, but excitement. Doing so can elevate you out of some of the debilitating effects of anxiety; increasing your attention, your reaction time and your performance, so you can smash that interview or speech. This simple method, of reframing your anxious sensations in a positive light, has been proven in a number of studies and is called *anxious reappraisal*.[9]

Anxiety strikes when you feel threatened in some way. It is your body employing your fight or flight response. When this happens, your nervous system triggers physical symptoms in an effort to keep you safe: your heart pounds in order to prepare you to sprint away from danger, your stomach hosts a butterfly orgy in order to slow down your digestion. In these moments of anxiety we often try to calm ourselves. But going from this intensely jittery and active *fight or flight* state, to a relaxed, *rest and digest* state – where the parasympathetic nervous system slows down your heart rate and returns your digestion to normal – is a big leap in biological states, and is quite difficult to do. This can only really happen if we're able to truly convince ourselves that we're no longer in any 'danger', be that physical or psychosocial, be that real or imagined. It *can* be achieved through hacking your parasympathetic nervous system (i.e. by performing slow breathing techniques in order to 'trick' your body into thinking you are calm), *but* it's a much shorter leap from anxiety to excitement, biologically, and it's becoming clear that reframing your nervousness by calling it what it is, another kind of excitement, can boost your confidence levels and is, consequently, a better plan for dealing with anxiety in certain situations.

In one study, that I particularly enjoyed, by psychologist Alison Wood Brooks, participants had their karaoke skills tested on the Nintendo Wii. One by one, participants were asked to perform Journey's classic 'Don't Stop Believin''; but before beginning their turn at the mic, they were asked to say one of the following phrases out loud: 'I am anxious' or 'I am excited' (or, as a control, nothing at all).

Following their performance, interviews with the participants – as well as analysis of heart rate, vocal pitch, and volume – found that those who had verbally stated their excitement beforehand actually performed better, regardless of how nervous they were to start with. The excitement reappraisal didn't actually make the subjects less anxious, nor did it lower their heart rate, it just shifted their explanation for their underlying biological state from anxiety to excitement:

> By stating 'I am excited' out loud, individuals reappraised their anxiety as excitement and improved their subsequent singing performance.[10]

In this way, convincing yourself that your anxiety is actually just excitement is not lying to yourself whatsoever, anxiety and excitement are just two sides of the same coin.[11]

Wood Brooks suggests that instead of our anxiety slogan being 'Keep Calm and Carry On', a phrase more like 'Get Amped and Don't Screw Up' would actually be more beneficial.[12] There you go, this book has finally turned into a self-help book! I hope the anxious reappraisal technique helps you in your life. It's certainly a technique I've used in mine.

So, even though the heart of the story in **Satellites** is concentrated on social inequality and the difficulties associated with sexual orientation and gender identity, I didn't want to create a purely dark, sombre or tense song, I wanted to properly represent the feelings of someone in a newly forming relationship. I wanted the music to feel exciting, upbeat and hopeful, as these are the feelings that are present and powerful for anybody meeting a new love interest, *as well as* anxiety. This battle between excitement about a new relationship, and anxiety heightened by being justifiably afraid about publicly revealing that relationship, is evident in the lyrics:

> 'Cos I think it could be love
> But I can't show you enough
> I wanna burn through the atmosphere
> Soar like a meteor tonight

The love they feel is stunted. To some degree, its trapped inside them, unable to be let out through fear of public repercussions, be that ridicule or worse.

The correlation between anxiety and excitement is represented by the song's high tempo, too. It mimics the high heart rate associated to both emotions (a normal resting heart rate is between 60 and 100 beats per minute; the **Satellites** tempo is a very fast 180bpm). These two basic emotional states that, on the face of it, appear to contradict each other, became the two binding fundamental themes that the song was built on.

Public Attitude Towards Homosexuality

When meeting a new love interest, the reappraisal technique can help us function properly. It works because you can go from viewing the situation as a threat, to viewing it as an opportunity; a simple switch of focus from the negative to the positive.

The reappraisal technique *does* have its limits though. It is not of assistance when your situation *actually* has the capacity to be dangerous – as with the fear my friend felt about being a target of abuse – and when it's not possible to be reframed as an opportunity. For situations like these we must instead look at the root of the problem: ignorance and indoctrination.

In May 1990, the World Health Organization declassified homosexuality as a disease. Yes, in 1990 it was finally agreed that being gay was no longer a mental health disorder. (If that isn't a warning from history to always question the traditions, rules and perceived knowledge of your society, then I don't know what is!) The International Day against Homophobia, Transphobia and Biphobia commemorates this decision yearly on 17 May.

Shortly before that, in 1987, according to the British Social Attitudes Survey, 90% of people thought there was something wrong with sexual relations between same-sex adults. Thankfully, this figure has fallen year after year, as people's education and experience has increased. And it kept falling ... until 2018. In 2018, the UK had reached the point where only 33% of people thought there was something wrong with gay sex, but it was here that it began to plateau. NatCen, the independent social research agency who carried out the research, suggested that 'Liberalisation of attitudes does seem to be slowing down'.[13]

Perhaps, upon sensing a decline in their numbers, the ignorant and indoctrinated groups became more determined to make their socially conservative views heard? Religious and politically conservative groups have been increasingly vocal in their resistance to social liberalism (as we've already looked at, with the intolerance of the religious parents who protested outside primary schools in Birmingham, in Chapter 4).

The Closet

In the third verse of the song I imagine being brought up in one of these more socially conservative families:

> Surely all my family and my friends,
> My god and my ends
> They cannot all be wrong
> So I play along

The cognitive dissonance must be almost impossible to navigate. A jarring war between, on one hand; your closest and most trusted confidants and influencers; your loved ones, your beliefs, and your wider environment of influence (for international readers: 'ends' is slang for the part of city or town where you are from, used regularly here in London, deriving from Jamaican slang); and, on the other hand; your own feelings.

The pressure to conform to the accepted norms of your environment, to not upset your family or your church, to not be ridiculed by your friends, or heckled in public, can all prevent someone from 'coming out', or, when out, from being comfortable with public displays of affection.

> We refrain from touch
> We are satellites
> In a cosmic dance
> Amongst the northern lights
> And we orbit fast
> But I wish we could collide
> I'm sick of concealing
> I'm sick of the feeling
> I no longer want to hide

The stress of hiding your sexuality, of withholding your emotions and affections, of fearing the judgement and violent reactions of others, can all have a devastating effect on one's mental health. In fact, tragically, gay people are (depending on which study you quote) between 2 and 10 times more likely than straight people to take their own lives,[14] and twice as likely to have a major depressive episode.[15]

The researcher Travis Salway has spent the past 5 years trying to figure out why gay men are more prone to anxiety, depression and suicide: 'The defining feature of gay men used to be the loneliness of the closet, [...] But now you've got millions of gay men who have come out of the closet and they still feel the same isolation.'[16] It seems that it is not just when 'in the closet' that things can be difficult for gay people. William Elder, a sexual trauma researcher and psychologist, says:

> The trauma for gay men is the prolonged nature of it [...] If you experience one traumatic event, you have the kind of PTSD that can be resolved in four to six months of therapy. But if you experience years and years of small stressors – little things where you think, 'Was that because of my sexuality?' – that can be even worse.[17]

During adolescence, it is common for LGBT+ people to have their stress systems so activated, that they end up producing less cortisol, the hormone that regulates stress.[18]

This has a broad range of effects on physical health too. Homosexuals everywhere, at every age, have higher rates of cardiovascular disease, cancer, incontinence, erectile dysfunction, allergies and asthma – 'you name it, we got it' as the writer Michael Hobbes says in his excellent article which has informed much of this section of the book.[19]

> I still drag the closet
> All my limbs, they ache inside

This is all a type of *minority stress*: a chronically high level of stress experienced by members of a stigmatised minority group. It is these groups, who have had to put up with so much and still do, that we must strive to understand and to support, in any way we can. Please do not for a minute think that this is me demanding that any straight readers 'check your privilege', this lazy meme is not only inflammatory and ultimately unhelpful, but also it puts the focus on *you*, on your life as the 'privileged', instead of focusing on the minority group, stimulating empathy, understanding and support for them (i.e. this phrase aims to pull *you* down, rather than raise *others* up.)

Michael Hobbes' article talks about the critical constitutional amendments, passed in 2004 and 2005 by 14 US states, which define marriage as being between a man and a woman *only*. They caused an immediate upsurge in anxiety and depression among gay men – *even though* gay marriage wasn't legal anyway in those states to begin with. 'Gay men in those states showed a 37% increase in mood disorders, a 42% increase in alcoholism and a 248% increase in generalised anxiety disorder.'[20]

And these rates of anxiety and depression didn't just rise in those states alone, they rose throughout the *whole country*. Homosexual couples couldn't get married before or after this amendment, this was just those states giving their citizens a chilling reminder that they do not consider homosexuality acceptable or normal.

Minority stress is very real, to the point that even purely symbolic laws such as these have a very real and serious effect on the mental health of millions.

Transgender People

So far, throughout this section of the book, I've been focusing on the history and the continuing struggle for gay rights today, but I must make it clear; I of course acknowledge and celebrate the huge progress that we've seen over the years. At the time of the 1969 Stonewall uprising in New York City, every state – with the notable exception of Illinois – outlawed gay sex. Psychiatric experts classified homosexuality as a mental disorder, and most gay people stayed in the closet for fear of losing jobs, family or friends. Today things have undoubtedly improved dramatically, for many people.[21]

Now, though, it is transgender and non-binary people that more widely experience the curtailing of rights, or who are on the receiving end of regular waves of targeted public hostility. Seeing the vile online comments they have to tolerate, from those completely ignorant of gender dysphoria or the difference between 'sex' and 'gender', coupled with seeing the crusades against their rights by populist politicians,[22] inspired the lyrics of the middle eight section:

> Now online they discuss
> Whether I exist
> And in the court they decide
> Who I can kiss

The fight for free love still continues. The fight to be accepted for who you are still exists. The fight for more empathy carries on. And that fight is supported and thrust forward by allies.

The Importance Of Allyship And Solidarity

In the mid-1960s, a psychotherapist named George Weinberg noticed that some of his colleagues displayed discomfort around gay men or women. Upon learning that a friend Weinberg had planned on bringing to a work-related event was lesbian, they asked that he disinvite her. Weinberg concluded that they didn't just dislike her, they actually also feared her. The fear appeared so extreme to him, that Weinberg felt they displayed similar behaviour to people afflicted by phobias. He invented a word to describe this peculiar behaviour: homophobia.[23]

In a sexuality research study conducted in 2004, the psychologist Gregory M. Herek wrote:

> The invention of homophobia was a milestone. It crystallized the experiences of rejection, hostility, and invisibility that homosexual men and women in mid-20th century North America had experienced throughout their lives. The term stood a central assumption of heterosexual society on its head by locating the 'problem' of homosexuality not in homosexual people, but in heterosexuals who were intolerant of gay men and lesbians.[24]

From that moment onwards, Weinberg became a dedicated and very public advocate of gay rights. He was an active supporter of New York's fledgling gay movement, an opponent of psychiatric attempts to 'cure' homosexuality, and he helped lead the campaign that ultimately convinced the American Psychiatric Association to remove homosexuality from the handbook of psychological disorders. In fact, Weinberg helped turn the tables completely, when, in 2016 – the last year of his life, and still fighting the good fight – he suggested that 'the next big step should be to add 'homophobia' to the official list of mental disorders'.[25] having previously made it clear that 'I would never consider a patient healthy unless he had overcome his prejudice against homosexuality.'[26]

Freedom

Freedom is great, right?! Who doesn't love freedom?! For William Wallace, as portrayed in the 1995 film *Braveheart*, 'freeeeedom!' meant literal liberation from his English oppressors. But while freedom today is often used in equally impassioned battle cries, it can also be quite meaningless.

You see, the whole concept of freedom can be nebulous, and almost, well, bullshit. It can merely be a piece of political rhetoric that politicians use to get an emotional reaction from you – remember Aristotle's remark about how some speakers are all emotion and no substance? – it's often too broad, too all-encompassing, to have any real definition. In the US, shouting the word 'freedom' along with 'Merica', have become memes that ridicule a particular brand of flag-shagging, American Conservatism that ironically isn't talking about the freedom to 'conserve', only the freedom to exploit.

I was always sceptical towards the use of the word freedom, but it has slowly begun to dawn on me that the word is often deployed in even *more* cynical and malicious ways than I had previously realised.

Freedom is not absolute. That is to say, some freedoms can restrict, limit, or destroy other freedoms. Or, as the writer George Monbiot puts it, 'one person's freedom is another's captivity'.[27]

Religious Freedom Is Not Absolute

For example: religious freedom (the freedom to practise and promote religious doctrine and ideas), is of course a vital part of a fair and just society, but religious freedom can sometimes impede upon *other* freedoms – as is the case in the restriction of gay rights. In this way, some sects of Christianity, Islam and Judaism are openly homophobic, and their dogmas restrict the lives of LGBT+ people.

Conversely, a person's personal freedom to love and live with their consenting partner, whatever sex or gender they may be, does *not* impede upon anyone else's freedoms. Two people having gay sex certainly doesn't prevent you from praying and praising your lord saviour. Freedoms such as this, that do *not* detract from anyone else's liberty, pose no injury to others; these freedoms *are* absolute.

Any restriction of gay rights is not just damn-well mean, but also illogical. If gay rights pose no threat to other freedoms, you cannot oppose gay rights on an intellectual basis. You need the influence of dogma instead; you require the argument that the freedom and rights of LGBT+ people somehow offend some higher power, or go against some long held tradition; you need the influence of archaic religious or cultural indoctrination.

Philosophically, as soon as your argument relies on nothing else but cherry-picked quotes from inconsistent and capricious doctrines – doctrines somehow full of both bloodshed and intellectual banality – written by mediocrities living millennia ago, you're clearly losing the moral high ground.

Religion's Beginnings And Stagnancy

The fundamental weakness of religion is that it is static or set in stone; it has a very limited capacity for revision and development. There is a scripture, and that scripture is then fixed and hallowed. No ifs, no buts. At almost the exact opposite end of the spectrum, philosophy and science strive only to develop *themselves*. That is their core purpose, in fact, and why I firmly believe they are better tools by which to live your life. Science is like a living organism; it changes, it adapts, it advances.

Religion, generally, remains archaic. Stuck representing the era in which it was birthed. It *just about* keeps up with moral progress, though it has to be reluctantly dragged along by society, kicking and screaming like a petulant child.

Homo sapiens went from roaming the Earth in small tight-knit tribes, to relatively suddenly (from an evolutionary perspective) finding themselves in heavily populated city-states, getting used to the idea of private property and inequality. Organised religion served as a useful tool to scare the inhabitants into keeping the peace.

With this context in mind we can begin to see how commonplace and ordinary its teachings were. 'You shall not covet your neighbour's wife, or his manservant, or his maidservant, or his ox, or his ass', reads one of the Ten Commandments. It wasn't revelatory, it was merely the best moral teachings of the time – personal property was a new concept, so saying 'don't steal', was a way of establishing the new non-egalitarian order. (You're a lot more inclined to accept someone being an owner of some land simply because they stood upon it first and claimed it for their own, if you believe there is an all-seeing creator who endorses the concept of real estate and watches your every move. Not to mention this creator will happily refuse you entry to his kingdom of Heaven and send you plummeting into eternal hellfire should you demand the owner share or attempt to steal from him.)

Often religion was so unremarkable and morally unimaginative that it simply adopted the laws that already existed, as is the case with Islam's adoption of the prohibition of same-sex relations, which by around the 8th century CE (when a great deal of the Islamic texts were written), was an almost universal orthodoxy.[28]

Doctrine is pertinent to the era it was written, and then swiftly ages (or morally decays), as human understanding outgrows it. Scripture, by definition, is fairly resistant to moral development, it is static. This is why so often throughout history religion has used the tools of brute force and fear to maintain its relevance instead.

Sadly, the crude moral musings of ignorant people working out how to order and govern post-hunter–gatherer societies are still treated as relevant by many today, and its indoctrinated homophobia still has a residual effect on society. Even for those who are unreligious, homophobia is still 'contracted' by the wake that organised religion has left behind.

The Science

Scientifically there is, of course, no refuge for the homophobic argument either. Ask any anti-gay devotee why they oppose gay rights and they will most likely say that that it is 'unnatural'.

OK. Firstly, homosexuality has been known to occur throughout the whole animal kingdom. Bruce Bagemihl published the first comprehensive study of the subject in 1999 with his book *Biological Exuberance*. He collated clear evidence of homosexuality in more than 450 species of mammals, birds, reptiles, insects, and other animals worldwide.[29]

Regardless of its clear prevalence in nature, those who call homosexuality 'unnatural' most probably have a fundamental confusion about the very concept of 'nature' itself. From a biological perspective, there is no such thing as something being 'unnatural'. Whatever life forms evolved on this planet, and whatever behaviours those life forms partake in, (even homosexual sex!), simply *are* natural. What else could they be? Nature is life and the evolution of life on our planet. What these poor confused people actually mean when they claim that a behaviour is 'unnatural' is that it isn't what *their* God intended, or isn't what *their* tradition accepts. Again, it is a fundamental lack of empathy. Here's the historian Yuval Noah Harari:

> Christian theologians argued that God created the human body, intending each limb and organ to serve a particular purpose. [...] To use them differently than God intends is unnatural. But evolution has no purpose. Organs have not evolved with a purpose, and the way they are used is in constant flux.[30]

Evolution endows a species with small and gradual changes over vast amounts of time, so at first a small change may serve one particular helpful purpose, but it can quickly evolve further to serve another purpose entirely. Therefore anything that we can do, is perfectly natural in the biological sense. We come well-equipped, overly-equipped even, for a whole variety of behaviours. Harari uses a great example:

> Insect wings evolved millions of years ago from body protrusions on flightless bugs. Bugs with bumps had a larger surface area than those without bumps, and this enabled them to absorb more sunlight and thus stay warmer. In a slow evolutionary process, these solar heaters grew larger. The same structure that was good for maximum sunlight absorption – lots of surface area, little weight – also, by coincidence, gave the insects a bit

of a lift when they skipped and jumped. [...] Some insects started using the things to glide, and from there it was a small step to wings that could actually propel the bug through the air. Next time a mosquito buzzes in your ear, accuse her of unnatural behaviour. If she were well behaved and content with what God gave her, she'd use her wings only as solar panels.[31]

To call homosexual behaviour unnatural is not a truthful assessment of reality, it is a cultural decision; a mythical dogma. And if we do not update our mythical dogmas in order to reflect reality, we fail to exercise our empathy properly.

Restricting someone's ability to love and be loved is a moral disaster, and sighting 'God's will' as your reasoning, is to show you profoundly misunderstand the biological basis of life and how it evolved.

It is for this reason that I 'write a prayer to Venus', the Roman goddess of love, in the second verse of **Satellites**. I'm asking her 'What is life without affection?'. I'm demanding an explanation for the pain that many higher powers have ostensibly caused throughout the ages, and for the drivel that people *still* spout in their name. But of course, higher powers – at least how we have so far imagined them – are not real. It is indoctrinated humans who we have to question and enlighten.

Homophobia is an inability to see the world through another's eyes, it is a tragic lack of empathy. As we looked at above, it is a prime example of how empathy can be hacked, employed only in a limited and biased sense; the religious homophobe restricts his empathy, using it only towards heterosexuals like themselves. It is in moments such as these, when lead blindly by religious or cultural allegiance, that our rationality and compassion disappears.

Foundations Of Modern Homophobia

In the 1970s, Americans considered just *one* minority group more harmful than homosexuals. Can you guess which? It was ... atheists![32] Religion was clearly still the main port of call in establishing the moral order then, and the main obstacle to LGBT+ people living a free and safe life.

Though the influence of religion is diminishing today, it still has a lingering effect on the formation of people's values and sense of normality. Furthermore, when those who remain devout see the increase in the relative acceptance and empathy of modernity, they view it as an attack on their cherished – but narrow-minded – way of life. Homophobes, spurred on by their ignorance or inability to see other perspectives, then feel like they are acting to preserve all that is 'decent' and 'right', and this motivates them further. The psychologist Bob Altemeyer puts it like this:

> [Homophobes] see homosexuality as a sign that society is disintegrating and as a threat to their sense of morality, [...] Their self-righteousness makes them feel they are acting morally when they attack homosexuals. It overcomes the normal inhibitions against aggression.[33]

As discussed in Chapter 4, this is *tribal anger and moral outrage*. The tribe teaches that the purity of the heteronormative relationship is sacred. This indoctrinated belief is then held with such emotional intensity (due to its members identifying emotionally to the tribe and their beliefs) that when the belief is not adhered to, it motivates *moral outrage* in them. So, like many of the worst things in life, homophobia is due to a mixture of ignorance and arrogance.

Our old friend, and inventor of the word 'homophobia', George Weinberg realised homophobia was spurred by 'a fear of reducing the things one fought for – home and family. It was a religious fear, and it had led to great brutality, as fear always does.'[34]

The religious assertion that normality contains only one type of relationship – the heterosexual, monogamous family unit – has caused unfathomable amounts of pain in people's lives throughout history (think of all the failed arranged marriages. The frightened, closeted homosexuals acting straight. The dysfunctional or toxic relationships stubbornly continued, just to avoid the public 'shame' of 'failure'). Religion was simply unimaginative, it had no idea of the innate variability, motivations and desires of human nature. Yet it mindlessly dictated that everyone live by one specific heteronormative relationship framework, and ordered followers to punish anyone that didn't fit into this narrow order.

When You're Certain You're Right

In the early 1990s Bob Altemeyer would tell his university students that he was gay at the start of the educational year: 'For most, over the course of the year it makes their attitudes toward gays more positive, but if their hostility toward gays is based on religion, their views are hardest to change.'[35] The devout harness no rationality here. They rely purely on emotional argument, all noise and stubbornness as they limit their empathic response, 'their emotionality makes them prone to simplistic thinking. It is such emotionality that makes anti-gay stereotypes so hard to change'.[36]

As we looked at with tribalised political allegiances, people can also fall for *confirmation bias* when it comes to their fear or hatred of homosexuals. In 1990, the psychologist Mark Snyder offered this explanation:

> If your attitude is negative, it snowballs, and you only notice and remember facts that are negative, until it becomes a full-blown prejudice, and you tend to assume everyone feels as you do. As you become more convinced, you are more likely to take the next step and put your beliefs into actions like outright discrimination or violence, whether it's against blacks or gays.[37]

When you're emboldened by faith and by filter bubbles, you feel certain in your beliefs and have a misplaced sense that everyone agrees with you. Your homophobia then only strengthens. Homophobes begin to see themselves as guardians of all that is good or moral. Keepers of the faith.

Homophobia is an extreme example of how easily our empathy and sense of morality can be lead astray, but there are many subtler ideologies that can be equally damaging and radicalising. It is therefore a solid idea to get into the routine of asking yourself, during any debate or analysis, 'are there any group allegiances that are limiting *my* empathy?' 'Is my rationality and compassion being impaired in any way?' Keeping an eye on our own biases is a good safeguard against having our empathic response hijacked and controlled by bigots and ideologues. Put bluntly; it's a good safeguard against becoming a dickhead.

Additionally – The Spark's Vulnerability Theme

Before we leave this subject, I just want to relay one interesting point that struck me during my research. A point that further corroborates the central theme of our last album, *The Spark*. The album's core tenet, as reflected upon with the giraffe quote in Chapter 4, was that we *must* see ourselves as we naturally are: a vulnerable and fragile species. Furthermore, we must realise that this is *not* a weakness, it is essential to our capacity to learn, to communicate, to empathise, to cooperate; everything that makes us exceptional.

The misjudged discipline of the Victorian era – the 'stiff upper lip' mindset – ingrained self-restraint and detachment into the British psyche. The showing of emotion, or fragility, or femininity, was taught to be showing weakness. Sadly, today, males are *still* discouraged from sensitivity or ridiculed for admitting fragility. This archaic view of masculinity causes serious psychological suffering, contributing to the substantially higher suicide rate in males.[38]

On the subject of the motivations behind homophobic abuse and violence, the psychiatrist Dr Richard Isay says, 'Seeing a feminine man evokes a tremendous amount of anxiety in many men; it triggers an awareness of their own feminine qualities, such as passivity or sensitivity, which they see as being a sign of weakness.'[39] In this way, it seems that homophobia may also be related to the inability of men to accept their innate vulnerability as human beings. It is a miserable rally against reality.

Do not be ashamed by femininity, or sensitivity, or gentleness, or a measured degree of passivity; these are all human traits, they are natural, they are within us *all* and, what's more, they are beneficial to us! They should not cause shame, they should be encouraged and exercised.

/ / / / / / / / /

In 1969, two friends of George Weinberg, the gay activists Jack Nichols and Lige Clarke, were the first people to use Weinberg's term 'homophobia', in print. Another ally, Al Goldstein, the editor of the tabloid *Screw* magazine, had given them a regular column to discuss gay matters, a bold move given that it was a 'decidedly heterosexual publication' at the time.[40] Goldstein gave Nichols and Clarke control over the content of their columns but, as with the majority of publications, in his role as editor he composed the headlines himself.

On 23 May 1969, they wrote their column on the subject of homophobia, describing it, among other things, as a fear that limited men's experiences by declaring 'sissified' things like poetry, art, movement, and touching, as off limits. This article offered a whole new perspective on masculinity, showing just how ridiculous and restricting homophobia was. Goldstein decided on the rather brilliant headline:

He-Man Horse Shit.[41]

I couldn't agree more. Here's to accepting vulnerability and sensitivity and art and affection. And here's to empathy and allyship.

5.3 The Pressure's On

Big History

I've mentioned *perspective* a lot throughout this book. One of modern society's most consistent failings is that we are not encouraged to regularly broaden our perspective. So, I thought that, just for a moment, I could encourage *you* to try and take what we could call a *supra-human perspective*. The prefix supra- just means 'above' or 'beyond', so I'm asking you to attempt to view humanity through the eyes of another species. Maybe an alien visitor, or even a god. Let us look down upon the Earth together, analyse human behaviour and broaden our perspective.

Just a small ask, then!

Let's try it from this angle …

In 1990, just over one year since passing the orbit of Neptune, the space probe Voyager 1 had far surpassed its primary mission and was heading out into interstellar space at a speed of around 40,000 mph. It was (and still is) the most distant human-made object from Earth. During this time, eminent American astronomer Carl Sagan suggested that Voyager take one last picture, pointed back towards Earth. Sagan believed it would provide a meaningful perspective on humanity's place in the universe. It took a bit of persuasion and, even after the project was given the green light, was met with many delays. But, eventually, the frames were taken. With the radio signal travelling at the speed of light, the images took nearly five and a half hours to reach home. The photographs featured, almost entirely, empty black space. Except for one tiny blue speck, smaller than one pixel, among the vast empty vacuum of blank infinity. *That* was Earth.

Never had our planet seemed so fragile. Never had humanity seemed so delicate. Never had our human differences seemed so trivial, our disunity so inconsequential, and our commitment to self-interest so perilous. And – to *my* mind – pathetic.

This image and resulting mindset was, in part, the inspiration for Enter Shikari's 2008 track **We Can Breathe In Space, They Just Don't Want Us To Escape**:

> All our empires, our philosophies,
> Our practised faiths, our revolutions, our proud sciences,
> Are but a flicker in one day of the lives of the stars

When you look at *big history*, and view human life from a comprehensive perspective, our commitment to self-interest, economic growth, and consumerism begins to appear bewilderingly misguided. Much as our hostile politics and factionalised fervour appears petty and provincial when we recognise that it all takes place on a fragile and finite 'pale blue dot' (as Voyager's photograph and, as a result, the Earth itself, came to be known).

I find it fascinating that – when our perspective is narrow and focused on the *micro* and the immediate – we are capable of becoming riddled with tribal anger. Yet, if we transcend out into space and take the *macro* view, our hate seems to be burnt away by the sun's rays as they sweep out across the solar system.

Sadly, while reifying and epiphanic images such as the pale blue dot *have* worked in collectively inspiring deep reflection, not much has transpired in terms of systemic change from these observations. Nor, for that matter, has anything else. We have now reached a precipice, where the future seems less and less likely to harbour human civilisation. Yet we grow increasingly (and wilfully) ignorant to that fact; ignoring the root causes and stubbornly digging our heels in. Too focused on provincial, short-term self-interest to realise that what we are actually digging our heels into is sinking sand.

This broader perspective – taking into account the fragility of our planet and our species – needs to be the very starting point for the makings of a new social design. Our precarious situation, cosmic circumstance, and, indeed, our broader reality, all need to be the first considerations in its formation.

Music Expands Our Circles

We've already been through *some* of the list of historical advances which have helped to develop and expand human empathy: language, literature and drama, along with increased mobility.

From folk to rock, from soul to hip hop, music has a broader reach than literature, spurs a more immediate emotional impact, *and* does so with greater ease. Music itself has an astonishing power to deeply affect us; greater than any other art form. If a singer is honest and bold with their lyrical content, and the music backing those lyrics is well crafted, they can open up the minds of their listeners with minimal effort. Instrumental music is equally capable of expressing emotion with great precision and power. Just as with the tragic dramas of Ancient Greece, music today can be a great healer; another art form to help achieve Aristotle's catharsis. We experience someone else's difficult emotions and it helps us understand our own. It helps us realise that we are not alone in feeling those emotions.

Music opened up our world and the scope of our understanding, and I see it as my duty – as a songwriter today – to challenge and broaden your perspective still, as well as strengthen your compassionate response. Anything that increases our ability, as a species, to see life through someone else's eyes, or imagine ourselves in someone else's position, increases our moral consideration for others, and this is essential to our ongoing survival.

The Pressure's On

Well, we've covered a lot of ground already. We've looked at the true scale of the problems that face humanity. We've looked at their interconnectivity and at the trends which highlight the immediacy in which we need to act at a structural level. Our species stands at a crossroads. We are paused and poised at this crucial point in our history: **The Great Unknown**. There has never been a point in human history where the stakes have been so high, where our power has been so great, or our next steps so pivotal.

The pressure truly is *on*.

Anyone who dares scale the vast mountain range of problems we face does so with an immense weight upon their psyche. Existential dread is one thing but, alas, most of us have enough on our plates as it is, with the problems we face in our personal lives. For the majority of us, modern living has become enough of a test of character, strength, and perseverance already, before we even get to our bigger picture problems.

The Pressure's On is a song that addresses loneliness, stress, depression and anxiety. It's a song about the existential threats we've already discussed, but also being so burdened by worries and problems in our personal lives that we fail to even address our own existential dread! Essentially, it's a song that encapsulates the overwhelming nature of life right now.

Afflictions Of Civilisation

Did you know that for the vast bulk of human existence – 99% of it in fact – we lived as hunter–gatherers?[1] Since the very first human species, *Homo habilis*, or even as far back as *Australopithecus* (around 3 million years ago), we have travelled in groups, hunting when we were hungry, sleeping when we were tired, and then –

when the land was stripped of all fruit, nuts and meat – we ventured on, giving it a chance to restore and regrow.

How do you think these pre-industrial, pre-agricultural humans faired mentally? Do you think they were crippled with loneliness, stress, anxiety and depression, just as we are today?

Early humans were most likely completely free from these afflictions. They lived in tight groups, which provided secure social bonds, they kept their physical fitness through all the – you guessed it – hunting and gathering, and they preserved their health through balanced diets.

We can hypothesise about early human mental health by studying hunter–gatherer societies surviving today, who show very few examples of these ailments. In his book *The Depression Cure*, psychologist Stephen Ilardi writes:

> Modern-day hunter–gatherer bands – such as the Kaluli people of the New Guinea highlands – have been assessed by Western researchers for the presence of mental illness. Remarkably, clinical depression is almost completely nonexistent among such groups, whose way of life is similar to that of our remote ancestors. Despite living very hard lives – with none of the material comforts or medical advances we take for granted – they're largely immune to the plague of depressive illness that we see ruining lives all around us.[2]

In our own society today, we see a continuing rise in mood disorders and mental health problems. In fact, depression is the leading cause of ill health and disability worldwide.[3] One of the reasons for this is quite obvious, when you think about it; our lifestyle has simply changed so dramatically, and so *quickly*, from that which we were built to experience as *Homo sapiens*.

There is now a profound difference between the way of life our genomes were evolved for, and the contemporary environment we actually find ourselves in now. In biology this is called an *evolutionary mismatch*. We evolved to be suited to a hunting and gathering lifestyle, but as we moved (in such a short space of time, evolutionary speaking) towards a stationary agricultural lifestyle, our genes got left behind, so to speak. We're trying to run vastly different software from that which the hardware (our body) was built for. We freeze, we glitch, we break.

Taking an evolutionary approach to understanding the conflict between our biology and our modern way of life has only become an area of study in the last few decades. Yet this is the crucial perspective needed to help us understand and fight the diseases that are exacerbated by our modern lifestyle (and that's everything from obesity, cardiovascular disease, depression, and many forms of cancer). It is this pivotal outlook that also must inform us when redesigning our social systems to better suit our nature.[4]

'I Can't Quite Believe The Time That's Gone Flying By'

10,000–12,000 BCE

Population of humanity on planet Earth = 10 million
Percentage of humans that are hunter–gatherers = 100%

During this period, we saw the beginnings of what we now call the *agricultural revolution*. We began to settle down, choosing one geological spot to call home and, as a result, our lives became dramatically more inactive. We invented the concept of 'property' and began to amass resources, rather than sharing them (yes, interestingly, it was at this point that we first begin to see inequality rear its ugly head. Prior to this, hunter–gatherer societies had been egalitarian and shared resources). Our previously diverse diets began to narrow, gradually becoming fundamentally altered from the nutritional characteristics of our ancestral hominins.[5]

1500 CE

Population of humanity on planet Earth = 350 million
Percentage of humans that are hunter–gatherers = 1%

A dramatic difference. The development of agriculture had changed everything. Hunter–gatherer lifestyles survived only in small pockets around the world.

Following on from this period – around 200 years ago – we observe the next big change in the way of life for *Homo sapiens*, the Industrial Revolution. Here, we see a modern lifestyle emerge that was even *further* disconnected from that which we were evolved to experience.

How much has the human genome changed in the couple of centuries since the Industrial Revolution? It hasn't. 200 years is only eight generations, give or take a generation or two; nowhere near enough time for selection to take place. Our lifestyle changed dramatically, but our hardware remained the same.

Population of humanity on planet Earth = 3 billion
Percentage of humans that were hunter–gatherers = 0.001%[6]

And here, to top it all off, since the late 1970s the neoliberal economic consensus has continued the trend that has moved us away from our original active, cooperative, social lifestyle – the lifestyle our bodies and minds are assembled for – with its vehement distrust of anything remotely *collectivist*.[7]

Stephen Ilardi puts it best: 'We were never designed for the sedentary, indoor, socially isolated, fast-food-laden, sleep-deprived, frenzied pace of modern life.'[8]

To summerise, the lives of our ancestors were lived in strongly bonded hunter–gatherer tribes. Changes in the environment (e.g., in diet and other lifestyle conditions) that began 10,000 years ago occurred too recently on an evolutionary time scale for the human genome to adjust to them. Changes in the social structure have also occurred. Tribes lived and worked together to meet the challenges of survival. In contrast, today we live in weakly bonded, extremely fractured societies, working against each other to meet the challenges of our own survival. All of this creates multiple problems for our physical and mental health, making way for many chronic diseases that have been birthed out of the diet, lifestyle, and environment of Western civilisation. These diseases have been called *diseases of civilisation*.[9]

When We Lack Connection To Others ...

I step out the door and it's dark and I'm on my own

This is what it often feels like in our modern world of rampant individualism. There are so few structures of community support left, and so few incentives for new ones to be built. Consequently, we feel more and more lonely. Britain has a serious loneliness problem – to the point where it is sometimes seen as the loneliness capital of Europe.[10] – and over in the USA, it's believed that between 61% and 75% (depending on which studies you consult) of Americans are lonely.[11] It's pretty clear that loneliness is a major problem for the more individualist countries ...

Traditionally, it has been the older generations who have suffered from loneliness,[12] but more recent trends lean towards it being the *younger* generations who are the most lonely of all the age groups.[13] For millennials, and even more so for

Generation Z, a great deal of life takes place online. In case it's not obvious; the amount of *friends* or *followers* you have does not leave you feeling socially fulfilled, it's only physical relationships that actually count.[14] But as we discussed in Chapter 4, social engagement and connectedness has been in decline for decades. So much happens online now, yet the online world rarely satisfies our natural thirst for contact, connection and collaboration.

This may go some way to explaining why every new generation has increasingly higher rates of depression than the one which preceded it.[15] Indeed, loneliness is both a cause *and* an effect of mental health problems.[16] Our socially fractured way of life is not *only* associated with depression and anxiety, but dementia, stroke and heart disease, too.[17] In fact, researchers warn that 'Loneliness is more dangerous than obesity and as damaging to health as smoking 15 cigarettes a day'.[18] We cannot cope alone. We're simply not built for it.

Due to the COVID-19 pandemic, and the examinable effects of social distancing, we've recently been gaining a lot more insight into loneliness. Studies are showing us that our need to connect is as fundamental to our survival as our need to *eat*! We *literally* hunger for social contact. (I honestly felt that myself during lockdown, and I'm quite a well-practised introvert!)[19]

When We Lack Connection To Nature ...

I breathe in the scent of the pine and the conifer cones

This line could have been taken straight out of **Shinrin-yoku**, our ode to nature from *The Spark*.

Sometimes my only source of beauty, calm and tranquillity comes from nature.[20] A walk in the woods. A swim in the sea. A jog through a park. Nature provides us with an easy way to help remedy our evolutionary mismatch. It has long been proven to have excellent health benefits, and can be a strong restorative antidote when battling mood disorders.[21]

It's no wonder that when we force ourselves out from behind our desks and back into nature we feel revitalised. It is where our bodies were built to be. The environment we were adapted for. It is us getting back to our roots! (If you'll excuse the pun.)

Our bodies were not evolved for overworked, overstressed, concrete-covered modern living. The majority of humans still lived rurally as recently as 1950, when only a third lived in cities. Today though, over 50% of us live in cities (or *megacities*; those cities with over 10 million inhabitants). By 2050, two thirds of us are estimated to be living in these built up, urban areas.[22]

What is most sad about this gradual urbanisation is that it has been accompanied by a rise in isolation and loneliness. Living surrounded by people doesn't mean you actually get to know them, of course. Especially if there's no structure that encourages it.

We are drifting away from nature and drifting away from each other, and this new, more disconnected, lifestyle is impacting upon our mental and physical health.

Prosociality Is In Our Bones

> I feel like I've fallen down a staircase and broken my bones

Our bodies, built for one scenario, have been thrust into a completely unrelated one. We yearn for connection but are served mostly separation. For 99% of our species's existence we have been dependent on each other. Trusting each other. Cooperating with each other. Yet, now, our socioeconomic system disincentives those essential human characteristics. Cooperation and compassion are in our bones, but those bones are breaking under the pressure of a mismatched lifestyle.

Struggling? It's Your Own Fault

Today, our sense of separation from one another is fermented by what we could call the *cult of personal culpability*. It is a pervasive system of belief that primes you – with all the excited vigour of a self-help guru – to 'take responsibility for your own life!' because, in doing so, you 'free' yourself from any dependence on others, thereby ridding yourself of potential weakness! It almost sounds motivational. Until you realise that this is not helpful advice for us as individuals or as a society.

In the 1950s and '60s the word 'responsibility' was directed more at our duty *to* society; how we interact and cooperate and help each other. Remember JFK's famous speech? 'Ask not what your country can do for you; ask what you can do for your country' – responsibility was something beyond the self, it was towards your family, your community and your country.

Later, in the 1980s, the concept of responsibility began to narrow dramatically. Ronald Reagan promised to make 'free enterprise and personal responsibility' a central theme of his presidency.[23] This was a core tenet of the newly accepted neoliberal worldview, it replaced collective responsibility and social solidarity with self-sufficiency and accountability. Economically, it was decided that we have no commitments to each other; it was every man for themselves.

This idea soon became a widely accepted notion. It transcended politics and became common sense, and paved the way for big changes in how we define our society or civilisation. Ultimately, it has led to the consistent underfunding of key social services and safety nets throughout Western democracies – what need for social support if everyone takes responsibility for themselves ...?

It's when you have bad fortune, though, that the *cult of personal culpability* really starts to reveal its underlying brutality. An individual's specific circumstances, their bad luck, or their vulnerability are ignored, and society convinces them that *they* are solely responsible for their own misfortune. During times of hardship – be that related to finance, health, employment, or any number of situations that could befall a person through no fault of their own – you are left to fend for yourself and told that you only have yourself to blame.

Social support has been cut dramatically over the decades. In 1996, Bill Clinton followed in Reagan's footsteps, with Congress resolving to 'end welfare as we know it'. With bipartisan support, the state now punished people for failing to live up to their responsibilities, even if they were raising children or couldn't find a job due to recession. (In my mind, this act only serves to solidify the notion of the broken two-party political system, as, in effect, despite any surface differences, both the Republican and Democrat parties adhered to the same core economic programme.)[24]

The neoliberal wet dream then, essentially, came true. The deregulation of the workplace, the decline of unions, as well as the slashing of unemployment, welfare, and social security benefits, forced the American people (and, ultimately, the rest of the 'Western world') to heed this individualist sense of personal responsibility.

The welfare state, with its vital safety nets providing social and economic support to those who need it the most, has been continuously slashed.[25] Universal healthcare has been consistently underfunded and restricted, education has become prohibitively expensive for most, and secure jobs that actually provide a liveable salary have become harder to get. This has stunted social mobility (social mobility = making poor people richer) and helped inequality grow to the obscene levels it has reached today.

At this point you may be saying, 'Hold on Rou, I see examples of people who "came from nothing" and ended up rich and famous all the time!' I know, I know, so do I. And yes, these stories make us all believe that people truly *can* scale the ladder and go from poverty to great wealth, if they act with personal responsibility. But remember, the media focuses on things that are extraordinary, or rare, this is just another example of *availability bias*. If truth be told, the 'rags to riches' stories we hear are few and far between; those people are the lucky ones, the anomalies. The game is well and truly rigged *against* those whose only mistake was to be born to poor parents. Something that they, I'm sure you'll agree, cannot be held personally responsible for.

> And this isn't what I planned
> I wish you could understand
> I throw myself into the day
> But I just seem to ricochet ...

The uncomfortable truth is that if you're born into a poor family, or are somehow vulnerable, you will most likely stay poor and struggle to make ends meet.[26] Whereas if you're born into a rich family and can afford all the life-comforting trimmings of health insurance, financial support, an expensive and vibrant education, *and* extra-curricular education etc. you will most likely thrive, even if you're incompetent.[27] This is not exactly a revelatory analysis, the same internal market logic was clear even to Matthew when he wrote his gospel in the Bible:

> For to everyone who has, more shall be given, and he will have an abundance; but from the one who does not have, even what he does have shall be taken away.[28]

The director of a study that analysed a huge amount of data from the National Center for Education Statistics said this:

> To succeed in America, it's better to be born rich than smart, [...] What we found in this study is that people with talent that come from disadvantaged households don't do as well as people with very little talent from advantaged households.[29]

Well, that explains Boris Johnson.

No matter your effort, natural ability, and perseverance, if you're unlucky enough to be born poor, it seems it's your own fault, and you must simply 'learn your lesson'. In reality, fortune rarely favours the bold, it mainly favours the wealthy.

Free Will

The philosopher and neuroscientist Sam Harris, in his excellent book *Free Will*, dismantles the common assumption that we all have personal agency or control over our actions:

> You did not pick your parents or the time and place of your birth. You didn't choose your gender or most of your life experiences. You had no control whatsoever over your genome or the development of your brain. And now your brain is making choices on the basis of preferences and beliefs that have been hammered into it over a lifetime – by your genes, your physical development since the moment you were conceived, and the interactions you have had with other people, events, and ideas.[30]

How can you be solely responsible for your life's failings if you are not responsible for your own genetic and environmental influences? Today, it is somehow assumed that everyone is born equal, and if you fail ... well then, you only have yourself to blame! We punish people for circumstances they are not responsible for.

The *cult of personal culpability* ignores reality. It ignores the stifling levels of inequality of wealth and of opportunity. It takes away community solidarity and replaces it with blinkered, overblown and rigid individualism.

Even when you contemplate the nature of *luck* – how quickly our fate can turn, and often through no fault of our own – you realise the *cult of personal culpability* is one of the sickest and most sadistic mindsets you could employ when structuring a society. Indeed, what is the point of civilisation if it is not to support *all* people, especially the less fortunate? Civilisation without social solidarity is just a highly populated, noisy and brutally competitive stock exchange.

'A War Of All Against All'

Ironically, the seminal 17th century philosopher Thomas Hobbes said that 'the state of men without civil society [...] is nothing else but a mere war of all against all'.[31] How very backwards this statement is in today's world, where civil society now actively *encourages* a 'war of all against all'. In fact, look at the full Hobbes quote: 'the state of men without civil society (which state we may properly call the state of nature) is nothing else but a mere war of all against all'. Hobbes (though of course a fantastic philosopher) was, here, even more incorrect still. Through modern scientific inquiry, it is becoming more and more apparent, that our state of nature – our ancient hunter-gatherer state – seems to be one that tends more towards group cooperation and compassion, not a 'war of all against all'. See this note for a more detailed technical analysis of Hobbes' 'state of nature', scarcity and ownership.[32]

The Retreat Of Real Civilisation

The saddest thing about 'freeing' ourselves from any dependence *on,* or responsibility *to* others, is that it actually shuts us off from the world; it is the worst possible way to live a human life. It should be thought ridiculous to try and persuade a species whose success was built on acts of connection, cooperation and reciprocal altruism, that each individual should be solely responsible for themselves and have little responsibility toward one another. Just as it is equally ridiculous to say that society does not have any responsibility towards individuals in return.

The saddest consequence of a decline of social support and safety nets, is that caring for others begins to become perceived as a risk that isn't worth taking. Being independent becomes a defence mechanism we employ to protect ourselves against the 'burden' of the other. Our natural willingness to cooperate and be compassionate withers, replaced by the mantra 'every man for themselves!'

For **The Pressure's On** chorus, I chose to highlight this shirking of social responsibility by utilising the shoulder-shrugging recitation: '*you* better figure it out now' – effectively 'I don't care, that's *your* problem, mate' – rather than the more unifying call to arms: '*we* better figure it out now'.

This *every man for themselves* attitude of self-interest is the fundamental core of all our major problems today. It is the nucleus of social destabilisation. It is the very root of our heartless existence.

When a society has embraced a selfish mindset to free itself from the burden of care for others, then it easy to see how the demonisation of immigrants becomes a logical next step; 'We can't afford to look after our *own,* let alone *them!*' come the cries from citizens whose social services have been starved and dismantled. Their anger at their own lack of means gets retargeted towards the other, rather than the political architects who have dismantled the structures which should provide social solidarity and stability.

We *can,* of course, look after *everyone.* That is not some misty-eyed, utopian pipe dream, we just have to structure society in a way that matches our more cooperative and compassionate instincts. At the moment, the main structural incentive is for each individual to achieve as much wealth as possible. We believe that this will bring us contentment and satisfaction. But, as I'm about to argue, this is not the case.

The End Goal Of Individualism = Personal Wealth
Personal Wealth ≠ Happiness

In these individualistic, competitive cultures, where citizens strive to be a successful self-made person, what exactly *is* the end goal? Is success simply measured by how much money you have or power you amass? Is that all there is? It would seem so. So, the question *then* becomes, 'does that even lead to a more socially fulfilled, happier life?'

Well, I guess we'd have to ask the people at the top. Those who, by any metric, have 'made it'. What do those in the top 1% say, when analysing their lives and their mental health?

A survey of high-net-worth American individuals (possessing, on average, around $78 million each) found, for all their success in amassing wealth, they had not successfully freed themselves from life's worries. They were actually just as beset with anxiety, dissatisfaction and loneliness as the rest of us.[33] Most telling of all the findings was that the respondents were dissatisfied *even* with their own immense wealth! Financial anxiety was present to a large degree. These people are in the wealthiest percentile of Americans, yet most of them *still* don't consider themselves financially secure or content with what they have. On average they believed they'd need to have about 25% *more* money in order to feel financially secure.

This, as wild and ridiculous as it seems, is most likely due to our ability as humans to quickly acclimatise to new states of being; with more wealth, the things we previously considered to be luxuries, become normalised, and then our sights get set higher still. And when *that* next financial milestone is reached, we look higher again. We simply believe our next goal is another 25% more wealth, *regardless* of how much we have. It. Never. Ends.

Robert A. Kenny, one of the architects of the Boston survey, said:

> Sometimes I think that the only people in this country who worry more about money than the poor, are the very wealthy [...] They worry about losing it, they worry about how it's invested, they worry about the effect it's going to have. And as the zeroes increase, the dilemmas get bigger.[34]

I know, I know, right now you're playing the world's tiniest violin while shedding a sarcastic tear for the super-wealthy. This all seems preposterous, and I'm not informing you of all this to try to convince you that the super-wealthy deserve our sympathy and support, no. I am telling you this because I want to make it clear; The very core of the individualistic, competitive and self-interest obsessed way of life, where the main goal is to increase your own personal wealth, does *not* lead to fulfilment. The central tenet to modern living is to consume, to amass, to accrue, yet it brings us no core satisfaction and does not free us from loneliness. If you don't achieve your heart's desires, life can be coated in misery. But likewise, if you *do*, still, all the wealth in the world cannot banish misery. Wealth is but a veneer of happiness. It is connection, community, and purpose that counts.

I think this has been best recently summed up by the actor Jim Carrey, whose films made up a large proportion of my VHS and DVD collection as a kid:

> I wish people could realise all their dreams and wealth and fame, so that they could see that it's not where you're going to find your sense of completion.[35]

The fact that the wealthiest people, who have *so* much, *still* believe they need *more* and are *still* unsatisfied and unhappy, exemplifies the innate sickness of our culture.

In the past, the rich used to be known as 'pillars of the community'. They would sit beside other less well-off members at their local church, they would be involved in community groups, they would give liberally to the poor, they would fund various local initiatives and charities. They were part of their community. This consequently gave them a sense of belonging. Now, I would argue this is not so much the case. The wealthiest burrow themselves away behind the grand walls of their estates, shutting themselves out from their local communities, or what's left of them. It is no wonder the wealthy today are unhappy. They have their eyes fixated on the wrong prize.

Individualistic Countries Report More Loneliness

It is perhaps not surprising that cultures or countries most dedicated to staunch individualism – places where those in power have cut social services the most – report the most loneliness.[36] When people see the other as a burden, they are not encouraged to put value in friendship and community.

As a quick side, it is also worth pointing out that loneliness particularly affects young men. Today, 'manliness' is still measured by the archaic units of strength, success and wealth. Emotional secrecy and the concealment of vulnerability are still standard behaviour for young men. 'Men' are taught to be focused on personal success at the expense of true friendship and mutual support.

Alleviating Loneliness

> You try to tell me that everything will be fine
> I appreciate your belief
> But I'm not sure you're right

The truth is – if you'll allow me to momentarily be proper bleak, again – your life, whoever you are, however wealthy you are, most probably, won't be 'fine'. It will be far from it. It will veer off in erratic directions. It will be formidably different to your predictions, and full of difficulty because of it. It will be full of questions and few answers.

For every question that does get answered, and for every adversity you traverse, more questions will arise and more difficulties will emerge. These difficulties are infinitely harder if approached alone.

That is why, as decent human beings, we all hope we will be able to help friends, family, or even the occasional stranger, when life throws adversity their way. Sometimes, though, you don't need to try and fix a person's problems, or even make vain attempts to reassure them, you just need to be there beside them.

We are all quite aware that our lives will only contain short periods where 'everything' is 'fine'. These will be rare intervals of bliss among continuous degrees of adversity, for most of the time we will be struggling with some kind of problem.

So you just need to make sure you are available for people. You do not have to speak or act, but simply *be there*. Sometimes that's all that's necessary.

Life's difficulties are myriad and exhausting, yes, but facing those problems *alone* is utterly intolerable. If you can simply alleviate someone's loneliness, you're *often doing them* the best service possible.

The Music's Uplifting Answer

Lyrically, there is no resolve or pleasing resolution to this song. I wanted to hammer home this rather bleak outlook on life in order to express the potentially harsh reality we will likely experience. Why? Because in presenting no hope, no turn around, no victory, and certainly no Disney-style happy ending, the song instead suggests one of the most central moral imperatives to life for any principled human being – kindness. It suggests the answer lies in *you*, in your actions, in society's actions.

As the old cliché would have it: you never really know what other people are going through. It's most likely everyone you meet is experiencing something incredibly difficult, in fact they could well be at their absolute lowest moment and have little hope for resolution. Compassion is therefore paramount. In our personal lives, it means being there for others when they need it most. Within our societies, it means building a socioeconomic structure that supports people, especially when they are at their lowest points.

With the lyrics centred on the inevitability of adversity, I wanted to express hope within **The Pressure's On** some other way. I had the song build, harmonically and texturally, to a colossal and warming crescendo. Upon hearing, I would hope you can't help but visualise it being played live to a swarming mass of bodies, all moving as one, caught in the euphoria. The lyrics reflect the struggles of life, the music exemplifies the answer: compassion and community.

Structural Change

Before we move on, I just want to focus on the importance of structural change. Problems such as loneliness, anxiety and depression – and, indeed, all the other diseases of civilisation – are not *personal* problems. They are not *private* matters. They are *social* problems. As individuals, no matter how hard we try, or how lucky we are, these diseases will not disappear. This is the disaster of our modern age; systemic stagnation lays the groundwork for our perceived 'individual problems', *as well as* leading to the large-scale social problems of climate change, ecosystem decline and polarisation.

• Diseases of civilisation are only to be expected, when forests are worth less alive than they are chopped down, and where the mood-enhancing presence of nature is ignored and ecosystems are viewed only as resources to be exploited.

• Diseases of civilisation are only to be expected, when self-interest – a 'war of all against all' – is our central economic mechanism and basic assumption of human nature.

- Diseases of civilisation are only to be expected, when endless consumption and the accumulation of wealth are the perceived indicators of achievement.

The very things we need *most* in order to overcome the diseases of civilisation – compassion and empathy – are bludgeoned out of us by the lifestyle our current system advocates. Jamil Zaki says:

> Empathy evolved for a world in which we were interdependent, aligned, and visible to each other. And now, more than ever, we're isolated, tribal, and anonymous. It's almost like if you were to design a system to break human empathy, you really couldn't do that much better than we have.[37]

To treat the diseases of civilisation we need to *restructure* civilisation. We must recognise our modern lifestyle as unhealthy and unnatural. A study on depression in the *Journal of Affective Disorders* summarised it well:

> Modern populations are increasingly overfed, malnourished, sedentary, sunlight-deficient, sleep-deprived, and socially-isolated. These changes in lifestyle each contribute to poor physical health and affect the incidence and treatment of depression.[38]

- We are not a solely self-interested species; our greatest strengths actually reside in our cooperative and compassionate actions.

- We are not an urban species; we thrive in communities *aligned* with nature, not in concrete cityscapes living lifestyles that pollute it.

- We are not a solitary species; our lives are enriched and validated by contact, communication and cooperation, *not* isolation.

- We are not a sedentary species; our health is sustained through being agile and active, not stuck behind a desk half our lives.

And that reminds me; I've been sat down at my desk writing this section for far too long. I'm away for a walk! But I'll leave you with some final thoughts from Stephen Ilardi, the psychologist we met earlier. Ilardi found that by implementing just *six* key lifestyle changes, over 90% of people are able to tackle depression.[39] Even one lifestyle change – exercise – beats taking anti-depressants.[40]

Together, we need to have a serious conversation about how we can restructure our society. Until we do, we will just seem to ricochet, continuously. Blaming ourselves. Demonising others. Further dividing, while the existential threats discussed in

Chapter 2, loom closer and closer.

You're up on your feet now, aren't you? Fist in the air, you're ready for revolution! Ready for the scientific redesign of society! I can hear you shouting 'Let's do this, then! What on Earth's stopping us ...?!'

6 The Mechanics Of Control And Constraint

T.I.N.A. & Marionettes

Have we fallen into a mesmerized state that makes us accept as inevitable that which is inferior or detrimental, as though having lost the will or the vision to demand that which is good?

Rachel Carson (from *Silent Spring*, 1962)

What on Earth *is* stopping us from addressing the failures of our socioeconomic system as a whole?

A lot of the time, when you criticise an existing structure, you are faced with an immense backlash. There is anger, there is bewilderment, there is dismissal, there is ridicule, there is contempt. Even with the abundant evidence of environmental crises and social decline discussed throughout this book (and there are, of course, so many more equally relevant crises I haven't discussed),[1] there is *still* a steadfast commitment to protecting the status quo. These people, who attempt to prevent any real change, or even any *discussion* about real change – we shall call them *the self-appointed guardians of the status quo.*[2]

Even starting a conversation that highlights the blatant failures of our current socioeconomic system is often met with denial, personal attacks, or perhaps, if you're lucky, just disinterest. There appears to be widespread agreement that our established system is the *only* viable way of arranging society and that 'there is no alternative'. This phrase, famously attributed to Margaret Thatcher, a phrase heard so often, verbatim or otherwise implied, that it has come to be abbreviated as T.I.N.A.[3]

Conviction Versus Curiosity

One of my favourite philosophers, Bertrand Russell, wrote an essay in 1933 titled 'The Triumph of Stupidity'. It was about the then current rise of Nazism in Germany. Within it he said, 'The fundamental cause of the trouble is that in the modern world the stupid are cocksure while the intelligent are full of doubt.'[4]

I think, therefore, in order to test that you aren't 'cocksure' and 'stupid', or that you haven't fallen into fanaticism – like the Nazis, brainwashed by an ideology – it's a good idea to ask yourself the following question, regarding your beliefs: 'What would it take for me to concede that I'm wrong?'

If the answer is a fervent 'Nothing! I *know* I'm right', then congratulations my friend, you may very well be an idiot!

This is the state of mind that drives a lot of religious or ideological fervour. The religious homophobes we talked about in the **Satellites** section suffer from this dangerously self-assured over-confidence. They are *right* and others are *wrong*; they do not try to empathise with other views, or attempt to see the world from another perspective. Where they should stop and think, they only assert.

This highlights the interesting hazard of holding a steadfast conviction; a firmly held belief or opinion can limit your broader or deeper understanding of an issue. It can blind you to the truth through confirmation bias or motivated reasoning, so it's important to stay curious. Curiosity is not only key to creating civil conversations where before there has only been hostility (as we looked at in Chapter 4), but also to keeping an updated, correct view of the world, *and* avoiding fanaticism.

Curiosity opens up your world. Conviction closes it off.

That's not to say that, after deliberation, we shouldn't have *any* beliefs or confidence in those beliefs. We need boldness, to be heard in today's society, and we need a degree of self-assurance to be taken seriously, but we can present ideas boldly without leeching ourselves onto an ideology, or getting our identity tangled up within an unyielding tribal allegiance. We must devote ourselves to progress, not to ideologies or traditions. Don't get caught leechin'.

Another example of people plagued by cocksure, stubborn convictions are those who assert that the way things are today is the way things should be. The people who assert that our current career politicians are the best suited to lead us; that our current form of representative democracy (and the narrow two-party system it creates) is the best type of democracy; that the free market has all the answers to today's problems; that neoliberalism is a functional and logical economic structure.

Our political system, our media, our social network technologies, the core economic values of growth and self-maximisation; for too long we have held these to be acceptable systems, even satisfactory, appropriate or healthy.

Guardians Of The Status Quo

We must ask these staunch believers the same question; 'What would it take for you to concede that you are wrong?'

What would it take for them to admit that our current system is struggling, archaic and inept? Is there an amount of crises we have to endure for them to accept the impotence of our current framework? Is there a threshold to how much existential danger they're willing to accept in favour of preserving the status quo?

The most indoctrinated guardians of the status quo will answer in the manner of Russell's cocksure idiots; 'This is the best system we have!', they'll say, maybe then going on to compare our current system to other systems – 'Oh, so you must want communism then?' – this is the only option they're aware of outside the status quo; it's all they have in their narrow frame of reference. They'll gleefully remind you of the (self-proclaimed) communist regimes of Mao or Stalin, and the immense loss of life they brought about;[5] creating a convenient *straw man* argument as they rush to repeat the same old boring debate between capitalism and communism.

To be honest, not a great deal has changed since we released the song **Gandhi Mate, Gandhi** in 2012, the lyrics of which contain the following verse:

'You're a communist! You're a fucking Utopianist!'
Ah, there come the emotive labels
But their attempt just fails
'Cause man, we're so far out your comfort zone

And that's the problem. The guardians of the status quo rarely think outside the confines of the historical network of systems attempted so far. They seem quite incapable of thinking about how – as human understanding and capability evolves – we could now create a *new* system, better suited to our position today, than the narrow, faulty, contradictory, out of date systems we currently implement.

Neither Capitalism Nor Communism Are The Answer

Communism, like capitalism,[6] has no ability to deal with our modern problems. Karl Marx himself was born in 1818, when CO_2 was stable at around 265ppm in the atmosphere (it is now almost double that, at 410ppm, far higher than at any point in the last 800,000 years).[7] He was a child of the Enlightenment period, we are children of the Anthropocene; these two periods are drastically different in all manner of ways.

As I pointed out in Chapter 2, today we are no longer passengers on Spaceship Earth. We have taken the wheel. We are changing our planet's climate. We live in a completely different world. Marx's criticisms of capitalism were, of course, insightful and timeless, but they were also limited in scope to the context of the era. His work predates, by a long way, any understanding of the critical relationship between economics and ecology and so, like capitalism, does not hold a viable answer to today's problems. A new socioeconomic system today simply *must* be constructed in the 'real world'. In the natural world. It must recognise, structurally, the natural limits of our environment and incentivise, not the exploitation of the environment, but the conservation, for our own good. There is no human life on a destabilised and plundered hothouse Earth. Our system must realign us with nature.

The Management Of A Household

The word 'economy' comes from the Greek *oikonomia*; *oikos* meaning 'house' and *nemein* meaning 'manage'. Therefore an economy is the intelligent management of a household. Today, can we describe our current socioeconomic system as the intelligent management of our household, Earth?

How was your family's household managed when you were growing up? Did the wealthy and powerful (read: your parents) act in their own self-interest? Did they take more and more of the house for themselves? Did they eat more and more of the food themselves? Did they leave you to fend for yourself, teaching you 'personal responsibility'?

Hopefully they acted in ways completely opposite to this, or else you possibly had an horrific childhood (in which case, I apologise for bringing back the memories!). Hopefully they, instead, shared everything with you and showed you the patience, kindness and support that allowed you to develop into a healthy human being. Hopefully they instilled the importance of not being wasteful, selfish or greedy; in essence, to be *economical*. That is how you manage a successful household; with rationality, compassion and solidarity. Currently, our economy does not mimic the intelligent management of a household. It is quite dysfunctional, in fact. When you contemplate the endless short-term self-interest that it glorifies, perhaps it should not even be considered an economy at all? It's more a raid. We manage our household, the Earth, by gutting, ransacking and raiding it. We have the management style of a racoon in a trashcan.

The Madness Of Infinite Growth

I am part of the generation that learnt their politics during the era of the Occupy movement. The nauseating realisation that there was 1% of our population who were hoarding the majority of wealth was a huge wake up call. I learnt a lot from that movement, and I experienced a lot too! (I will certainly never forget DJing outside the Bank of England on New Year's Eve 2011, to support those occupying the square!)[8]

Things have moved on since then, but, unfortunately, in the *wrong* direction. The nauseating wealth and power of the 1% has been overshadowed by that of the 0.1%. In 2017 the World Inequality Report confirmed that the richest 0.1% of the world's population had 'increased their combined wealth by as much as the poorest 50% – 3.8 billion people – since 1980'.[9] We can only assume things have got worse since then, too. Even during the height of the COVID-19 pandemic – which meant lost jobs and livelihoods for many people – billionaires actually increased their wealth by more than 25%, in the space of a few months.[10] And boy ... don't even get me started on the 0.01%.[11]

This increase in wealth inequality is mainly due to the neoliberal policy of cutting tax for the richest in society. In 2019, for the first time in history, Donald Trump's tax cuts helped billionaires pay a *lower* rate than the poorest people in society.[12]

The other excellent point that the Occupy movement brought to light was probably best summarised by the great British filmmaker, natural historian and the man everyone wishes was their grandad, David Attenborough:

> We have a finite environment – the planet. Anyone who thinks that you can have infinite growth in a finite environment is either a madman or an economist.[13]

Our system has us raiding the planet's resources in the name of continuous short-term profit, with no concern for the future and no mechanism to fix our continuous resource overshoot. (Yes, 'humanity's demand for ecological resources and services in a given year exceeds what Earth can regenerate in that year.'[14])

Our extreme devotion to infinite growth really is a disease in itself, as Edward Abbey said: 'Growth for the sake of growth is the ideology of the cancer cell.'[15] It would be bad enough even if we were devoted to infinite growth *within* a wonderful world of socioeconomic equality, but it appears this dedication to continuous profiteering mostly just rewards the richest, adding to the unfathomable wealth of the 0.1%.

I say 'unfathomable' because it really is difficult to properly grasp how much money a billionaire *actually* has. I've found one of the best ways to get my head around the sheer enormity of the imposing numbers is to convert currency into time.

The average wealth of a household in the UK is just under £300,000; so, let's say instead that an average citizen has 300,000 seconds to spare. Now we'll convert those seconds into days:

- An average UK citizen has 3½ days.
- A millionaire has 11½ days.
- A billionaire has 31½ *years*!!!

Quite a fucking drastic escalation at the end there, right? The billionaire isn't just 'the new millionaire'. They have amassed an amount of wealth completely outside anything we have seen before. It is truly insane. In this way, our system today is just as morally dwarfed as in times past, we've just replaced the hoarding, and all-powerful kings and pharaohs, with billionaires.

How Is Wealth Inequality Sustained?

You may be thinking 'How on Earth is this extreme wealth inequality sustained? How do we accept it?'. Well, it certainly relies heavily on the economic philosophy of *infinite growth*. This is the *engine* that 'legitimises' wealth inequality; if we believe we can all create our own huge amounts of wealth because resources are ubiquitous and infinite, then what is wrong with huge amounts of wealth? Just get stuck in! There's enough for everybody! We can all get there if we work hard!

But of course we can't *all* amass huge amounts of wealth. As we looked at in Chapter 5; there is really no such thing as equality of opportunity or social mobility (making the poor, richer), they are borderline fictional.

If infinite growth serves as the philosophical engine that sustains wealth inequality, then the fuel and the pistons are the corporate press, the spin doctors and lobbyists. As George Monbiot says, 'If voters can be persuaded that insane levels of inequality are sane, reasonable and even necessary, then the concentration of income can keep growing.'[16]

It is our systematised dedication to infinite growth that legitimises not only inequality, but also individualism; if you can produce and consume indefinitely, then it's easy to argue that we can all just look after ourselves. If there's more than enough to go around, then what need for social solidarity? Just help yourself!

But, again, there is *not* 'more than enough to go around'. A clear way to exemplify that is to concentrate on money itself:

- There is $80 trillion in the world.
- Yet there is $200 trillion in debt.[17]

There is not enough money in circulation to cover all our debts.

This is a direct infliction on the less affluent. The more that wealth is concentrated in the upper percentile, the less and less there is for everyone else to squabble, swindle, and compete over. Poverty is built into this system.

Infinite growth and self-interest are the two defining pillars of our economic structure and they both rely on each other for legitimacy. Yet neither are aligned with nature. They are immensely socially and ecologically damaging.

Social Effects Of Wealth Inequality

The obscene levels of inequality that our economic system produces diminishes all that is good about civilisation. In my mind, one of the most important books ever written is *The Spirit Level* by Richard Wilkinson and Kate Picket. It documents clearly and extensively that the more inequality there is in a society, the worse that society's outcomes are, by almost *any* factor you could measure; physical and mental health, education, violence and imprisonment, social mobility, social trust and child wellbeing – all of these are adversely affected as inequality increases. The more unequal a society, the more dangerous it is, with less educated, less trusting and less healthy citizens.[18] On top of that, inequality is *also* a source of our most vile tribalistic frames of mind; it is a driving force in racism, nationalism, and other forms of bigotry. No matter how hard we all fight as dedicated anti-racists, if our focus is not on changing the economic system, then the racism will continue.[19]

Our dedication to the short-term profit motive and the wider mechanism of infinite growth has caused insurmountable suffering through inequality – a state that brings more pain, in every form, as it grows.

Economic Models Do Not Adapt

OK, so; in many ways, capitalism is a shocker of a system, clearly. But many people will still argue for its continuation. Some will say we just need to tweak some levers and dials on the machine. Some will say we haven't even had pure capitalism yet, and if we only gave complete control to the free market, all our woes will be fixed. Some will argue the opposite; that a fairer, gentler capitalism is possible through more socialist-orientated policies, and that giving more power to the state is the answer. But neither revision will get to the core of the problem of what the system incentivises. Capitalism rewards the worst aspects of our nature: *self-interest,* as well as the destruction *of* nature: *infinite growth.*

The struggle, also, is that the economic system is so colossal and stubborn, it is very difficult to change. Keynesianism – the prevailing economic model prior to neoliberalism – failed because it did not adapt. It worked really quite well for a while and is responsible for the post-Second World War boom, but then as the world moved forward at a fast pace, globalisation killed it. Now, neoliberalism is producing unseen levels of inequality and cannot adapt to the problems and nuances of today. It too will die. It is just a matter of how much pain it must cause first, before those ideologically leeched onto it admit we need something new.

Our current socioeconomic system is simply not the intelligent management of a household. It harms, rather than supports, public health, along with social and ecological stability. Let's briefly turn our sights back to communism, then, seeing as that's the only other alternative, apparently ...

(Hopefully, you can almost hear my eyes rolling in their sockets as you read that sentence.)

Neither Capitalism Nor Communism Are The Answer 2

For those who walked the Earth during the Enlightenment period of the 17th and 18th centuries, the impact that capitalism's commitment to growth would come to have on the environment was, of course, yet to become apparent. Marx saw nothing fundamentally wrong with infinite growth, indeed, it was intrinsic to the communist economic model of productivism too. Therefore, he could not appreciate that when capitalism eventually failed, it would actually be due to the finite nature of our planet's resources and the civilisation-destabilising effects of climate change.

It's sad, of course, that for many of us, it wasn't until we started influencing the climate that we realised capitalism was not healthy or sustainable. Especially as we've known about the numerous inherent contradictions within capitalism for years; those rigorously addressed by Marx and countless others.[20] It is only now, where our future hangs in the balance, that we are finally beginning to appreciate the systemic nature of societies ills.

We are still discouraged to take a systems perspective though; that is, we only see the small-scale problems – bad apples, specific faults – and very rarely do we correctly link them back to the socioeconomic structure; the *actual* cause that needs to be addressed. As I said in Chapter 4 we are focused on changing the *corrupt players*, not the *corrupting game* itself.

Systems are rigid, they hang on as relics of the past. They're too big and too clunky to efficiently and quickly adapt. At present we grip onto social and economic frameworks from bygone eras. As stated in the first verse of **T.I.N.A.**:

> F16s flying overhead
> The present is the past
> That we cannot shed

We are being restricted by our dedication to ideas whose time has passed.

'F16s flying overhead' is a reference to the violent extents some are willing to go to, to protect this system and ensure more profits. It was inspired by the Iraq War. The war itself was seen by some as an opportunity for business to capitalise on the resources in the territory. This is 'disaster capitalism' – a term coined by Naomi Klein in her book *The Shock Doctrine*, which outlines how exploitative economic policies are often snuck in while a population is too shocked and distracted by some natural or human-made disaster.[21] Klein describes the 2003 invasion of Iraq, using the tactic they called 'shock and awe', as the most comprehensive and full-scale implementation of the shock doctrine ever attempted.

Through military force, US companies were able to exploit Iraqi territories and their people (for example; Halliburton – a US oil field services corporation – made $39.5 billion from the Iraq war).[22] The supersonic fighter aircraft, the F16, was used throughout 'Operation Iraqi Freedom'.

This desire to exploit should be part of a dark 'past', yet this behaviour survives as humanity has not managed to rid itself of the system that incentivises the behaviour.

Adaptation

Even thinking generally; to believe that systems can continue indefinitely, unchanged – that we can just go on with the same damaging traditions, industries, and incentives – is colossally foolish. A sane civilisation would value and pursue flexibility. We must have a constant keen eye on how to progress and adapt as a society, if we are to survive as a species. As brilliantly put in Leon C. Megginson's neat summary of Darwin's theory of evolution:

> It is not the most intellectual of the species that survives; it is not the strongest that survives; but the species that survives is the one that is able best to adapt and adjust to the changing environment in which it finds itself.[23]

What *would* actually represent the intelligent management of a household, do you think?

What can we do better?

What alternatives are there?

These are the very questions we should be *encouraged* to think about from youth onwards.

We should be teaching systems theory, teaching the ability to understand layers of cause and effect, teaching the ability to broaden our perspective and solve our biggest problems... instead, we're teaching 'there is no alternative!'

We are curious, creative, problem-solving creatures. It's what we *do*! Building new worlds should not be discouraged.

In summary my friends: adaption is essential. Stasis is death.

> It's the essence of humanity
> To build an infinite reality

T.I.N.A. Definition

'There Is No Alternative' is the most stubborn and debilitating of mindsets; it seeks to obstruct change and even stunt creative thought itself. It belittles and ridicules anyone who wishes to consider that our lot could be improved. It is the biggest mental obstacle to progress today, the great aversion to development.

For the rich and powerful, T.I.N.A. is an *assertion*. Obviously, they are incentivised to keep things the way they are because they want to hold on to the comfort they have secured through status, wealth, and authority. Asserting the dogmatic mantra 'there is no alternative' louder and louder, while the current system brings only worsening sociological and ecological results, is their defence mechanism, their tantrum. They pledge loyalty to the status quo and attempt to squash anyone questioning it or offering anything different. (As we looked at in Chapter 4, the tobacco industry and the fossil fuel industry are two examples of this mindset on an industrial scale; both reacted to calls for change with dishonesty, attempts to mislead the public, and denial. All in order to protect their position.)

For the rest of society, T.I.N.A. is an *assumption*. For some of us, there is a tragic ignorance of our capability. There is a lack of imagination, confidence and courage in discussing new ideas and designing new possibilities. In effect, we assume this is the best we can do.

For others, there is a tragic ignorance of our species's mouldable nature. We believe society truly is a 'war of all against all'. We assume this is our human nature, rather than a behaviour, or psyche, which our socioeconomic culture has instilled in us, and if we believe we are naturally self-interested, a system built on self-interest actually makes perfect sense! Poverty is natural, and necessary, if there are to be winners and losers. Imprisonment, punishment and inequality; all are just and fair. We assume these outcomes are unavoidable realities of life, and that sticking to the status quo is the best we can do to overcome them.

A Crisis Of Creativity

To assert or assume that there is no alternative is to have a failure of imagination.

> It's a crisis of creativity
> We've forgotten our ability

David Flemming – one economist who *did* understand how economics and the environment are inextricably linked – said; 'if the mature market economy is to have a sequel, it will be the work, substantially, of *imagination*'.[24]

That seems clear, right?

In order to move on from our disastrous current system, we need to create a new one from scratch. Or, at least, make substantial adaptations to our current system (adaptions *so* substantial it wouldn't bare any resemblance to its original form!). This will all take *serious* imagination.

When writing this album, I kept hearing about a human 'crisis of creativity', or our 'incredible failure of imagination', on the subject of tackling climate change especially.[25] Upon further reading, I began to discover that this wasn't just the frustrated experience of a few disgruntled activists. The science was confirming a general decrease in imagination throughout populations.

The Torrance Tests of Creative Thinking are, as the name would suggest, tests to evaluate creativity. They have been conducted in the US consistently since the 1960s. When test results over the decades were collated and analysed in more recent years, some clear trends emerged; Imagination and IQ rose together until the mid-1990s, at which point they parted, and imagination went into a 'steady and persistent decline'.[26] 'How can this be?', I thought. Surely our imaginations fluctuate? Surely some folks are more imaginative than others? Some of us more imaginative at different times or after different experiences? How *can* a wholesale decline in human imagination be taking place?

Hippocampus

The answer to those questions lies in particular changes that have occurred in human society, changes that have, again, taken us further and further away from our natural hunter-gatherer state, with disabling consequences. I'll take you through a couple, shortly. But, first of all, let's take a little look inside your brain ...

The hippocampus is the part of your brain most linked to imagination, as well as memory. You have two hippocampi, they are shaped like seahorses (the name actually derives from the Greek for 'seahorse'), and they are buried deep in the middle your brain, one in each hemisphere. Typically, the hippocampus gets smaller once a person hits their mid-fifties, leading to memory loss, so it's important to try and keep this part of the brain especially healthy.

Now, a defining aspect of the modern world is stress. We're chronically stressed, stuck in fight or flight mode as we navigate life's difficulties and deal with our mountains of work, debt, or personal strife. Prolonged stress is a state that is incredibly toxic to the body, but especially to the hippocampus (which is particularly vulnerable to the stress hormone, cortisol). Stress causes atrophy in the brain, which you can think of as similar to tooth decay; it's effectively a slow and subtle form of brain damage. When we are chronically stressed, anxious, isolated or suffering from trauma, our hippocampus can shrink by as much as 20%![27] This then impedes our ability to think hopefully about the future, *and* in an imaginative capacity. This, it turns out, is what is happening in our current society; stress is everywhere and it's shrinking the very part of the brain pivotal to imagination.

Our system is abound with stressors: stress caused by the shrieking 24-hour negatively biased news media, stress caused by government-imposed austerity measures (a debunked economic policy,[28]) and stress caused by the innumerable pervasive effects of wealth inequality.

The very faculty we require most to innovate ourselves out of this stress-inducing mess is our imagination. Yet, ironically, as our system produces more and more stress, our imagination declines further.

Additionally, as our way of life causes increasing ecological destruction, it is destroying one of the facets of our planet capable of reducing stress ...

Nature

Researchers in Japan – birthplace of the *shinrin-yoku* (or forest-bathing) concept – have studied nature's effects on our health. In one experiment, participants took a walk while having their blood pressure, heart rate, and heart rate variability measured, as well as filling out questionnaires on their mood and stress levels etc. One group walked in a forest, the other in an urban centre, and the walks were all of equal length and difficulty. The results showed that those who walked in forests had significantly lower heart rates and higher heart rate variability (indicating more relaxation and less stress), and reported better moods and less anxiety, than those who walked in urban settings.[29]

Tragically, the one sure-fire way to reduce stress, simply being *in nature*, is being taken away from us as we increasingly live in urban centres and spend more and more time in front of screens, rather than in the countryside.

Our system also *incentivises* us to spend less and less time in nature; cities are where the money and jobs are, and the great outdoors is to be valued only as a commercial playground to be exploited. Nature is viewed as a commodity instead of a health and creativity-boosting resource. With less time spent in nature, our imagination and creativity are stunted as our hippocampi shrink. Anytime you're feeling stressed, just think of the little cowering and delicate seahorses in your brain, and promptly take them for a walk in nature! Or try meditation.[30]

Denying ourselves access to natural environments starves our brain. When among nature, we practice an effortless type of attention known as *soft fascination*,[31] which creates feelings of pleasure, the opposite of the tiring, dispiriting influence of urban environments.[32] The link is becoming clearer and clearer as more studies begin to confirm how our imagination is *strengthened* by spending time in nature.[33] With our lives increasingly centred around the stressful and fatiguing city environment, though, our imagination is suffering. As George Orwell put so succinctly: 'The imagination, like certain wild animals, will not breed in captivity.'[34]

Following the World Wide Web's invention in 1989, life changed extensively throughout the 1990s. The internet, of course, dramatically *improved* life in all manner of ways, but it also helped propel this general decline in our creative capacity. The psychologist Larry Rosen suggests that our imagination 'is probably on the decline exactly in the opposite trend of our time spent on smartphones'.[35] Just like with urbanisation, the digitalisation of our lives is also reducing our imaginative capacity.

You should pause here, and take a moment to congratulate yourself for actually reading a book – an activity that is, sadly, in sharp decline[36] – instead of endlessly scrolling through your social media feed!

But the really worrying effect of digitalisation can be found with children; the average American child is said to spend up to 7 minutes a day playing outdoors, yet spends over 7 *hours* a day in front of a screen.[37]

Play

It's not just being outdoors and away from screens that's pivotal to imagination. *Play* itself is, too. The pioneer play theorist Brian Sutton-Smith said that 'The opposite of play is not work, it is depression.'[38] He helped us realise that play involves 'the wilful belief in acting out one's own capacity for the future'.[39] whereas depression is characterised by a complete inability to see one's prospects improved in the future. Essentially, a loss of proactive hope.

And, guess what, children are playing less and less. And the trend is not only caused by the allure of technology.

Over the past 60 years in 'the West' there has been a gradual, but overall dramatic, decline in children's freedom to play with other children, without adult direction.[40] The Psychologist Peter Gray tells us that we're now living in a 'play deprivation experiment.' For children and adolescents, life is now much more stressful than in previous decades. Kids' days are rammed full of schooling, more schooling, then homework and sports.

'But sports!' you might exclaim, 'that surely counts as play, doesn't it?!'

Gray disagrees:

> One of the crucial defining characteristics of play is that it is directed by the children or players themselves. It's self-directed. Adult-directed games like sports, or activities in school where a teacher is telling children what to do, is not play by my definition.[41]

Taught forms of play, with rules and structures, are completely different from autonomous, imaginative, free-play. Sports, I'm afraid, are not the type of play that are pivotal to developing creativity.

For children, play is an education through discovery and innovation, the same growth is not found from a parent's shouts of encouragement on the sidelines of the football field.

Hunter–Gatherer Play

Isn't it interesting, though, that our society – one so centred around economic competition – has found its major pastime to be competitive sport? Hunter–gatherer societies didn't have this form of competitive play, they just had free-play, and loads of it.

Gray, who has studied surviving hunter–gatherer societies over the years, says:

> What I've learned is in these band hunter gatherer cultures, children play. They are free to play all day long. There's no such thing as anything like school. There's no sense that it's the adults job to educate children. Children learn on their own and they learn in play. They learn by watching, observing, and incorporating what they see in to their play. That's how children are designed to grow up.[42]

It turns out, these lifestyles of play produce some of the brightest, happy, cooperative, well adjusted, and resilient children that anthropologists have ever observed anywhere.[43]

The world has changed dramatically for children. Decades ago, they could play unsupervised in the streets, in the parks and in the woods. Today, on the other hand, our youth is the most stressed section of society. It is teenagers who are the *most* anxious, with most of them citing schooling as the main source of their anxiety.[44] The stressful, one-size-fits-all, test- and grade-obsessed education system, is damaging the imaginative capacity of the youth.

Play In Adult Life

To take a broader perspective, and refocus back on adults, play has been infantilised; framed as an immature, or worse, unproductive activity. Which feels like common sense, if we accept the idea that life *after* childhood is purely a structured and serious affair. It is no wonder, then, that we live for holidays where we get to explore and play, discovering new places and *ourselves* again; it is no wonder we live for our children who provide us with an *excuse* to play again; and it is no wonder we obsess over sex, the only area left in adult life where play is acceptable.

It is also no wonder that a break from work or school is referred to as recreational time, *re-creation*; they are the only moments we are given to be ourselves, free and imaginative, recharging our batteries once again, before we head back behind the desk. **Marionettes** (**II. The Ascent**) contains the lyric: 'By the sweat of one's brow, Thou shall eat bread'. This quote – taken from the Bible, Genesis 3:16 – epitomises, for me, the archaic notion of work as an assumed moral undertaking; an imperative, an obligation for all. Yet we are imaginative problem solvers. For a healthy society and a healthy life, we should seek freedom from tedious and strenuous work in every way possible. With the invention of machinery and technology we have the means to take away the drudgery. Machines, in fact, are set to do 'half of all work tasks by 2025' according to a World Economic Forum report in 2020.[45]

Disastrously, this will just increase poverty and inequality as millions more lose their jobs. Again, the problem here is with an archaic structure. Menial jobs that can be done by machines *should* be done by machines, therefore freeing humans from modern day slave labour, and giving them time to spend on more imaginative, interesting, problem solving work. Obviously this then must be supported through some form of universal basic income or citizen's dividend, in order to give people financial stability. Structuring society by this Biblical notion of 'earning' a living through dull and routine hard work is unwarranted in the 21st century.

The more time we can spend being imaginative, social, and compassionate, seeking knowledge, exploration, experience, and companionship, the better.

I am eternally grateful that much of my 'work' is not of the tedious or strenuous variety and requires the constant exercising of my imagination. For many though, life contains a lot of drudgery. And we certainly *all* suffer from a lack of play.

Play *fights* depression, it allows us to feel joyous and in control.

Play *fights* narcissism, it teaches us to cooperate with others and see things from their point of view.

And, of course, play *fights* a lack of imagination. It is, by definition, creative and innovative.

By spending time doing things that are pleasurable, voluntary and imaginative, you'll be giving your hippocampus a helping hand, and you'll have a better capacity for memory, empathy, and imagination, as well as more hope about the future, because of it.

Rob Hopkin's book *From What Is to What If* documents the gradual decline in human imagination, and supplies a whole host of ideas of how we can reverse the trend:

> The neglect of the imagination is generally overlooked, seen as a frivolous distraction from the overarching aim of building economic growth and technological progress [...] our imagination isn't accidentally dwindling; it is being co-opted, suffocated, corrupted and starved of the oxygen it needs.[46]

There it is again; that blinkered obsession with growth, pushing every other healthy human purpose, or reason for living, out the way, like an insufferable bully stealing our lunch money (in this case; our natural resources), and spoiling our playtime! Humanity and ecology *must* come before economic growth, in whatever socioeconomic system comes next.

As we looked at in Chapter 2, if we are focused on technological advancement with barely any attention to an equal advancement in our morality or wisdom, we end up in a precarious situation with social and ecological instability, and multiple existential threats.

The guardians of the status quo point to graphs that show a continuous, steady climb in economic growth, and they tell us we're doing just fabulously. But, of course, they're tragically failing to acknowledge that the very thing they believe to be a measure of 'success' is, in fact, a measure of looming ecological disaster. Yet, when this is pointed out to them, they have the audacity to tell us 'yeah, well, there is no alternative'. Perhaps their hippocampi have shrunk beyond all measure!

Our Sad Commitment To Justifying Our Normality

Voltaire said, 'it is difficult to free fools from the chains they revere'.

Why *do* we desperately cling on to systems that cause so much damage?

I think a substantial part of the answer is that, as human beings, we have a psychological need to maintain a positive view of what we see around us. It's why we convince ourselves that the groups we join (or see ourselves as part of) are the best, or that the country we are a citizen of is the greatest. It's why those who joined Dorothy Martin's doomsday cult (which we looked at in Chapter 4) stayed true to her for so long, even after it was clear she was wrong. It's why the most hardened Trump supporters tell you that he *did* have more people at his inauguration than Obama had at his. Our group, our society, our norms must be supported and upheld because we're motivated to keep them that way; for our own self-esteem, and also to prove our loyalty to our tribe (again, we're scared of being ostracised or outcast; we're subconsciously taken back to the savannahs of Africa where we'd almost certainly not survive even one night alone).

We big up our tribe, we hold it in high esteem, because we are motivated to stay safely embedded *in* that tribe.

This plays out on an even larger scale with our systems, in a psychological concept called *system justification* – 'the strong tendency to perceive existing social relations as fair, legitimate, and desirable, even in contexts in which those relations substantively disadvantage the person involved'.[47]

You may have seen the 2013 webcomic *On Fire*, or the resulting 'this is fine' meme, where a dog sits in a room that is on fire, sipping coffee, desperately trying to convince itself everything is OK. There are some people who don't know about the awful 'fires' our current systems produce, so they support them through ignorance. There are some people who *do* know about the fires, yet *still* continue to go about their day supporting the systems that caused them, convincing themselves that all is normal and preferable. This is because they do not want to be cast outside the house. I mean, who knows what's out there?! We rate stability and order over that which is novel and therefore possibly threatening. We accept known difficulties over unknown difficulties. Familiarity over unfamiliarity.

System Rigidity

Before you think I'm looking down on those who uphold our current socioeconomic and political system, let it be known; I vote. I contribute to, and live within, our economy. I, too, participate. Which goes some way (regardless how minute) to authenticating it.

This is our habit of social constructionism. We all mentally invest in the current apparatus of our existence. Our political system, our economic system, even money itself, are all social constructs. They're beliefs that we have all agreed to share or, at least, which we have reluctantly accepted that we *have* to share. There's no escaping them. There's no ability to 'go off-grid'. The grid is inescapable. Simply, if you want to live, it seems you must subscribe to social constructs.

This acceptance was the inspiration behind the line in **T.I.N.A.** about 'a secret trapdoor that we cannot shut'. I had the image of *all* of us, walking down a hallway, and then, like lemmings, one after another, proceeding to fall through a trapdoor.

We all follow in line, *believing* that we have no other alternative. Our system appears as natural and solid to us as the very earth we walk on, yet it does not have a basis in nature or in physical reality. It is a structure that humans have invented. It's not like *gravity* or *photosynthesis* – a natural process or a fact of life – it is a construct that *we* have created, and one that should be *constantly* analysed and improved upon.

Unfortunately, though, as I said in the introduction of this book; when it comes to serious structural improvement, we have very little apparatus in place to achieve progress. Democracy, in its current form, keeps politicians focused on the short-term – the next election, to be precise – it has little incentive for means of long-term structural improvement. The immediate issues take up all of our attention, and therefore the politician who bears no responsibility for longer-term problems and future outcomes is not punished at the polling booth. At the same time, the free market keeps investors focused on short-term profits, with little consideration for the ecological *or* social harm caused in the long-term. Neither our democratic system or our economic system have the capacity for long-term planning, and neither can be relied upon to produce structural change.

The future isn't really represented at all in our policy making and economics. Whether we are talking about the political and economic interests of our children today, or their children to come, our descendants are not represented. Children of course have no vote, nor is there any adult at the table to represent their generation's interests. And unfortunately those in the future have no time-travelling lobbyists who travel back to visit us, making sure their generations' interests are represented. Those in the future are powerless to our whims and will. The author of the *Precipice* whom we met in Chapter 2, Toby Ord, describes this situation well: 'One might think of this as a tyranny of the present over the future'.

A sane and prudent species would have an advisory board of people speaking up from the perspective of the future and even the far future, but unfortunately this broad perspective is rarely incentivised politically or economically.

It's actually worse than that, though. I'm being far too kind. We are actively *disincentivised* from long-term thinking. For example; if there is a natural disaster – let's say, a flood; money and resources are made available and our systems react reasonably well. But the politician who wants to *prepare* for a flood receives little to no support. There are usually more pressing things that take people's attention. Other things a politician must be seen to be focusing on. Likewise, the market disincentivises prudence too; there is little profit in flood prevention. The profit only starts flowing in once the water starts flowing in, when public or private money is offered up to aid and assist. This is why a lot of activism or progressive laws that are passed could be called *sandbagging*. Like erecting temporary, last-minute defences against rising waters by placing sandbags around your property, sandbagging is the process of concentrating on the symptoms and not the cause, it is reactionary instead of preventative. The focus is almost always on the bad apples, the quick fixes, the immediate visually striking problems, the flooding. The focus is rarely on the root causes of the flood.

Pandemics And Engineered Pandemics

Thank fuck COVID-19 was a *relatively* tame virus. If it was, say, an avian flu, with a 60% death rate,[48] we would have seen societal collapse like never before. It would have been a civilisation-destroying event. Pandemics (especially engineered pandemics) *are* an existential threat.[49]

Unfortunately, and over the last few years especially, neoliberalism's commitment to smaller government meant no one was listening to the epidemiologist's warnings, because there was no reason to; no profit, no reward, no incentive (Trump actually disbanded the US pandemic response team[50] and ended Project Predict[51] – the early warning program designed to find potential pandemics – not long before COVID-19 hit).

How we act during inter-pandemic years is just as pivotal as how we act within a pandemic itself. The UK and the US (two countries who seem to have fared really badly in broad comparison to others) had a distinct, and tragic, lack of preparation.[52] It will be interesting to see what changes are made in preparation for the next pandemic, as they *are* likely to become more frequent, due to climate change, increasing industrial expansion, habitat destruction, and the treatment and consumption of wildlife.[53]

/ / / / / / / / /

Capitalism Appears As Part Of The Natural Order Of Things

The scientific analysis of our broader systems, and their outcomes, is virtually non-existent. Our current systems are self-reinforcing. They disincentivise and obstruct change. This is achieved *structurally* by keeping us focused on the short term, and *individually* by keeping us stressed; to the detriment of our imagination.

It's very difficult to see things from a systems perspective. As Orwell suggests in *1984*, we are 'like the ant, which can see small objects but not large ones'. Most of us fail to realise how interlinked things are; how the problems that we encounter have deeper, systemic causes. We see the way our world is structured as a fixed entity, so established in our lives as to be almost unnoticeable:

> I never noticed you were in disguise
> But now I see you T.I.N.A.

Our imagination is sucked dry by it:

> You were a barrier around my mind
> Yeah I see through you T.I.N.A.

We see our systems as almost divine. Ordained by the gods, rather than something built by humans hundreds of years ago. Mortal humans, just like you and me. As a collective, we are far smarter than the architects of our systems were. They had no knowledge of the problems that we would come to face now. So we must reframe our social and economic structures, they are not infallible or unsurpassable. Or as the lyrics in **Marionettes (II: The Ascent)** state:

> The world that you created is not mightier
> Than our means to remake it!

Cult Of Incapability

To hold this position that our current system is the best we can come up with, is to subscribe to what we could call a *cult of incapability*. We look around and assume that we cannot do better than this. We believe to revise, recreate, and redesign would be somehow too difficult for us. We believe that human capability peaked with the invention of the free market.

We all know in our gut this is wrong, we all know in our gut we were not built for the lifestyle our current system steers us toward; stressed and self-obsessed. And deep down, I think even the most devout guardians of the status quo realise that we must start protecting, and realigning with nature.

One thematic thread that runs through everything I've ever written has been a sense of frustration. Frustration in knowing what humanity is capable of – in terms of our rationality, our compassion and our ingenuity – and seeing it held back by the restrictions of our current socioeconomic paradigm. I am not, for one moment, saying I have all the answers – or, indeed, *any* of them – but I know that we, as a species, can find the answers together. So long as we are not held back from *trying* to find them.

Impatience

Marionettes is a story of frustration and discovery, in two parts. The frustration of feeling held back serves as the initial impetus for **Marionettes (I. The Discovery of Strings)**, which begins with the verse:

> Master,
> I think you owe them an answer
> You've become so complacent
> And they're becoming impatient

Impatience is a very strong motivator. My generation, and those younger, know that all too well. We're spoilt by the ability to buy anything we want and have it on our doorstep within 24 hours. Or, at the click of a button, we can watch any movie, order any meal, or search for any information, no matter how obscure the topic. We *expect* immediacy. If only we could harness this expectancy for system recalibration and redesign. This is why – after finishing this book of social analysis and criticism you hold in your hands right now – I shall be concentrating my efforts on seeking out and promoting the answers, solutions and positive possibilities. I want to make us all more impatient in this respect. Frustrated people make a lot of noise, and impatience is very contagious. A dash of impatience, birthed from the knowledge of the amazing progress humanity is capable of, might just end up being the special ingredient that triggers a revolution.

Marionettes tells the story of puppets questioning their nature, and the nature of the systems of power and control that they live under. It tells the story of rebelling against that which holds your wellbeing, and your natural environment, in contempt. It tells the story of the endless and arduous search for truth when so much around you is a lie.

After experiencing the complacent and reckless behaviour of their puppet master, a drunk and uncaring authority, they become inquisitive and energised:

Vandal,
You left their strings in a tangle
Since you turned to the liquor
Their eyes are starting to flicker ...

The 'vandalism' is a metaphor for the serious mistreatment of citizens and the environment, that our socioeconomic system inflicts through the pursuit of profit. This verse was partly influenced by the 2008 financial crisis, an economic crash largely caused by excessive risk-taking by the banking sector. We kept hearing how people within the sector were 'drunk on power', addicted to the mammoth amounts of wealth they were accruing through the reckless dishing-out of subprime mortgages (or whatever the hell it was – I can't remember the extensive jargon, and this isn't the time or place to be taking you down that dark alley, anyway, dear reader ... go watch *The Big Short* if you want the full dramatised story!)[54] The comparison of the bankers' behaviour to the hasty and self-destructive behaviour of an alcoholic felt suitable.

Just as the financial crash gave rise to the Occupy movement and influenced many more people to question our economic model, the puppet master's irresponsible and selfish behaviour causes the marionettes to begin to question authority and hold power to account:

Thunder,
They look up and they wonder
Are they controlled by the heavens?
They start to question their essence

They then discover their strings. This nightmarish realisation felt analogous to us discovering how we are moulded and manipulated by our socioeconomic structure, as it fosters and incentivises self-interest and destroys trust and imagination and everything we have been talking about.

The marionettes then see that they have been controlled by invisible, omnipresent forces, and become committed to testing the truths they have subscribed to their whole lives. Eager to find the source of these controlling factors, they begin to 'climb, climb, search and seek', paralleling the rise in the importance of fact-checking, and real, investigative, independent journalism in our post-truth world – 'we will test this "truth" you speak'.

I've spoken about the importance of curiosity at length. But mainly from the perspective of inquiry about individuals and the causes of individual behaviour. Curiosity also spurs us on to question our power structures; our institutions, traditions, and systems of influence. It is curiosity that spurs the marionettes forwards:

> Curiosity began to creep
> From underneath the bed
> Of toil and doctrine
> And the marionettes awaken
> Into a nightmare ...

When we're able to escape our preoccupations – be that our work issues, or the general stresses that makes up our everyday life – perhaps losing ourselves in music or going on holiday, it can be like waking from a nightmare. A serene release from everyday toil. Yet, this sweet release can disappear if our focus shifts toward the bigger picture, from the personal to the social. Grasping the scale of the mess we're in as a civilisation can instead feel like the contradictory notion of waking *into* a nightmare.

It is through curiosity that we achieve understanding and clarity. And this remains the case even when a difficult truth brings us suffering, such as when our previously held sheltered beliefs are proven false. In these moments, where we are thrust out of our sanctums of ignorance, the jarring and upsetting truths can be tough to accept or digest, but deeper understanding is almost always in your interest. This idea of learning being simultaneously difficult as well as liberating, inspired the refrain: 'Truth hurts / Truth frees'.

As we looked at in Chapter 4, our socioeconomic system assumes that modern humans are *Homo economicus*; a self-interest-obsessed perversion of a human being. In short; a monster. In the lyrics, I equate the system's architects with Victor Frankenstein, as they mould us into their own Frankenstein's monster. We must turn against the manipulative and polluting system that creates our perversion, just as the monster turns against his maker in Mary Shelley's novel:

> Now we see the warning sign
> We'll disobey our Frankenstein

The chorus of **Marionettes II** looks at our positive potential as human beings. If we're committed to curiosity over tribal allegiances, and compassion over self-interest, then we are capable of such light, such warmth – 'Our minds are firewood'. We cannot allow these traits to be neglected, or our species will be kept in a state of perpetual immaturity: 'Escape this childhood'. This harks back to the idea we looked at back in Chapter 2, that if we play our cards right, we are still only in our adolescences as a species. Such incredible feats await! As long as we hold onto and cultivate our better instincts. The theme of unending immaturity is also echoed in **T.I.N.A.**, where I describe our loyalty to the system as an 'Umbilical cord that we cannot cut'.

As Jean-Jacques Rousseau said to the guardians of the status quo in his day: 'You trust in the present order of society without imagining that this order is subject to inevitable revolutions.'[55]

Downfalls Of Debate

It is not the lyrical focus of *Nothing Is True & Everything Is Possible* to dictate *where* humanity goes next. Only to state the case that we simply *must* travel.

Within the album's lyrics, and throughout this book, I've tried to present some of the evidence that proves our current ideologies and structures are, in fact, not just outdated, but dangerous. Unfortunately, it is difficult to destroy the falsehood that our social structure is competent and permanent when to merely suggest that 'a new direction is needed' usually provokes an immediate aggressive questioning, as if you are some kind of traitor or deserter. This is an interesting step because it immediately preserves the Us versus Them standard of debate.

What we must *insist* is that we look at the available data *together*. Analyse the effects of our socioeconomic system *together*. Look for sustainable and life-supporting alternatives *together*. Imagine and create *together*. We're so indoctrinated by our self-interested and hostile world, we assume, that when discussing new ideas, they must always be presented through competitive argument, rather than through a cooperative and constructive conversation.

This isn't a debate, a competition, or a fight – we simply must realign with nature, so let's discuss what is possible. Let us look at the evidence, with a humble grasp of our own biases, and attempt to build a better world. Together.

We're drawn to heated debate over calm conversation, because it is emotional, competitive and, therefore, entertaining. But the thing is, with debate we strive mainly for *victory* over our opponents – and, if possible, to make them look stupid while we're at it – rather than to further our understanding of the topic in question, *or* of each other. Every interaction becomes a contest, each correspondence solely about *winning*. We set out only to shame and dominate.

Heated debates are not well-considered, nutritious, nor convincing. Debate rarely achieves anything more than stoking emotion and confirming biases, while allowing those involved to promote, prove and defend their tribal allegiances. Where you may personally 'win' a debate, a society engrossed in this form of communication will ultimately lose.

It strikes me that debate, being a form of self-interested competition, is perhaps a biased form of information exchange *innately*. By definition, debate reinforces the notion that there are to be winners and losers, that there is an *Us* and a *Them*. When you realign with nature and are led by science, there isn't an Us versus Them, there are only up-to-date values and out-of-date values.

Here in the UK, the Brexit campaign – and, along with it, the subsequent years of political turmoil – illustrated the awful limitations of heated debate very clearly. The British online academic journal *Conversation* criticised MPs for having 'gloated, jeered, heckled and booed' as well as 'indulged in gleeful laughter, smug condescension and personal attacks' throughout the Brexit campaign; it depressingly (but correctly) concluded, 'while providing enormous entertainment value to those not directly affected by Brexit, to most of the British public, the events [were] a tragedy'.[56] It created a whirlwind of brash emotion, it obscured truth and destroyed public trust in politicians, global institutions and, perhaps worst of all, each other.

This lack of will for a proper calm, curious and compassionate conversation is what the song **T.I.N.A.** is targeting. Remember, at its core, politics is the discussion of how we should inhabit this world together. Let us lay down the swords of tribal emotion and work together on a new way to achieve this.

T.I.N.A. – A Sinister Constraint

We've looked at how prosociality was the key aspect to our survival, evolution, and success as a species. The job of civilisation in return, then, *should* be to harbour and protect that prosociality. Civilisation should encourage and develop our greatest strength but, regrettably, as we've seen, it seems to only hinder it. This is weakening our trust in each other, our compassion for each other, and our sense of community. Our most precious and pivotal trait is being eroded by an uncompromising dedication to the status quo.

We can be as broad as you wish here – neoliberalism, capitalism, market based economics, or the whole concept of monetary based competitive trade altogether – however far you wish to zoom in or out and whatever label you wish to use; at every level, an economy predicated on self-maximisation, that has no concept of the limits of the finite planet upon which it operates, that has no bearings or vocabulary in our modern world of climate change, ecosystem decline, and pandemics, is, by definition, doomed.

To summarise; the mantra of 'There Is No Alternative' is a sinister constraint on our creative prospects and even on *possibility* itself. The conversation about real alternatives is sidelined and gagged by an intellectual orthodoxy and vested economic interests, as well as assumptions that this all simply 'natural', or 'the best we can do'.

I find it discouraging to see people so hostile to new ideas; it's the old ones we should be hostile toward.

As I said in the introduction; I chose the phrase 'everything is possible' because it sounded more negative and unnerving than 'anything is possible'. It seemed to better reflect the current state of the world. But it is important to remember, among all the doom and gloom, that everything is *also* possible in a *positive* sense. *If* we can come together and use the only tool we really have: conversation.

One of our first human compulsions is for compassion and cooperation (remember the experiments by Felix Warneken, and the toddlers whose first instinct was to help strangers in need?). If we were to build a system that supports these instincts, then we'd barely need to be concerned by the ominous tone of the phrase 'everything is possible' at all. That's not some far-fetched utopian ideal. If you dramatically change what behaviours are supported and rewarded by society, you'll dramatically change the outcomes of that society. *That* is the key to structural progress.

Everything Is Possible

Towards the end of the album's recording, during a long, long band meeting, surrounded by coffee cups and scrunched up bits of paper – containing only bad ideas – the four of us and our management finally agreed upon an album title.

Shortly after the decision, I began to have a distant flashback of hearing the phrase 'everything is possible' in a *positive* sense. I kept shrugging it off though as I was convinced that the phrase was not a hopeful one in *any* way, shape or form, for the semantic reasons I explained in Chapter 1. But the memory kept niggling away at me. (Damn you, hippocampus.)

After going back through some old notes, I found a TED video where I had first heard the phrase 'everything is possible' and re-watched it. It turns out it *was* used in a positive context. And the story is worth telling.

Jose Miguel Sokoloff begins his TED talk stating: 'In my lifetime I have never lived one day of peace in my country'.[57] Deep in Colombia's jungles, far from the major cities, there has been an ongoing war since 1958. More than 5 million people have been displaced over the decades since the war started, and over 220,000 lives have been lost (81.5% of whom were civilians).[58] You may not have heard of it because it has been a gruelling, slow, ongoing tragedy. It has a long, convoluted, history, steeped in the 'war on drugs', with many guerrilla groups, crime syndicates, and far-right parliamentary militias all in conflict.

One of the groups in this complex entangled web, is the *Revolutionary Armed Forces of Columbia*, abbreviated colloquially as FARC. It 'is the oldest and largest group among Colombia's left-wing rebels and is one of the world's richest guerrilla armies'.[59] They have financed themselves through kidnapping, extortion, drug trade and illegal mining.

The Colombian government was keen to try new options to bring this conflict to an end. They had a military, political and legal strategy but no communication strategy. Which is where Sokoloff came in. He was hired to attempt communication with the guerrillas. Not to spy on them. Not to infiltrate them. Not to sew seeds of discord and mistrust among them. No. Instead, to try persuade them to demobilise. To lay down their arms, and enter peace talks with the government.

Sokoloff set about his mission and began by speaking to as many ex-guerrillas as possible. He wanted to understand them.

In time, his team discovered that there was a trend which demobilisations tended to follow; there was a subtle peak during Christmas time. This helped Sokoloff reach the conclusion that they needed to speak to 'the human being, not the solider. We needed to step away from talking from army to army and we needed to talk about the universal values and we needed to talk about humanity'.[60] The plan they devised is quite surprising.

The first high-ranking official to offer support for Sokoloff's plan was Captain Juan Manuel Valdez of the Colombian Army. It was a mission that, I expect, was *very* different to any mission that he or his men had carried out before. That mission was codenamed 'Operation Christmas'.

Using Blackhawk helicopters, the elite troops of the Colombian army placed nine

75-foot Christmas trees, festooned with fairy lights, at strategic points along pathways throughout the jungle.[61]

The Colombian army also agreed not to attack guerrillas during the campaign. When nocturnal guerrilla activity brought them close enough to one of the trees, their presence triggered motion sensors and the trees lit up to reveal a sign beside them that read:

> If Christmas can come to the jungle, you can come home.
> Demobilise.
> At Christmas, everything is possible.

Here was the phrase that I had adamantly deemed negative and disconcerting, finding a positive use as part of an astonishingly imaginative and warm-hearted campaign.

The memories of Christmas that the campaign evoked had a profound effect on the lifelong fighters, helping them to re-evaluate and, ultimately, abandon their violent lives.

Sokoloff said: 'We need to remember that soldiers and guerrillas are not different. We are the same people.'[62]

That Christmas, 331 guerrillas came home.

Sokoloff and his team continued the success of their first year, with equally surprising and wonderful campaigns each following Christmas. By the close of 2016, after more than 50 years of war (the longest in the history of the Americas), FARC agreed to end the conflict. By that time, 18,000 guerrillas had demobilised,[63] forcing guerrilla leaders to put down their arms and instead attempt *diplomacy*. Which is, of course, just a fancy word for what I referred to above as the only tool we really have: conversation.

Today there are still factions of FARC dissidents intent on fighting, as well as multiple other groups and crime syndicates, and some guerrillas have had trouble reintegrating into civilian society (only to be expected, having lived the life of a guerrilla since childhood).[64] But much bloodshed was spared by Operation Christmas; showing just how fragile our hostile tribal allegiances *can* be, when confronted by a hand held out in peace and compassion.

Just as with Westboro's Megan Phelps-Roper, or former White Aryan Resistance member Tony McAleer, if we approach others with kindness, and as human beings, even the most seemingly 'hopeless case' has the potential to be persuaded to leave violent organisations or renounce hateful ideologies.

Sokoloff found that the main obstacle preventing the guerrillas from demobilising was the fear that if they left, they would be rejected; by their loved ones or by society itself. This is why our world of division and demonisation is so tragic. We are persuaded that we are only accepted and respected – only *human* – in our respective groups, however damaging or vile our group may be.

If we wish to calm online incivility, remove hostility from politics, or even reduce military conflict, we must be willing to approach our 'enemies' with curiosity, rather than animosity.

We must be willing to check into **The Dreamer's Hotel**.

And that is how we will become better placed to face **The Great Unknown**.

Epilogue

A survey into the public's perception of global threats to humanity revealed that half of respondents who believed the statement 'the world's future looks grim' also endorsed the statement 'so we have to focus on looking after ourselves'.[1]

As crises begin to really stack up, and times get tougher, people will increasingly narrow their focus upon themselves. Which is understandable, of course. When our resources, energy or means are diminished, we concentrate on ourselves and we 'look after our own'. This means that the economic narrative of self-interest grows stronger, even as it produces grimmer results.

It's worth noting that 'the game' is played the same no matter which side you're on. The rich, the elite, the 'winners' – who have no desire to lose their wealth or power – act with increasing self-interest to sustain their social standing. The poor, or the 'losers' in society's game – slipping further behind (even into destitution) – act with increasing self-interest, purely as a survival mechanism. Whatever your personal outcome in this game, it's the *same* behaviour being incentivised: self-interest. The game itself *relies* upon it.

The system is impressively self-reinforcing, even when creating extreme social damage. Adversity helps maintain the very status quo that *causes* adversity. It's similar to Stockholm syndrome: we grow reliant upon – *devoted to*, even – the very mechanism that hurts us in the first place. When adversity grows, we turn inwards, and away from the very thing that helps humanity progress: prosociality.

/ / / / / / / / / /

During the first COVID-19 lockdown in March 2020, the UK experienced a sudden and frenzied rise in the acquisition of toilet paper. Everyone was stocking up on it, in mortal fear that supermarkets would have issues with their supply.

Whatever the reason for *toilet paper*, of all things, becoming the hallowed essential, the result of this peculiar frenzy was a nationwide shortage. There were even fights in supermarket aisles of over remaining packets of the stuff. People saw – or perceived – others acting out of self-interest, and it spurred them to do the same, even if only as a precaution.

This is the crux of it: if we burrow down, retreat behind our borders or walls, and act only with self-interest (whether that's on a personal, local, or national level), how on earth are we going to face our existential threats? How are we going to address the multiple social and ecological crises we face?

This is the domino effect of self-centred behaviour. We cannot find collective will and proactive hope cowering behind our own walls and looking out only for ourselves. That form of individualism is cowardice. A failure to our fellow humans, as well as those humans still to come. If the 'world's future looks grim' then focusing 'on looking after ourselves' is only going to make it grimmer.

There is an old African proverb that sums up the problem of individualism:

If you want to go fast, go alone. If you want to go far, go together.

I don't know about you, but I want to go *far*. What's the point of going fast if it doesn't get you anywhere?

Ironically, and somewhat paradoxically, acting with self-interest is not even in our own interest in the long run. To face existential threats as self-interested individuals is to ensure failure. Leaving poorer countries to face climate change on their own will just guarantee a refugee crisis like the world has never known.

Self-interest will only ensure difficulties *everywhere* and will bring no escape from adversity in the long run.

For our own preservation, we *cannot* shut ourselves off from each other. We're foolish to even try.

/ / / / / / / / / /

Humans have long dreamt up a 'purpose' for our existence. Be that through religion and spirituality, power and wealth, or any number of man-made answers to 'the meaning of life'. Today, though, we have a defined sense of purpose larger than ourselves. One we no longer need to fabricate. That larger purpose is *the survival of our species.*

If we get our act together, humanity's long-term potential is virtually infinite. And infinitely beautiful. To secure this future we need personal change and structural change. We must revolutionise ourselves and our systems simultaneously.

Ourselves

We must, wherever possible, use and utilise compassion, cooperation and consideration. We must do our bit to spread a contagion of kindness throughout society.

We must exercise our creative muscle and our empathic muscle. We must work to understand our own biases and our own minds. Learn how to acknowledge the complexity and causality of human behaviour, and be better equipped for curiosity and forgiveness.

Our World

Personal progress means little without a framework that backs it up. We must utilise and fight for natural habitats and forests; the world's lungs. Not only does nature boost our creativity and lower our stress, it stimulates a more open and meditative mindset, and makes us happier and more generous.[2]

We can all do our bit to personally improve the world through learning about ourselves and others, and through stoking our compassion and activism. But, in reality, that must also be joined by a Second World War-scale paradigm shift. A Manhattan project for ecological and ethical social redesign. An immense effort to transform society. And should we achieve a change to our environment, we will see an equal change in humanity.

The inventor and systems theorist Buckminster Fuller once said: 'I must commit myself to reforming the environment and not man; being absolutely confident that if you give man the right environment he will behave favorably.'[3]

I love the age in which I find myself. What a thoroughly, bewilderingly exciting time to be alive! Alive at the time when our species is reaching **The Great Unknown**. Where we have to work out how to survive our own capacity for self-destruction. Where a confluence of crises have to be addressed. And very, very soon.

Combine all the risks and negative trajectories we have looked at in this book – our existential risks, our worsening ecological prospects, our rising hostility, our tribalism and polarisation, and our declining levels of trust and imagination – and we find ourselves in an unprecedented position of brittle fragility. A perilous situation which calls upon the greatness of humanity, more than at any other time in our history. It calls upon our creativity and our cooperation. It calls upon our composure and our compassion. And through saving ourselves, we will *rediscover* ourselves.

We are more than capable of achieving this safer and more sustainable future. Our position is far from hopeless. Yes, this book *has* concentrated on the core *problems*. But those problems – whether they're our journalism, our social media, our economic system, our dominant values and behaviours – they *can* all be reformed and renewed.

Neither the system nor the human is incorrigible, irredeemable, or hopeless. We *can* build a more compassionate socioeconomic system that produces far less ecological destruction and social instability.

As a species, we are either in our infancy, navigating our way through the perils of immaturity, walking the tightrope of discovery and mounting power, or we are in the twilight of our lives – perched precariously on the edge of our deathbed.

We must not let fatigue or fatalism convince us to lie back and shut our eyes forever.

/ / / / / / / / / /

Systems look mighty, fixed, and abiding. Simply the natural order of things. Until they suddenly break.

Whether they implode upon themselves, or whether they are overthrown, it is only afterwards, when the historians analyse, that they see that collapse was inevitable. With the benefit of hindsight: 'It was obvious if you look back at it!' 'All the signs were there!' And so on ...

All the signs are here now. Our system of self-interest and perpetual economic growth must be destroyed, before it destroys us. Let us hear, one last time, from Carl Sagan:

> There are some who look on our global problems here on Earth – at our vast national antagonisms, our nuclear arsenals, our growing populations, the disparity between the poor and the affluent, shortages of food and resources, and our inadvertent alterations of the natural environment of our planet – and conclude that we live in a system which has suddenly become unstable, a system which is destined soon to collapse. There are others

who believe that our problems are soluble, that humanity is still in its childhood, that one day soon we will grow up.[4]

Both outlooks Sagan describes here are true. The system *is* unstable, it *is* destined soon to collapse. Yet, our problems *are* soluble and humanity *is* still in its childhood. The two positions are not mutually exclusive. In fact, to hold one of these positions exclusively is to only hold half of the truth. If we are to survive as a species we *must* address the system that destines us for collapse.

Currently, all future trajectories are negative. This not only makes revolution imperative, but also, more than anything, *inevitable*. We will come to see that we *must* adapt. Bertolt Brecht's apt and elegant aphorism comes to mind here: 'Because things are the way they are, things will not remain the way they are.'

I shall leave you with a quote from Martin Luther King, Jr, who, back in 1967, told us about another dream he had for society, one that didn't become as famous, due to its obviously subversive content:

> For years I labored with the idea of reforming the existing institutions of the South, a little change here, a little change there, [...] Now I feel quite differently. I think you've got to have a reconstruction of the entire society, a revolution of values.[5]

Notes

Preface

1   Sir Bernard Crick, 'Voice of a Long Generation', *BBC History* (17 February 2011)
2   There are a few inspirations behind this overarching style of investigation. Firstly, systems theory. I feel more comfortable with a subject once I have some grounding in how it fits the bigger picture. Secondly, from the works of many people you will meet in the citations throughout the book; Peter Joseph and George Monbiot to name two. They have always motivated me to look at the broader perspective and research thoroughly. Thirdly, through my generally nosy and inquisitive nature. I try to live by the idea that achieving a broader perspective means receiving a deeper understanding.
3   Mark Twain, *The Innocents Abroad, or the New Pilgrims' Progress* (1869)
4   To watch my reading of his famous poem 'Dulce et decorum est', see www.youtube.com/watch?v=HxBg01-BXRc
5   Charlie Connelly, 'Wilfred Owen – the Voice of the Fallen', *The New European* (7 November 2020)

Introduction
Nothing Is True & Everything Is Possible

1   Kailash Chand, '2016 was the Worst Year in NHS History', *The Guardian* (4 January 2017)
2   '£350 Million EU Claim 'a Clear Misuse of Official Statistics'', *Full Fact* (19 September 2017)
3   Jack Peat, 'Recap: To the Moment Tory MPs Cheered after Blocking a Pay Rise for Nurses', *The London Economic* (23 March 2020)
4   Ashley Cowburn, 'Brexiteers Condemned for Not Backing £350m NHS Amendment to EU Withdrawal Bill', *The Independent* (8 February 2017)
5   '"Post-truth" Declared Word of the Year by Oxford Dictionaries', *BBC News* (16 November 2016)
6   'Fact Check: The Controversy over Trump's Inauguration Crowd Size' *USA Today* (24 January 2017)
7   The league table is as follows:
Locke: 309 words
Aristotle: 188 words
Kant: 174 words
Bentham: 164 words
Mill: 161 words
Stephen Hicks, 'Philosophy's Longest Sentences – New Kant Entry' (30 September 2013), www.stephenhicks.org/2013/09/30/philosophys-longest-sentences-new-kant-entry
8   'Atomic Education Urged by Einstein', *The New York Times* (25 May 1946). In 1945, as America was dropping atomic bombs on Japan, one of my favourite philosophers, Bertrand Russell, wrote: 'As I write, I learn that a second bomb has been dropped on Nagasaki. The prospect for the human race is sombre beyond all precedent. Mankind are faced with a clear-cut alternative: either we shall all perish, or we shall have to acquire some slight degree of common sense. A great deal of new political thinking will be necessary if utter disaster is to be averted.' See: Bertrand Russell, *The Bomb and Civilization* (1945)
9   William J. Perry and Tom Z. Collina, 'Who Can We Trust with the Nuclear Button? No One', *The New York Times* (22 June 2020)

10   Will Durant, *The Story of Philosophy* (Simon & Schuster, 1926).

11   Robert Sapolsky, *The Trouble with Testosterone and Other Essays on the Biology of the Human Predicament* (Scribner, 1997)

12   The Intergovernmental Science-Policy Platform on Biodiversity and Ecosystem Services (IPBES) states: 'the potential for future pandemics is vast'; Professor Josef Settele, 'COVID-19 Stimulus Measures Must Save Lives, Protect Livelihoods, and Safeguard Nature to Reduce the Risk of Future Pandemics' (27 April 2020)

13   IPBES (ibid.) states: 'There is a single species that is responsible for the COVID-19 pandemic – us. As with the climate and biodiversity crises, recent pandemics are a direct consequence of human activity.'

An Overview Of Our Predicament And Our Emotional Response
2.1 The Great Unknown

1   IPBES, 'Summary for Policymakers Global Assessment' (6 May 2019), according to the UN global assessment report

2   NASA, 'The Effects of Climate Change', https://climate.nasa.gov/effects

3   'New Report: Freedom in the World 2020 finds established democracies are in decline', *Freedom House* (4 March 2020)

4   Nafeez Ahmed, https://www.vice.com/en/article/3anbmy/covid-19-is-a-symptom-of-a-planet-thats-been-pushed-past-a-tipping-point

5   Matt Simon, 'Fantastically Wrong: That Time People Thought a Comet Would Gas Us All to Death', *Wired* (1 July 2015)

6   Mark Strauss, 'Ten Notable Apocalypses That (Obviously) Didn't Happen', *Smithsonian Magazine* (12 November 2009)

7   Thomas Babington Macaulay, 'Southey's Colloquies on Society', *The Library of Economics and Liberty* (1830), www.econlib.org/library/Essays/macS.html

8   Marc Trussler and Stuart Soroka, 'Consumer Demand for Cynical and Negative News Frames', *The International Journal of Press/Politics* (18 March 2014)

9   It is now just under 4% of children who die in the first 5 years of their life, compared with 36% in 1900. 'Child and Infant Mortality', *Our World In Data* (November 2019), https://ourworldindata.org/child-mortality

10   *Availability bias* was first noticed by Amos Tversky and Daniel Kahneman in the 1970s. See Amos Tversky and Daniel Kahneman, 'Availability: A Heuristic for Judging Frequency and Probability', *Cognitive Psychology* 5 (1973)

11   Hans Rosling, in his book *Factfulness: Ten Reasons We're Wrong About the World – and Why Things Are Better Than You Think* (Sceptre, 2018), puts it like this: 'In the media the "news-worthy" events exaggerate the unusual.'

12   Kalev H. Leetaru, 'Culturomics 2.0: Forecasting Large-Scale Human Behaviour Using Global News Media Tone in Time and Space', *First Monday* (5 September 2011), available at https://firstmonday.org/ojs/index.php/fm/article/view/3663

13   Steven Pinker, *Enlightenment Now: The Case for Reason, Science, Humanism, and Progress* (Penguin, 2018)

14   Just one month before handing over to Trump, Obama permanently banned new oil and gas drilling in most US-owned waters in the Arctic and Atlantic oceans, a last minute stab at upholding environmental protections. David Smith, 'Barack Obama Bans Oil And Gas Drilling in Most of Arctic and Atlantic Oceans', *The Guardian* (20 December 2016). But, of course, Trump took us back to square one as he seemingly worked to dismantle any and all environmental protections, during his presidency. Sabrina Shankman, '3 Arctic Wilderness Areas to Watch as Trump Tries to Expand Oil & Gas Drilling', *Inside Climate News* (9 January 2020)

15   Simon Calder, 'Airline Safety: 2017 Was Safest Year in History for Passengers around

World, Research Shows', *The Independent* (1 January 2018)

16   Macaulay, 'Southey's Colloquies on Society' (see note 7 above).

17   Toby Ord, *The Precipice: Existential Risk and the Future of Humanity* (Bloomsbury, 2020)

18   Anders Sandberg and Nick Bostrom, 'Global Catastrophic Risks Survey: Technical Report 2008-1' (2008)

19   Nafeez Ahmed, 'Theoretical Physicists Say 90% Chance of Societal Collapse Within Several Decades', *Vice* (28 July 2020)

20   Carl Sagan, *Cosmos* (Random House, 1980)

21   If we take the 300,000 figure for how old Homo sapiens are, then:
300,000 / 1 billion = 0.03%
0.03% of this book = page 0.07

22   Carl Sagan, 'The Quest for Extraterrestrial Intelligence, Cosmic Search Vol 1', *Smithsonian Magazine* (May 1978), www.bigear.org/vol1no2/sagan.htm

23   Steven Pinker has an article on the wealth of great books that document the positive and improving aspects of the world – 'Steven Pinker recommends books to make you an optimist', *The Guardian* (26 Feb 2018). His fellow rational optimist, Matt Ridley, is more problematic. His optimistic position comes from a mindset of market fundamentalism. Much of his journalism, and his book *The Rational Optimist* (Harper, 2010), suggests that if we just leave pure unhindered capitalism to itself, we will see the greatest benefit to society. Interestingly, when putting his theory into practice as the chairman of UK bank Northern Rock, the bank pursued high-risk, reckless strategies (in areas where the government failed to regulate and intervene) and we saw how that ended ... catastrophically, with the bank getting a £27 billion UK government bailout and the eventual nationalising of the bank. The unrestricted private market failed completely and had to rely on state intervention. His reasoning for rational optimism (in that we need *more* capitalism, not less) in my mind, appears utterly delusional. And it seems even his own experience has proven that.

24   The UN forecasts estimate that there could be anywhere between 25 million and 1 billion environmental migrants by 2050. Francesco Bassetti, 'Environmental Migrants: Up to 1 Billion by 2050', *Foresight* (22 May 2019), www.climateforesight.eu/migrations-inequalities/environmental-migrants-up-to-1-billion-by-2050

25   With most nuclear weapons worldwide remaining on 'hair trigger alert' – an incredibly dangerous affair that significantly increases risk – we still live in an undoubtedly unsafe world. The *doomsday clock* is a symbolic clock that puts a countdown on the likelihood of man-made global catastrophe. It has been maintained since 1947 by the members of the Bulletin of the Atomic Scientists. The closer it gets to midnight, the higher they perceive the risk of catastrophe. On January 23, 2020, it was moved forward to 100 seconds (1 minute 40 seconds) before midnight, based on the increased threats to global stability posed by 'a nuclear blunder', exacerbated by the rate of climate change. See: https://thebulletin.org/doomsday-clock/

26   Professor Stephen Hawking said that AI could 'spell the end of the human race'. See Kevin Rawlinson, 'Microsoft's Bill Gates Insists AI is a Threat', *BBC News* (29 January 2015. In 2016, a survey of leading AI researchers showed that half of the researchers questioned estimated that the probability of the long-term impact of artificial general intelligence being 'extremely bad (e.g. human extinction)' was *at least* 5%. Of course, 5% doesn't sound like much, but when we're talking *human extinction*, would you want to take those odds? Half of them said that research on minimising the risks of AI should be prioritised by society *more* than it currently is. See: Katja Grace et al., 'When Will AI Exceed Human Performance? Evidence from AI Experts' (May 2018), available at https://arxiv.org/pdf/1705.08807.pdf

27   Centre for Effective Altruism, 'Fireside Chat: Q&A with Toby Ord' (21 July 2020)

28   Sagan, 'The Quest for Extraterrestrial Intelligence' (see note 22 above).
29   There are many subtler links between *The Spark* and *Nothing Is True …*, and I won't give them all away, but one important one is that **The Great Unknown** as a concept, and lyric, was introduced in **The Sights**, the opening track of the album: 'Now I boldly go, into the great unknown, and like Jean-Jacques Rousseau, I give my mind to be blown.' Rousseau's philosophy was also one of the biggest inspirations behind many of the concepts on both albums.
30   Nye Bevan, *In Place of Fear* (Quartet Books, 1952/1979)
31   Mark Z. Jacobson, *100% Clean, Renewable Energy and Storage for Everything* (Cambridge University Press, 2020)
32   Paul Wolf, 'Creativity and chronic disease Vincent van Gogh (1853-1890)', *Western Journal of Medicine* (November 2001)
33   Ibid.

An Overview Of Our Predicament And Our Emotional Response
2.2 Modern Living

1   Gallup, 'Gallup 2019 Global Emotions Report' (2019)
2   Not a joke. It'll be 20 times more powerful than the atomic bomb dropped on Hiroshima, and the US Air Force plans to order more than 600 of them. See: Elisabeth Eaves, 'Why is America getting a new $100 billion nuclear weapon?', *Bulletin of the Atomic Scientists* (8 February 2021)
3   For further reading, see the Wikipedia page 'Self System', https://en.wikipedia.org/wiki/Self_system
4   A topic discussed in more detail in our song **Undercover Agents**, a track from our 2015 album *The Spark*.
5   Elle Hunt, 'Faking It: How Selfie Dysmorphia Is Driving People to Seek Surgery', *The Guardian* (23 January 2019)
6   Ibid.
7   William Blake, 'London', in *Songs of Experience* (1794)
8   See Wikipedia, 'List of nuclear close calls'. There have been an alarming amount of 'close calls', some truly terrifying. My personal 'favourite' though, in account of it's sheer ridiculousness, took place in 1962 (during the height of tensions due to the Cuban missile crisis). An intruder was spotted climbing a fence at an American airbase, guards sounded the alarms, which, due to a fault, sounded the klaxon that signalled the deployment of nuclear-armed aircraft at another base nearby. The pilots of these aircraft had previously been told there were to be no drills, and by all accounts it was believed that a nuclear war was, in fact, beginning. Luckily, the error was realised before the planes could take off, and an officer in the command center drove his car out onto the runway, and flashed his lights, signalling to the aircraft to stop, just in time. It later turned out that the 'intruder' had been a bear.Scott Douglas Sagan,' The Limits of Safety: Organizations, Accidents, and Nuclear Weapons' (1993) Furthermore, it's worth stating, that most people do not understand the sheer power of nukes: In 1954, a fission-fusion-fission superbomb was tested. 'The energy released in the explosion of this bomb was greater than that of all of the explosives used in all of the wars that have taken place during the entire history of the world, including the First World War and the Second World War.' (Yes that includes the bombs dropped on Hiroshima & Nagasaki) an abysmal amount of power. Linus Pauling, 'Nobel Lecture', *The Nobel Peace Prize* (11 December 1963) https://www.nobelprize.org/prizes/peace/1962/pauling/lecture/
9   Remember, news outlets write seductively reductive headlines in order to get you to click their links. Each hit they get makes their page more appealing to advertisers. This

is another example of the profit motive creating a toxic atmosphere, and we'll look at it in more detail in Chapter 4.

10   Jill Suttie, 'How to Overcome 'Apocalypse Fatigue' Around Climate Change', *Berkeley Greater Good Magazine* (23 February 2018)

11   Declining from 71% just a year prior. For example, see Ted Nordhaus and Michael Shellenberger, 'Apocalypse Fatigue: Losing the Public on Climate Change', *The Guardian* (17 November 2009). Luckily, more recently, the majority are back to believing climate change is occurring, and thankfully, the majority of people worldwide, roughly 70%, believe that climate change is now a major threat. Moira Fagan and Christine Huang, 'A Look at How People Around the World View Climate Change' (18 April 2019), www.pewresearch.org/fact-tank/2019/04/18/a-look-at-how-people-around-the-world-view-climate-change

12   For example, see: Lauren Gambino, 'Donald Trump Boasts that His Nuclear Button is Bigger than Kim Jong-un's', *The Guardian* (3 January 2018)

13   Voltaire, *Candide* (1759). In a letter to a friend in 1756, Voltaire also wrote: 'Optimism is dismaying. It is a cruel philosophy under a consoling name'. Sara Stone, 'Critically Discuss the Significance of Optimism in Candide', *Words From a Stone* (3 May 2017)

14   Terry Eagleton, *Hope Without Optimism* (University of Virginia Press, 2015)

15   Ibid.

16   A review quoted on the University of Virginia Press website, www.upress.virginia.edu/title/4948

17   Mia M. Bennett, 'Ruins of the Anthropocene: The Aesthetics of Arctic Climate Change', *Annals of The American Association of Geographers* (10 December 2020), available at https://doi.org/10.1080/24694452.2020.1835457

18   Ibid.

19   Ibid.

20   Srećko Horvat, *Poetry from the Future: Why a Global Liberation Movement Is Our Civilisation's Last Chance* (Allen Lane, 2019)

21   Eagleton, *Hope Without Optimism* (see note 14 above)

The Anthropocene
Crossing The Rubicon & Elegy For Extinction

1   Eliza Barclay and Brian Resnick, 'How Big Was the Global Climate Strike? 4 Million People, Activists Estimate', *Vox* (22 September 2019), www.vox.com/energy-and-environment/2019/9/20/20876143/climate-strike-2019-september-20-crowd-estimate

2   'Enter Shikari – *The Appeal & The Mindsweep* (plus intro) – Brooklyn, NYC. Sept 2019' (8 November 2019), www.youtube.com/watch?v=Za6VagjiI00

3   'UN Chief Warns of "Point of No Return" on Climate Change', *Politico* (12 January 2019)

4   'In the absence of policies, global warming is expected to reach 4.1°C – 4.8°C above pre-industrial by the end of the century.' http://climateactiontracker.org/global/temperatures/"climateactiontracker.org/global/temperatures/

5   The total amount of human emissions (from all agriculture and industry) is 660 gigatons of carbon (GtC). Sounds like a lot doesn't it? But it's hard to know how much that actually is, right? Well, for comparison, the total amount of carbon in all living organisms on the Earth right now equals 550 GtC. See: 'All life on Earth, in one staggering chart', *Vox* (29 May 2018)

6   Richard B. Rood, 'If We Stopped Emitting Greenhouse Gases Right Now, Would We Stop Climate Change?', *The Conversation* (7 July 2017)

7   For further reading, see 'Alea iacta est' on Wikipedia, https://en.wikipedia.org/wiki/

Alea_iacta_est

8   'If We Immediately Stopped Emitting Greenhouses Gases, Would Global Warming Stop?', (2 July 2007), https://earthobservatory.nasa.gov/blogs/climateqa/would-gw-stop-with-greenhouse-gases/

9   Also referred to as *positive feedback loops*. This term can cause confusion though, especially when relaying climate science to the layman, as there is nothing 'positive' about these loops. They are, of course, only 'positive' in the technical sense, but intricacies are often lost in translation. I have chosen to use the more obvious term *amplifying* as it is more intuitive. For a definition of positive and negative climate feedbacks see: 'The Study of Earth as an Integrated System', *NASA Earth System Science* https://climate.nasa.gov/nasa_science/science/

10 Fiona Harvey, 'Global ice loss accelerating at record rate, study finds', *The Guardian* (25 January 2021)

11 Tom Yulsman 'With Sea Level Rise, We've Already Hurtled Past a Point of No Return', *Discover Magazine* (6 December 2019)

12 George Orwell, *The Road To Wigan Pier* (Victor Gollancz, 1937)

13 This is a song I'm currently working on. I'm excited for it to see the light of day at some point. But if you imagine us drunkenly at the wheel of our Spaceship Earth ploughing through space without care or prudence, you get an idea of what it'll sound like.

14 Quote from the executive summary of *Global Biodiversity Outlook 3* (2010), www.cbd.int/gbo3/?pub=6667&section=6673

15 Gloria Dicke, 'Global Biodiversity Is in Free Fall', *Scientific American* (15 September 2020), www.scientificamerican.com/article/global-biodiversity-is-in-free-fall/

16 'Revolution Now! With Peter Joseph' (22 September 2020), www.revolutionnow.live/episodes/episode-06-staycationing-9jlk7-pcw4k-rctmc-rg7sy

17 IPCC, 'Global Warming of 1.5°' (2018), available at https://report.ipcc.ch/sr15/pdf/sr15_spm_final.pdf

18 Matt McGrath, 'Coronavirus Forces Postponement of COP26 Meeting in Glasgow', *BBC News* (1 April 2020), www.bbc.co.uk/news/science-environment-52122450

19 Fiona Harvey, 'World Has Six Months to Avert Climate Crisis, Says Energy Expert', *The Guardian* (18 June 2020)

20 'A Warning Sign from Our Planet: Nature Needs Life Support' (30 October 2018), www.wwf.org.uk/updates/living-planet-report-2018

21 Damian Carrington, 'Humanity Has Wiped Out 60% of Animal Populations since 1970, Report Finds', *The Guardian* (30 October 2018)

22 Timothy M. Lenton, 'Climate Tipping Points – Too Risky to Bet Against', *Nature* (27 November 2019), www.nature.com/articles/d41586-019-03595-0

23 Ibid.

24 Will Steffan et al. 'Trajectories of the Earth System in the Anthropocene', *PNAS* (14 August 2018), available at www.pnas.org/content/115/33/8252

25 Christina Nunez, 'Sea Level Rise, Explained', *National Geographic* (19 February 2019), www.nationalgeographic.com/environment/global-warming/sea-level-rise

26 The line in **Mothership**: 'Your answers were always lying on the ocean bed' is a reference to one of the first signs of climate change – the destruction of coral reefs. Climate change dramatically affects coral reefs through sea level rise, sea temperature rise and ocean acidification, amongst other things. Sea surface temperature has increased by about 1°C since reliable observations began in 1880. See: 'Extended reconstructed sea surface temperature', NOAA (2016). And since 1750 the ocean has become more acidic by 0.1ph. See: 'IPCC Fifth Assessment Report', IPCC (2014). This has had a deadly effect on coral reefs.

27 Stephen Leahy, 'Climate Change Driving Entire Planet to Dangerous "Tipping Point"', *National Geographic* (30 November 2019)

28   Anthony Cronin, *Samuel Beckett: The Last Modernist* (HarperCollins, 1996), p.565
29   Samuel Beckett, *Worstward Ho* (John Calder, 1983)
30   Mark O'Connell, 'The Stunning Success of 'Fail Better'', *Slate* (29 January 2014), https://slate.com/culture/2014/01/samuel-becketts-quote-fail-better-becomes-the-mantra-of-silicon-valley.html
31   'Isaac Newton letter to Robert Hooke, 1675', available at https://discover.hsp.org/Record/dc-9792/Description#tabnav

Human Nature, Social Structure, Communication And Mass Media
The Dreamer's Hotel & Waltzing Off The Face Of The Earth

1   I think it's important to clarify my definition of civility, seeing as I'll be using it so much throughout the book. Civility is not just being respectful, for instance we may use civility even when speaking with someone who we consider completely undeserving of our respect. Using civility just means we respect dialogue over arguments, feuds and violence. Civility is not the same as 'being nice', because being nice means sometimes not telling someone what you really think. We must endeavour to say what we really think to our adversaries face, not behind their back, but we must do all this with calm and clarity. We must not give in to the temptation of anger and spite. To achieve this, civility should be led by curiosity. We must attempt to find out how our opponents came to conclusions *so* different from our own, and then analyse them for the root causes. Civility is the only way to find out more about each other and our world, and it is therefore the only way to progress. Resorting to ridicule, violence, domination and subjugation to achieve your ends, regardless of being morally negligent, will rarely change things with any longevity. Civility is being able to explore disagreements with honesty and clarity while being able to stay calm, and all whilst in the same 'room' as your opponent. As soon as you are in different rooms, shouting through the walls at each other, you may mishear, misinterpret and exaggerate their words.

2   Barbara Gutierrez, 'Have We Lost the Art of Civility?' *University of Education & Human Development* (15 November 2018), available at https://sites.education.miami.edu/have-we-lost-the-art-of-civility

3   Jon Ronson's book *So You've Been Publicly Shamed* (Riverhead Books, 2015) is the best exploration of this kind of experience.

4   Takuya Sawaoka, 'The Paradox of Viral Outrage' *Psychological Science* 29(10) (2018), https://journals.sagepub.com/doi/full/10.1177/0956797618780658

5   Robert D. Putnam, *Bowling Alone: The Collapse and Revival of American Community* (New York: Simon & Schuster; 2000)

6   Quoted in Gutierrez, 'Have We Lost the Art of Civility?' (see note 2 above)

7   Soren Holmberg & Bo Rothstein, 'Trusting other people', *Journal of public affairs* (30 December 2016)

8   Rutger Bregman, *Humankind: A Hopeful History* (Bloomsbury, 2019)

9   Dacher Keltner, 'The Compassionate Instinct', *Berkeley Greater Good Magazine* (1 March 2004)

10   Sara H. Konrath, 'Changes in Dispositional Empathy in American College Students Over Time: A Meta-Analysis', *SAGE* (August 2010)

11   Jonathan Haidt and Tobias Rose-Stockwell, 'The Dark Psychology of Social Networks', *The Atlantic* (December 2019), available at www.theatlantic.com/magazine/archive/2019/12/social-media-democracy/600763

12   Boris's commitment to his own advancement is pretty well documented. Even his answer to the question 'Can you give an example in your political life when you've set your own self-interest aside for the benefit of the country?' was incredibly telling: 'I

would [...] make more money by not being a full-time politician. I don't want to put too fine a point on it, but, err, you know, you have to make sacrifices sometimes, and that is the right thing to do.' Yes, the only example he could think of was that if he wasn't in politics he'd be even more loaded than he is as an MP. He chose power over money. Oh, such sacrifice! (Interview on *Channel 4 News*, 5 July 2019)

13   Clayton Critcher and David Dunning, 'No Good Deed Goes Unquestioned: Cynical Reconstruals Maintain Belief in the Power of Self interest', *Journal of Experimental Social Psychology* (November 2011), www.researchgate.net/publication/251472815_No_good_deed_goes_unquestioned_Cynical_reconstruals_maintain_belief_in_the_power_of_self-interest

14   For example, see 'Why We Help', *Scientific American* (1 November 2012), www.scientificamerican.com/article/why-we-help

15   Dacher Keltner, 'Social Scientists Build Case for "Survival of the Kindest"', *ScienceDaily* (9 December 2009), www.sciencedaily.com/releases/2009/12/091208155309.htm

16   Rou Reynolds and Enter Shikari, *Dear Future Historians* (Faber Music, 2017)

17   Charles Darwin, *The Descent of Man, and Selection in Relation to Sex* (John Murray, 1871)

18   Paul Ekman, 'Darwin's Compassionate View of Human Nature', *JAMA Network* (10 February 2010), www.paulekman.com/wp-content/uploads/2013/07/Darwins-Compassionate-View-Of-Human-Nature-2010.pdf

19   For example: 'Compassion and benevolence, this research suggests, are an evolved part of human nature, rooted in our brain and biology' (Keltner, 'The Compassionate Instinct'; see note 9); or: 'Research shows that compassion is very natural for us ... We have as many, if not more, impulses to act kindly and with compassion' (Eric Nelson, 'Darwin Revisited: Compassion Key to Our Survival', https://charterforcompassion.org/becoming-compassionate/darwin-revisited-compassion-key-to-our-survival); or see S. Bowles and H. Gintis, *A Cooperative Species: Human Reciprocity and its Evolution* (Princeton University Press, 2011)

20   Emiliana R. Simon-Thomas, 'The Cooperative Instinct', *Berkeley Great Good Magazine* (21 September 2012)

21   Felix Warneken, 'Need Help? Ask a Two Year Old' (22 April 2014), www.youtube.com/watch?v=-qul57hcu4I

22   Ibid.

23   Ibid.

24   Keltner, 'The Compassionate Instinct' (see note 9).

25   Bregman, *Humankind* (see note 8).

26   Keltner, 'The Compassionate Instinct' (see note 9).

27   Ibid.

28   I use these terms by Mark Blyth and Eric Lonergan from their book *Angrynomics* (Agenda Publishing, 2020)

29   Larry Elliot, 'World's 26 Richest People Own as Much as Poorest 50%, says Oxfam', *The Guardian* (21 January 2019)

30   Dr. Charles Stangor, Principles Of Social Psychology, 'Ingroup Favoritism and Prejudice', available at https://opentextbc.ca/socialpsychology/chapter/ingroup-favoritism-and-prejudice

31   Michael Billig & Henri Tajfel, 'Social Categorization and Similarity in Intergroup Behaviour', *European Journal of Social Psychology* (January–March 1973), available at https://onlinelibrary.wiley.com/doi/abs/10.1002/ejsp.2420030103

32   Ibid.

33   E. O. Wilson, 'Tribalism, Groupism, Globalism', *The Globalist* (7 January 2013), www.theglobalist.com/tribalism-groupism-globalism

34   Amy Chua, *Political Tribes: Group Instinct and the Fate of Nations* (Penguin, 2018)

35   'Whites Believe They Are Victims of Racism More Often Than Blacks' (23 May 2011), https://now.tufts.edu/news-releases/whites-believe-they-are-victims-racism-more-o

36   Theo E. J. Wilson, 'A Black Man Goes Undercover in the Alt-Right', available on https://www.ted.com/talks

37   Ibid.

38   Chua, *Political Tribes* (see note 34 above)

39   Thomas J. Scheff, 'Hidden Shame as a Cause of Violence', *International Journal of Emergency Mental Health* (January 2015)

40   Rebecca Klaar, 'Herman Cain Account Tweets Coronavirus "Not as Deadly" as Claimed after His Death from COVID-19', *The Hill* (31 August 2020)

41   Pew Research Center, 'Partisanship and Political Animosity in 2016' (22 June 2016), www.pewresearch.org/politics/2016/06/22/partisanship-and-political-animosity-in-2016

42   Ibid.

43   Ellie Lisitsa, 'The Four Horseman: Contempt', *The Gottman Institute* (13 May 2013), www.gottman.com/blog/the-four-horsemen-contempt/

44   United Nations Human Rights Office of the High Commissioner, 'Joint Open Letter on Concerns about the Global Increase in Hate Speech', www.ohchr.org/EN/NewsEvents/Pages/DisplayNews.aspx?NewsID=25036&LangID=E

45   In the tenth instalment of *The Federalist Papers*, James Madison defines a faction as 'a number of citizens, whether amounting to a minority or majority of the whole, who are united and actuated by some common impulse of passion, or of interest, adverse to the rights of other citizens, or to the permanent and aggregate interests of the community.'

46   Gaia Vince, 'Why good people turn bad online – and how to defeat your inner troll', *The Independent* (2 April 2018)

47   Justin Rosenstein in Jeff Orlowski's (dir.), *The Social Dilemma* (Netflix, 2010)

48   For example, see: Guillaume Chaslot, 'The Toxic Potential of YouTube's Feedback Loop', *Wired* (13 July 2019), www.wired.com/story/the-toxic-potential-of-youtubes-feedback-loop

49   Barbara Oakley, 'A Mind for Numbers: How to Excel at Math and Science (Even if You Flunked Algebra)' (2014)

50   John Stuart Mill, *On Liberty* (John W. Parker & Son, 1859)

51   Ibid.

52   David Folkenflik, 'You Literally Can't Believe the Facts Tucker Carlson Tells You. So Say Fox's Lawyers', *NPR* (29 September 2020)

53   Peter Dizikes, 'Study: On Twitter, False News Travels Faster than True Stories', *MIT News* (8 March 2018), https://news.mit.edu/2018/study-twitter-false-news-travels-faster-true-stories-0308

54   Kirsten Weir, 'Why We Believe Alternative Facts', *American Psychological Association* (May 2017), www.apa.org/monitor/2017/05/alternative-facts

55   Some examples from Germany, UK and USA: 'German Police Officers Suspended for Sharing Neo-Nazi Content', *The Guardian* (17 September 2020), 'Met Police Officer Accused of Being Member of Neo-Nazi Terrorist Group and Child Sex Offences Appears in Court', *The Independent* (14 August 2020), 'White Supremacists and Militias Have Infiltrated Police Across US, Report Says', *The Guardian* (27 August 2020)

56   Guillaume Chaslot in Orlowski, *The Social Dilemma* (see note 47 above)

57   Angelo Antoci, 'Civility vs. Incivility in Online Social Interactions: An Evolutionary Approach', *PLoS ONE* (1 November 2016)

58   Ibid.

59   Tristan Harris in Orlowski, *The Social Dilemma* (see note 47 above)

60   Juliana Schroeder, 'The Humanizing Voice: Speech Reveals, and Text Conceals, a More Thoughtful Mind in the Midst of Disagreement', *Association for Psychological Science* (2017), http://faculty.haas.berkeley.edu/jschroeder/Publications/

SchroederKardasEpley%20Humanizing%20Voice%20Psych%20Science.pdf

61 Juliana Schroeder, 'Hearing an Opinion Spoken Aloud Humanizes the Person Behind It', *Association for Psychological Science* (6 November 2017)

62 We've had evidence for this even before the internet: in 1986 a pioneering experiment comparing face-to-face and computer mediated conversations found that the latter were more aggressive. Participants were more impulsive and assertive, and less bound by societal norms of civility. See 'Group Processes in Computer-Mediated Communication', *Organizational Behaviour and Human Decision Processes* (April 1986), available at www.sciencedirect.com

63 William J. Brady, 'Emotion Shapes the Diffusion of Moralized Content in Social Networks', *PNAS* (11 July 2017), www.pnas.org/content/114/28/7313

64 George Orwell, *Animal Farm* (Secker & Warburg, 1945)

65 Matthew Sparkes, 'Making a conspiracy theorist', *New Scientist* (27 January 2021)

66 Keith Perry, 'One in Five Children just Want to be Rich When They Grow up', *The Telegraph* (5 August 2014)

67 David Heath, 'Contesting the Science of Smoking', *The Atlantic* (4 May 2016), www.theatlantic.com/politics/archive/2016/05/low-tar-cigarettes/481116

68 Greenpeace, 'Koch Industries: Secretly Funding the Climate Denial Machine'

69 Niall McCarthy, 'Oil and Gas Giants Spend Millions Lobbying to Block Climate Change Policies', *Forbes* (25 March 2019)

70 'Big Oil's Real Agenda on Climate Change' (March 2019), https://influencemap.org/report/How-Big-Oil-Continues-to-Oppose-the-Paris-Agreement-38212275958aa2119 6dae3b76220bddc, this is an example of the Pollution Paradox: The more damaging the activity, the more money it must spend in politics to ensure it's not regulated or banned. As a result, politics becomes completely infested by the most harmful companies and oligarchs. And then there's also 'dark money'; see Douglas Fischer, '"Dark Money" Funds Climate Change Denial Effort', *Scientific American* (23 December 2013), www.scientificamerican.com/article/dark-money-funds-climate-change-denial-effort

71 For example, see Suzanne Goldenberg, 'Oil Company Records from 1960s Reveal Patents to Reduce CO_2 Emissions in Cars', *The Guardian* (20 May 2016)

72 I learnt this at the seminar, 'Climate Scepticism – Is it Primarily Found in the English-Speaking World, and if so, Why?', London School of Economics & Political Science (24 May 2012), www.lse.ac.uk/granthaminstitute/events/climate-scepticism-is-it-primarily-found-in-the-english-speaking-world-and-if-so-why

73 Chris Mooney, 'The Strange Relationship between Global Warming Denial and ... Speaking English', *The Guardian* (23 July 2014)

74 In America, it is *the* most preventable cause of death: see 'Smoking and Tobacco Use', www.cdc.gov/tobacco/data_statistics/fact_sheets/fast_facts/index.htm. Worldwide, most estimates put it a close second to hypertension.

75 In 2014, the World Health Organization (WHO) estimated that climate change would lead to about 250,000 additional deaths each year between 2030 and 2050, from factors such as malnutrition, heat stress and malaria. See WHO, 'Climate Change and Health' (1 February 2018), www.who.int/news-room/fact-sheets/detail/climate-change-and-health. They didn't account for the effect of many combining feedback loops though, nor the effect of civil unrest, social destabilisation, and the reaction of future far-right governments to climate refugees. The latter here being infinitely depressing: 'Future far-right governments, having consolidated power by undermining democratic infrastructures', will explore new ways of preventing immigration – possibly with fatal consequences for enormous numbers of people', according to Richard Parncutt, 'The Human Cost of Anthropogenic Global Warming: Semi-Quantitative Prediction and the 1,000-Tonne Rule', *Environmental Psychology* (16 October 2019)

76   See NowThisNews, https://www.youtube.com/watch?v=2rkQn-43ixs

77   Edith Honan, 'Walmart Says it Sells 20% of Ammunition in US, Defends Gun Sales after Mass Shootings', *ABC News* (15 August 2019)

78   Sarah Nassauer, 'Walmart Workers' New Security Threat Is Active Shooters, Not Shoplifters', *The Wall Street Journal* (5 August 2019),

79   Bill Allison, 'NRA Spent Record Amount Lobbying Congress, With Little to Show', *Bloomberg* (5 February 2019)

80   Katy Fallon, 'Three Years on from Alan Kurdi's Death and Life Is No Better for Child Refugees in Europe', *The Independent* (2 September 2018)

81   At land, see 'Thousands of Refugees and Migrants Suffer Extreme Rights Abuses on Journeys to Africa's Mediterranean Coast, New UNHCR/MMC Report Shows' (29 July 2020), www.unhcr.org/uk/news/press/2020/7/5f1ee9314/thousands-refugees-migrants-suffer-extreme-rights-abuses-journeys-africas.html; at sea, see 'Coastguard Seen Apparently Trying to Capsize Boat Full of Refugees before Attacking Them with Stick, as Child Drowns off Coast', *The Independent* (2 March 2020), www.independent.co.uk/news/world/europe/migrant-child-killed-greek-coast-lesbos-syria-refugee-deaths-a9369826.html

82   Catrin Nye, 'Children "Attempting Suicide" at Greek Refugee Camp', *BBC News* (28 August 2018), www.bbc.co.uk/news/world-europe-45271194. Since I wrote this part, the notoriously overcrowded refugee camp has been burnt to the ground during a huge fire, displacing 13,000 people. See 'In Pictures: Huge Fire Reduces Moria Refugee Camp to Embers', *Al Jazeera* (9 September 2020), www.aljazeera.com/indepth/inpictures/pictures-huge-fire-reduces-moria-refugee-camp-embers-200909065407992.html

83   Department For Education, 'Relationships Education (Primary)', available at www.gov.uk

84   73% of the public says that most Republican and Democratic voters not only disagree over plans and policies, but also disagree on 'basic facts'. See Pew Research Center, 'Partisan Antipathy: More Intense, More Personal' (10 October 2019). Only 28% of people think that people agree on basic facts even if they disagree politically. See Pew Research Center, 'In Views of US Democracy, Widening Partisan Divides Over Freedom to Peacefully Protest', (2 September 2020)

85   Julie Beck, 'The Christmas the Aliens Didn't Come', *The Atlantic* (18 December 2015), www.theatlantic.com/health/archive/2015/12/the-christmas-the-aliens-didnt-come/421122

86   Leon Festinger, Henry W. Riecken and Stanley Schachter, *When Prophecy Fails* (Harper-Torchbooks, 1956)

87   Ibid.

88   Nicholas Epley and Thomas Gilovich, 'The Mechanics of Motivated Reasoning', *American Economic Association* (Summer 2016)

89   Dan Kahan, 'Weekend Update: You'd Have to Be Science Illiterate to Think "Belief in Evolution" Measures Science Literacy', *The Cultural Cognition Project at Yale Law School* (24 May 2014), www.culturalcognition.net/blog/2014/5/24/weekend-update-youd-have-to-be-science-illiterate-to-think-b.html

90   Robinson Meyer, 'Republicans Can Understand Science and Still Deny Climate Change', *The Atlantic* (5 October 2016)

91   'Effective Messages in Vaccine Promotion: A Randomized Trial', *Pediatrics* (March 2014), https://pediatrics.aappublications.org/content/early/2014/02/25/peds.2013-2365

92   Brian F. Schaffner and Samantha Luks, 'Misinformation or Expressive Responding? What an Inauguration Crowd Can Tell Us about the Source of Political Misinformation in Surveys', *Public Opinion Quarterly* 82(1) (17 February 2018), pp.135–147

93   Ibid.

94   Julie Beck, 'This Article Won't Change Your Mind', *The Atlantic* (11 December

2019), www.theatlantic.com/science/archive/2017/03/this-article-wont-change-your-mind/519093

95   Kirsten Weir, 'Why We Believe Alternative Facts', *American Psychological Association* (March 2017), www.apa.org/monitor/2017/05/alternative-facts

96   For a clear, science-based, gibberish-free introduction to mindfulness meditation, I have a free podcast called 'Here, Now, Together', available on all platforms.

97   Jonathan Haidt and Tobias Rose-Stockwell, 'The Dark Psychology of Social Networks', *The Atlantic* (December 2019)

98   Keltner, 'The Compassionate Instinct' (see note 9)

99   A rule against this sort of behaviour comes to us in the form of Hanlon's Razor: never attribute to malice what could be attributed to something else (e.g. stupidity or ignorance). So, when someone appears to act badly towards you, do not assume it is with an intention to wrong or hurt you, it is more likely they are being thoughtless, or somehow unaware of their effect. We often assume the worst in people or jump too quickly to feeling targeted or victimised.

100 Baruch Spinoza, *Tractatus Theologico-Politicus* (1677)

101 Ron Carucci, 'How to Avoid Fueling Affective Polarization' *Ethical Systems* (29 June 2020), www.ethicalsystems.org/how-to-avoid-fueling-affective-polarization

102 The author and journalist Will Storr explains this train of thought well: 'When I was in my teenage years I was a classic angry skeptical kind of guy. [I was] angry at my parents for being Catholic. I was angry at Christians in general for being so stupid and for causing all of the wars. And it's actually been a journey of ... I've gained humility. What happens when you go and meet these people with an open-mind, is that before you've met them you think they're idiots or hateful or they're whatever ... and then you meet them, and after you meet them sincerely and show a genuine interest in their story, trying to find out why they believe what they believe, even if you don't end up agreeing with them, you can understand why/how they've ended up where they are. You can understand the story of their lives; the story of how they've' got there. And you leave much more empathetic.' From Skeptiko podcast, episode 262, 'Science Has its Enemies, but They May Not Be Who You Think', https://skeptiko.com/262-will-storr-enemies-of-science

103 Richard Appignanesi, *Introducing Melanie Klein* (Icon Books, 2006)

104 Robin Skynner and John Cleese, *Families and How to Survive Them* (Methuen, 1983).

105 Alain, 'Propos impertinents' (c.1921–1936), trans. Brenda Almond, *The Philosopher* (1 September 2007)

106 A good place to start with Piff's work is his TED talk: Paul Piff, 'Does Money Make You Mean?', (October 2013)

107 Quoted in Anne Manne, 'The Age of Entitlement: How Wealth Breeds Narcissism', *The Guardian* (7 July 2014)

108 Quoted in Anthony Cunningham, *The Heart of What Matters: The Role for Literature in Moral Philosophy* (University of California Press, 2001)

109 Martin Luther King Jr, *Strength To Love* (Harper & Row, 1963)

110 Megan Phelps-Roper, 'I Grew Up in the Westboro Baptist Church. Here's Why I Left', (February 2017)

111 In Matthew Ornstein (dir.), *Accidental Courtesy: Daryl Davis, Race & America* (PBS, 2016), https://accidentalcourtesy.com

112 Founded in 2011, the group encourages and helps people to leave hate groups and begin new lives. In January 2017, the Obama administration awarded the group $400,000 as part of a government grant. However, aides of President Trump decided to discontinue the grant in June 2017.

113 Jason Wilson, 'Life after White Supremacy: The Former Neo-Fascist Now Working to Fight Hate', *The Guardian* (4 April 2017)

114 Matthew Brown, 'He was a Neo-Nazi Leader. Now He's Standing in a Synagogue Seeking One Thing from His Jewish Audience', *Deseret News* (15 September 2019)
115 Ibid.
116 Nicole F. Roberts, 'Emotional & Physical Pain Are Almost The Same – To Your Brain', *Forbes* (14 Feb 2020)
117 Evan L. Ardiel, 'The importance of touch in development', *Paediatrics & Child Health* (March 2010)
118 Dana G. Smith, 'Neuroscientists Make a Case against Solitary Confinement', *Scientific American* (9 November 2018)

Human Complexity
5.1 The King

1   See, for example, Tim Radford, 'The Untold Story of Evolution', *The Guardian* (25 April 2011), 'around 40,000 years ago, modern humans must have shared the planet with at least four other human cousins: *Homo erectus*, the Neanderthals, a strange, small-brained human found only on the island of Flores in Indonesia, affectionately known as the Hobbit; and most recent of all, species X: a separate human genetic lineage identified in 2010 only by DNA extracted from a finger bone found in a Siberian cave.'
2   Ben Guarino, 'Ancient Humans Had Sex With More Than Just Neanderthals, Scientists Find', *The Washington Post* (11 January 2019)
3   Pascale Hughes, '"Neanderthal" No Longer Works as an Insult', *iNews* (30 November 2018)
4   Pat Lee Shipman, 'Do the Eyes Have It?', *American Scientist* (May–June 2012), www.americanscientist.org/article/do-the-eyes-have-it; Michael Tomasello, 'Reliance on head versus eyes in the gaze following of great apes and human infants: the cooperative eye hypothesis', *National Library Of Medicine* (20 October 2006), https://pubmed.ncbi.nlm.nih.gov/17140637
5   For example see: Alban Lemasson, 'Social Learning of Vocal Structure in a Nonhuman Primate?', *BMC Evolutionary Biology* (16 December 2011)
6   Altruism must be deeply seated in our species's ancestors as even our closest living relatives today contain some degree of altruistic behaviour. Again, for an introductory example, see Felix Warnekn's TED talk: 'Need Help? Ask a Two Year Old' (22 April 2014)
7   Examples of chimp douchebaggery (i.e. chimps not showing a preference for outcomes that benefit their groupmates) are available from the following studies: J. Silk et al., 'Chimpanzees are Indifferent to the Welfare of Unrelated Group Members', *Nature* 437 (2005), pp. 1357–1359, www.nature.com/articles/nature04243; K. Jensen et al., 'What's In It for Me? Self-regard Precludes Altruism and Spite in Chimpanzees', *Proceedings of the Royal Society B: Biological Sciences* 273(1589) (22 April 2006), pp. 1013–1021; J. Vonk et al., 'Chimpanzees Do Not Take Advantage of Very Low Cost Opportunities to Deliver Food to Unrelated Group Members', *Animal Behaviour* 75 (2008), pp. 1757–1770. Interestingly, even mothers will not voluntarily offer novel foods to their own infants unless the infants beg for them; see A. Ueno et al., 'Food Transfer between Chimpanzee Mothers and their Infants', *Primates* 45(4) (2004), pp. 231–239.
8   'Human beings routinely help others to achieve their goals, even when the helper receives no immediate benefit and the person helped is a stranger. Such altruistic behaviors (toward non-kin) are extremely rare evolutionarily, with some theorists even proposing that they are uniquely human', according to Felix Warneken, 'Altruistic Helping in Human Infants and Young Chimpanzees', *Science* (3 March 2006), https://science.sciencemag.org/content/311/5765/1301.abstract. See also Keith Jensen, 'The Emergence of Human Prosociality: Aligning with Others through Feelings, Concerns,

and Norms', *Frontiers in Psychology* (29 July 2014) 'The fact that humans cooperate with nonkin is something we take for granted, but this is an anomaly in the animal kingdom. Our species' ability to behave prosocially may be based on human-unique psychological mechanisms.'

9   'The reason we say that foragers were fiercely egalitarian is because they practiced reverse dominance hierarchy. [...] The goal of reverse hierarchy is to restrain physically powerful and aggressive men. Foraging societies use a variety of social mechanisms to prevent such 'upstarts' from bullying everybody, ranging from gossip and ridicule to expulsion and even capital punishment.' Peter Turchin, 'A Feminist Perspective on Human Social Evolution' (16 February 2019), http://peterturchin.com/cliodynamica/a-feminist-perspective-on-human-social-evolution

10   Hannah Devlin, 'Early Men and Women Were Equal, Say Scientists', *The Guardian* (14 May 2015) Sexual equality may have actually been a key part of our early human relationships and societies: 'It gives you a far more expansive social network with a wider choice of mates, so inbreeding would be less of an issue, [...] And you come into contact with more people and you can share innovations, which is something that humans do par excellence' (ibid.). See also M. Dybe, 'Sex Equality Can Explain the Unique Social Structure of Hunter–Gatherer Bands', *Science* (15 May 2015), https://science.sciencemag.org/content/348/6236/796

11   James Woodburn, 'Indigenous Discrimination: The Ideological Basis for Local Discrimination against Hunter-Gatherer Minorities in Sub-Saharan Africa', *Ethnic & Racial Studies* (1997)

12   Brian Hare, 'Survival of the Friendliest: *Homo Sapiens* Evolved via Selection for Prosociality', *Annual Review of Psychology* (January 2017)

13   Yuval Noah Harari, 'What Explains the Rise of Humans?' (June 2015), available at www.ted.com

14   Again, for a well-researched and rounded discussion of how we have forgotten our cooperative roots and now live in societies centred on hierarchy and competition, see Rutger Bregman's book *Humankind: A Hopeful History* (Bloomsbury, 2019)

15   Simon Baron-Cohen, 'Your Inventing Mind', *New Scientist* (5 December 2020)

16   Jamil Zaki, 'The War for Kindness: Building Empathy in a Fractured World' (20 February 2020), www.youtube.com/watch?v=7Y23qQjXmHs

17   Sean Illing, 'The Case against Empathy', *Vox* (16 January 2019)

18   Ibid.

19   Aristotle, *Rhetoric* (350 BCE), trans. W. Rhys Roberts

20   There are other problems with empathy too: 'It's innumerate, we feel empathy for the one and not for the hundred. We're more concerned about a little girl stuck in a well, than we are about a crisis like climate change. See 'Paul Bloom – Against Empathy: The Case for Rational Compassion' (27 January 2017). Empathy can also be exhausting and difficult. A therapist that properly empathises with her patients wouldn't last a week. A surgeon that properly empathises with their patient could not start through shaking with anxiety. For example, see *Making Sense* podcast no. 219, 'The Power Of Compassion' (9 October 2020), with surgeon James R. Doty

21   Bregman, *Humankind: A Hopeful History* (see note 14)

22   For example: 'Results showed that oxytocin drives a 'tend and defend' response in that it promoted in-group trust and cooperation, and defensive, but not offensive, aggression toward competing out-groups.' C. K. W. De Dreu et al., 'The Neuropeptide Oxytocin Regulates Parochial Altruism in Intergroup Conflict Among Humans', *Science* (11 June 2010)

23   Jill Suttie, 'Can We Find Morality in a Molecule?', *Greater Good Magazine* (10 July 2012)

24   Simon Baron-Cohen, *The Science of Evil: On Empathy and the Origins of Cruelty* (Basic Books, 2012)

25   If we can increase the scenarios where oxytocin is released naturally in people then we'll become more relaxed, empathic and trusting. Paul Zak thinks we should do this by 'passing laws or creating spaces where people have more face-to-face informal interactions, more exposure to diversity, less income disparity, and better education … things that promote trust' (Suttie, 'Can We Find Morality in a Molecule?'; see note 23 above). Don't forget though, the easiest way to release oxytocin is to simply hug someone!

26   Paul Bloom, 'Why Empathy Is Not the Best Way to Care', *Big Think YouTube* (18 January 2017)

27   Ibid.

28   See Peter Singer, *The Expanding Circle* (Princeton University Press, 1981)

29   Aeschylus, *Oresteia: The Libation Bearers* (5th century BCE), trans. George Theodoridis, www.poetryintranslation.com/PITBR/Greek/Choephori.php

30   Aeschylus, *Oresteia: Agamemnon* (5th century BCE)

31   Ibid.

32   Thomas J. Scheff, 'Hidden Shame as a Cause of Violence', *International Journal of Emergency Mental Health* (January 2015)

33   There is so much fundamental truth and guidance that lies in the wisdom of ancient philosophy that we now so easily ignore, so we placed an Ancient Greek bust on the cover to symbolise those great truths, and plastered a censor over his mouth to represent the suppression and ignoring of those truths. There has been an underlying general anti-science, anti-expert rhetoric that has been around since 2016, its increase made all the more dangerous by the prevalence of the era of post-truth. For example, leading up to the Brexit referendum, Conservative MP Michael Gove stated: 'I think the people of this country have had enough of experts' (Richard Portes, 'I Think the People of this Country Have Had Enough of Experts', 9 May 2017, www.london.edu/think/who-needs-experts). It is the cool-headed investigative and inquisitive focus of expertise, of science and philosophy that will defeat incivility and division, just as they will conquer our technical problems.

34   David J. Harding, 'Do Prisons Make Us Safer?', *Scientific American* (21 June 2019)

35   Wagner & Bertram, 'What Percent of the US is Incarcerated?', *Prison Policy Initiative* (16 January 2020), www.prisonpolicy.org/blog/2020/01/16/percent-incarcerated

36   'Imprisonment is an ineffective long-term intervention for violence prevention, as it has, on balance, no rehabilitative or deterrent effects after release.' David J. Harding et al., 'A Natural Experiment Study of the Effects of Imprisonment on Violence in the Community', *Nature* (July 2019), www.nature.com. If anything, harsher prison conditions lead to more post-release crime. For example, see M. Keith Chen, 'Do Harsher Prison Conditions Reduce Recidivism?' (16 April 2007). And Francis T. Cullen et al., 'Prisons Do Not Reduce Recidivism: The High Cost of Ignoring Science', *The Prison Journal* (19 July 2011), 'beyond crime saved through incapacitation, the use of custodial sanctions may have the unanticipated consequence of making society less safe'.

37   Ryan Berger, 'Kriminalomsorgen: A Look at the World's Most Humane Prison System in Norway' (10 December 2016), https://doi.org/10.2139/ssrn.2883512

38   Alper & Durose, '2018 Update on Prisoner Recidivism: A 9-Year Follow-up Period (2005–2014)', *US Department of Justice* (May 2018)

39   Denis Yukhnenko, 'A Systematic Review Of Criminal Recidivism Rates Worldwide: 3-Year Update', *Wellcome Open Research* (2020)

40   'Proven Reoffending Statistics: January 2016 to March 2016' (25 January 2018), available at www.gov.uk

41   'How Norway Turns Criminals into Good Neighbours', *BBC* (6 July 2019)

42   Ibid.

43   Eleanor Taylor-Nicholson and Barry Krisberg, *Contagion of Violence: Workshop Summary* (National Academies Press, February 2013)

44   Aeschylus, *Oresteia: Agamemnon* (5th century BCE)

45   Bregman, *Humankind: A Hopeful History* (see note 14)

46   Martha C. Nussbaum, 'Beyond Anger', *Aeon* (26 July 2016), https://aeon.co/essays/there-s-no-emotion-we-ought-to-think-harder-about-than-anger

47   Zelda La Grange, *Good Morning, Mr Mandela* (Penguin, 2014). This book is yet another story about how someone's most vehement beliefs can be changed through patience and compassion. The author had her life – her beliefs and prejudices – utterly transformed by Mandela, thanks to his willingness to see humans as humans, vulnerable and impressionable, and most of all, imperfect.

Human Complexity
5.2 Satellites

1   Sam Francis, 'Call for Law Change Over Increase in Homophobic Hate Crimes in London', *BBC News* (10 January 2020)

2   'London Bus Attack: Arrests after Gay Couple Who Refused to Kiss Beaten', *BBC News* (7 June 2019)

3   'LGBT in Britain – Hate Crime and Discrimination' (2017), www.stonewall.org.uk/lgbt-britain-hate-crime-and-discrimination

4   'Hugging Row: Kerala School to Review Student's Expulsion', *The Times of India* (20 December 2017)

5   'At least 6 of these implement the death penalty – Iran, Northern Nigeria, Saudi Arabia, Somalia and Yemen – and the death penalty is a legal possibility in Afghanistan, Brunei, Mauritania, Pakistan, Qatar and UAE.' Human Dignity Trust, 'Map of Countries that Criminalise LGBT People'

6   All Party Parliamentary Group on Global LGBT Rights, 'The UK's Stance on International Breaches of LGBT Rights' (April 2016)

7   Jamie Wareham, '6 In 10 LGBT+ Europeans Fear Assault If They Hold Hands In Public', *Forbes* (14 May 2020)

8   I see you raising your eyebrow, questioning my use of 'comet'. Yes, OK, a whole comet itself doesn't 'burn up into the night'. It is, of course, *fragments* of periodic comets or asteroids that enter the planet's atmosphere and burn up with the heat of atmospheric friction. These fragments make up what we call meteor showers. So perhaps I should have said 'I wish I was a meteor'. Or perhaps even 'meteorite', as the metaphor is about 'touching down' on the planet. But neither fit syllabically within the melody (go on, try singing it yourself), they both ruin the rhythm. So zip it, you! I'm exercising my poetic licence.

9   See Alison Wood Brooks, 'Get Excited: Reappraising Pre-Performance Anxiety as Excitement', *Journal of Experimental Psychology* (2014), or Jeremy P. Jamieson, 'Improving Acute Stress Responses: The Power of Reappraisal', (2012)

10   Brooks, 'Get Excited' (see note 9 above)

11   If you still think this is lying to yourself, it doesn't even have to be as overt as saying you are excited. When you feel anxious, you can also simply tell yourself that your anxiety will be a resource for improving your performance, instead of a sign of looming failure, and will improve your performance under pressure. What separates these two arousal emotions are the associations we make with them. Lee J. Moore, 'Reappraising Threat: How to Optimize Performance Under Pressure', *Journal of Sport and Exercise Psychology* (2015)

12   Olga Khazan, 'One Simple Phrase That Turns Anxiety Into Success', *The Atlantic* (23 March 2016)

13   Robert Booth, 'Acceptance of Gay Sex in Decline in UK for First Time since Aids Crisis', *The Guardian* (11 July 2019)

14   Travis Salway Hottes, 'Preventing Suicide Among Gay and Bisexual Men: New Research & Perspectives' (September 2016), available at www.academia.edu

15   Public Health England, 'Promoting the Health and Wellbeing of Gay, Bisexual and Other Men Who Have Sex with Men' (2014)

16   Michael Hobbes, 'Together Alone: The Epidemic of Gay Loneliness', *Huffington Post* (2 March 2017)

17   Ibid.

18   'Minority Stress Predicts Depression in Lesbian, Gay, and Bisexual Emerging Adults via Elevated Diurnal Cortisol', *Emerging Adulthood* 4(5), (January 2016), pp. 365–372, https://journals.sagepub.com/doi/abs/10.1177/2167696815626822

19   Hobbes, 'Together Alone' (see note 16)

20   Ibid.

21   CNN Editorial Research, 'LGBTQ Rights Milestones Fast Facts'

22   National Centre for Transgender Equality, 'The Discrimination Administration: Trump's record of action against transgender people', https://transequality.org/the-discrimination-administration

23   William Grimes, 'George Weinberg Dies at 87; Coined "Homophobia" After Seeing Fear of Gays', *New York Times* (22 March 2017)

24   Gregory M. Herek, 'Beyond "Homophobia": Thinking About Sexual Prejudice and Stigma in the Twenty-First Century', *Sexuality Research & Social Policy* (2014), https://psychology.ucdavis.edu/rainbow/html/Herek_2004_SRSP.pdf

25   'Homophobia: Don't Ban the Word – Put It in the Index of Mental Disorders', *Huffington Post* (12 June 2012)

26   Gregory Herek, 'The Father of "Homophobia": George Weinberg (1929–2017)' (24 March 2017)

27   George Monbiot, 'The Problem with Freedom' (7 April 2017), available at www.monbiot.com

28   'By the 4th century, the Theodosian Code, had effectively criminalised all forms of same-sex relationships, including same-sex marriage, on pain of death. Paganism and homosexuality had become indistinguishable.' Jonathan Cooper, 'Faith Has Long Been Used to Justify Anti-LGBT+ Discrimination – Here's Why this Dangerous Ploy Won't Work', *The Independent* (31 May 2019)

29   Bruce Bagemihl, 'Biological Exuberance: Animal Homosexuality and Natural Diversity' (1999)

30   Yuval Noah Harari's excellent rule of thumb here is: 'Biology enables, Culture forbids.' See his book *Sapiens* (Harper Collins, 2011)

31   Ibid.

32   Herek, 'The Father of "Homophobia"' (see note 26)

33   Daniel Goleman, 'Homophobia: Scientists Find Clues To Its Roots', *The New York Times* (10 July 1990)

34   Grimes, 'George Weinberg Dies at 87' (see note 23)

35   Goleman, 'Homophobia' (see note 33)

36   Ibid.

37   Ibid.

38   For example, see Ali Haggett, 'Looking Back: Masculinity and Mental Health – the Long View', *The Psychologist* (June 2014)

39   Goleman, 'Homophobia' (see note 33)

40   Herek, 'The Father of "Homophobia"' (see note 26)

41   Ibid.

Human Complexity
5.3 The Pressure's On

1   As opposed to agriculture: 'Hunting and gathering as activities have been with humans for all of human evolution up to today. For more than 99% of their time on Earth, humans have gained their sustenance through animal and plant food that they hunted and gathered.' Thomas Widlok, 'Hunting and Gathering', *The Cambridge Encyclopedia of Anthropology* (18 May 2020)

2   Stephen S. Ilardi, *The Depression Cure* (Penguin, 2009). Ilardi continues: 'In perhaps the most telling example, anthropologist Edward Schieffelin lived among the Kaluli for nearly a decade and carefully interviewed over two thousand men, women, and children regarding their experience of grief and depression; he found only one person who came close to meeting our full diagnostic criteria for depressive illness.'

3   World Health Organization, 'Depression: "Let's Talk" Says WHO, as Depression Tops List of Causes of Ill Health' (30 March 2017), www.who.int/news/item/30-03-2017--depression-let-s-talk-says-who-as-depression-tops-list-of-causes-of-ill-health

4   'By considering the nature of humans as adapted not for modern societies but for hunter–gatherer existence, and examining what humans were evolved for, new light can be shed on contemporary behaviours exposed by the medical inquiries into what is going wrong in acute health systems.' Jeffrey Braithwaite, 'Hunter–Gatherer Human Nature and Health System Safety: An Evolutionary Cleft Stick?', *International Journal for Quality in Healthcare* (20 June 2005)

5   '[F]ood staples and food-processing procedures introduced during the Neolithic and Industrial Periods have fundamentally altered 7 crucial nutritional characteristics of ancestral hominin diets'. Loren Cordain, 'Origins and Evolution of the Western Diet: Health Implications for the 21st Century', *The American Journal of Clinical Nutrition* (1 February 2005)

6   Richard B. Lee and Irene DeVore, *Man the Hunter* (Aldine de Gruyter, 1968)

7   See George Monbiot's excellent summary of how the early creators of neoliberalism saw any sort of collectivism on the same spectrum as Nazism and Communism, and always leading to a totalitarian state. They even saw Franklin Roosevelt's New Deal and the gradual development of Britain's welfare state as a great danger, and therefore set to making an economic alternative that favoured individualism, self-interest, and, as we've seen, a massive transfer of power and wealth to the super-rich. George Monbiot, 'Neoliberalism – the Ideology at the Root of All Our Problems', *The Guardian* (15 April 2016)

8   Stephen Ilardi, 'Depression is a Disease of Civilization' (23 May 2013)

9   Cordain, 'Origins and Evolution of the Western Diet' (see note 5 above)

10 Gillian Orr, 'Britain Has Been Voted the Loneliness Capital of Europe – so How Did We Become so Isolated?', *The Independent* (3 July 2014)

11 For 61%, see CIGNA, 'Loneliness is at Epidemic Levels in America – Loneliness and the Workplace: 2020 US report' (2020), for 75%, see Bradley J. Fikes, '3 out of 4 Americans Are Lonely, Study Says' (20 December 2018), https://phys.org/news/2018-12-americans-lonely.html

12 There's a lot of evidence for this. One particular sad statistic is that two-fifths of elderly people rely on the television for their main source of company. See Age UK, *Evidence Review: Loneliness in Later Life* (July 2014)

13 16- to 24-year-olds are the group most likely to report feeling lonely in the UK. See Office for National Statistics, 'Community Life Survey' (25 July 2019). 'Younger people (18–22) are lonelier than older people (72+)'. See CIGNA, 'Cigna Takes Action To Combat The Rise Of Loneliness And Improve Mental Wellness In America' (23 January 2020)

14   Douglas Nemecek, the chief medical officer for behavioural health at CIGNA, said: 'We hear all the time about social media and being connected. What our study actually found, however, is that the level of attachment with social media really did not impact loneliness one way or the other, [...] What that means really is that I could have a thousand or ten thousand friends on Facebook, but it's the meaningful in-person relationships that I have with other people that actually keep me from becoming lonely.' See 'Many Americans are Lonely, and Gen Z Most of All, Study Finds', *CBS News* (3 May 2018)

15   'The largest community-based, cross-sectional studies of mental illness [...] report a greater lifetime risk of mood disorders and, specifically, MDD [manic depressive disorder] in each successive generation.' Brandon H. Hidaka, 'Depression as a Disease of Modernity: Explanations for Increasing Prevalence', *Journal of Affective Disorders* (12 January 2012), www.ncbi.nlm.nih.gov/pmc/articles/PMC3330161

16   Jenny Edwards and Paul Farmer, 'The Most Terrible Poverty: Loneliness and Mental Health', *Campaign to End Loneliness* (16 June 2014)

17   Loneliness comes 'with a greater risk of cardiovascular disease, dementia, depression and anxiety'. Vivek Murthy, 'Work and the Loneliness Epidemic', *Harvard Business Review* (26 September 2017), https://hbr.org/2017/09/work-and-the-loneliness-epidemic. See also Nicole K. Valtorta, 'Loneliness and Social Isolation as Risk Factors for Coronary Heart Disease and Stroke', *BMJ Journals – Heart* (18 April 2016).

18   Health Resources & Services Administration 'The "Loneliness Epidemic"' (2019), www.hrsa.gov/enews/past-issues/2019/january-17/loneliness-epidemic

19   There's a 'shared neural signature between the two states'. See Lydia Denworth, 'The Loneliness of the "Social Distancer" Triggers Brain Cravings Akin to Hunger', *Scientific American* (2 April 2020)

20   OK, I have another source, my Siberian forest cat, Freya.

21   Harvard Medical School, 'Sour Mood Getting You Down? Get Back to Nature' (July 2018)

22   UN, 'World's Population Increasingly Urban with More than Half Living in Urban Areas' (10 July 2014), available at https://www.un.org/

23   Yascha Mounk, 'Responsibility Redefined' (2017), available at https://democracyjournal.org/

24   Ibid.

25   Welfare regimes have been under siege since the eighties. See Neil Gilbert, 'Transformation of the Welfare State: The Silent Surrender of Public Responsibility', Oxford Scholarship Online (April 2004)

26   For examples of this, see Andrew Grice, 'Born Poor, Stay Poor: The Scandal of Social Immobility', *The Independent* (22 May 2012), www.independent.co.uk/news/uk/home-news/born-poor-stay-poor-scandal-social-immobility-7771336.html; or Stephanie Mencimer, 'If You're Born Poor, You'll Probably Stay That Way', *Mother Jones* (3 June 2014), www.motherjones.com/politics/2014/06/the-long-shadow-poverty-baltimore-poor-children ('family determines almost everything, and that a child's fate is essentially fixed by how well off her parents were when she was born').

27   For example, see Matt O'Brien, 'Poor Kids Who Do Everything Right Don't Do Better than Rich Kids Who Do Everything Wrong', *The Washington Post* (18 October 2014)

28   Matthew 29, 'Parable of the Talents', https://biblehub.com/nasb/matthew/25.htm

29   Abigail Hess, 'Georgetown Study: 'To Succeed in America, it's Better to Be Born Rich than Smart'', *CNBC* (29 May 2019)

30   Sam Harris, *Free Will* (Deckle Edge, 2012)

31   Thomas Hobbes, *Leviathan* (1651)

32   Here's a small section exploring Thomas Hobbes' 'state of nature' as well as scarcity and ownership. It's a more technical analysis and may bore some of you senseless,

so feel free to skip. The phrase 'a Hobbesian state of nature' is thrown around a lot today. Hobbes' views on human nature have become memetic and therefore reductive. So I should point out that he may have *only* been referring specifically to pre-*state* societies, rather than pre-*civilisation* completely. If we take this interpretation, then his 'civil society' referred to the capitalist states of modernity and his 'state of nature' was the period from the agricultural revolution, 10,000 years ago, up to the formation of states, a few thousand years ago. In this case, yes, life in the centuries following the agricultural revolution 'involved more work, reduced nutrition and increased disease'. Counterintuitively, life actually got worse for most people after the agricultural revolution. There was widespread malnutrition and disease, resulting from 'seasonal hunger, reliance on single crops deficient in essential nutrients, crop blights, social inequalities and trade.' Most people were reduced to peasantry and there is a lot of anthropological evidence for violence.

But if we compare Hobbes' 'civil society' to our *true* 'state of nature', i.e. our pre-civilisational condition – the nomadic hunter-gatherer societies that have made up 99% of human life – then we see a lack of evidence for disease, poverty, war, mass violence, or even intertribal warfare. As well as a failure of evidence for metaphorical 'war' too.

Competition and self-interest were certainly *not* the main tenets of pre-civilisational life. Our state of nature was *not* a 'war of all against all'".

I think these massive shifts in human welfare and lifestyle were certainly caused, to some degree, by scarcity. Nomadic hunter-gatherer societies had an abundance of resources. They therefore had no need for war – literal or metaphorical – seen as war is almost always triggered by securing ownership or gaining access to scarce resources. As soon as we see the introduction of population densities – agricultural societies based on competitive trade – we *then* see artificial scarcity introduced through property and resource hoarding and the inequality it establishes. It is at this point that a utility value in self-interest arises. Life became about protecting and guarding your resources, as well as, ultimately, stockpiling them as an ultimate protective measure.

This brings us to the *Hobbesian trap*. The fear of attack or burglary motivates us to hoard and protect our resources, and even pre-emptively attack any perceived competitors. We see this in outbreaks of conflict whether between individuals or states. And we see this in the business world with monopolisation and the 'externalisation' of costs.

Although cooperation would be a better result for all sides, (in terms of innovation, equality, trust and ultimately, welfare) this mutual sense of distrust, and this fear of the other encourages strategies that negatively affect everyone.

The quotes in this note are from the following study: Mummert et al, 'Stature and robusticity during the agricultural transition: evidence from the bioarchaeological record', *National Library Of Medicine* (2011)

33   Graeme Wood, 'Secret Fears of the Super-Rich', *The Atlantic* (April 2011)
34   Ibid.
35   'Full Speech: Jim Carrey's Commencement Address at the 2014 MUM Graduation' (30 May 2014), www.youtube.com/watch?v=V80-gPkpH6M&feature=youtu.be
36   'People in individualistic (vs. collectivist) countries reported more loneliness.' Manuela Barretto, 'Loneliness around the World: Age, Gender, and Cultural Differences in Loneliness', *Personality & Individual Differences* (1 February 2021), www.sciencedirect.

com/science/article/pii/S0191886920302555?via%3Dihub (and by the way, it was of course the US and the UK – where neoliberalism has the tightest and most pervasive grip – that were rated the most individualist countries in this research).

37 Jamil Zaki, 'The War for Kindness: Building Empathy in a Fractured World' (20 February 2020), www.youtube.com/watch?v=7Y23qQjXmHs

38 Hidaka, 'Depression as a Disease of Modernity' (see note 15)

39 Those changes are Omega-3 fatty acid supplements, anti-rumination strategies, exercise, light exposure, social support and sleep hygiene. See Ilardi, *The Depression Cure* (see note 2)

40 'Simply exercising 3 times a week happened to beat taking the anti-depressant, Zoloft, in two separate trials.' Stephen Ilardi, 'Depression is a Disease of Civilization', www.youtube.com/watch?v=drv3BP0Fdi8

The Mechanics Of Control And Constraint
T.I.N.A. & Marionettes

1 Notably: structural racism and sexism, antibiotic resistance, topsoil degradation, food and water scarcity, technological unemployment, etc. All these problems have systemic routes.

2 For this brilliant phrase I am indebted to the author and filmmaker, Peter Joseph.

3 I first came across the acronym in Srećko Horvat's book, *Poetry from the Future: Why a Global Liberation Movement Is Our Civilisation's Last Chance* (Allen Lane, 2019)

4 Bertrand Russell, 'The Triumph of Stupidity', in *Mortals and Others: Bertrand Russell's American* Essays (1931–1935), volume II (Routledge, 1998)

5 See 'Mass Killings Under Communist Regimes', https://en.wikipedia.org/wiki/Mass_ killings_under_communist_regimes

6 Our track **The Bank of England** looks at the failings of capitalism specifically, criticising Adam Smith's 'invisible hand'.

7 Rebecca Lindsey, 'Climate Change: Atmospheric Carbon Dioxide' (14 August 2020), www.climate.gov/news-features/understanding-climate/climate-change-atmospheric-carbon-dioxide

8 Roughton Reynolds, 'The JBM's New Years 2011' (1 January 2012), www.youtube.com/ watch?v=wX5y2PsgMgI

9 Rupert Neate, 'World's Richest 0.1% Have Boosted Their Wealth by as Much as Poorest Half', *The Guardian* (14 December 2017)

10 'A report by Swiss bank UBS found that billionaires increased their wealth by more than a quarter (27.5%)'. Rupert Neate, 'Billionaires' Wealth Rises to $10.2 Trillion amid COVID Crisis', *The Guardian* (7 October 2020). From the start of the pandemic in March to the end of 2020, billionaires in the US increased their wealth by more than $1 trillion, and 29 billionaires saw their wealth double. See Institute for Policy Studies, 'Pandemic Profiteering'

11 For example, have a look at some of the graphs here if you want to do a little sick in your mouth: Howard R. Gold, 'Never Mind the 1% Let's Talk about the 0.01%', *Chicago Booth Review* (2017)

12 'The richest 400 families in the US paid an average effective tax rate of 23% while the bottom half of American households paid a rate of 24.2%.' Dominic Rushe, 'Trump's Tax Cuts Helped Billionaires Pay Less than the Working Class for First Time', *The Guardian* (9 October 2019)

13 Mark Riley Cardwell, 'Attenborough: Poorer Countries are just as Concerned about the Environment', *The Guardian* (16 October 2013)

14 See www.overshootday.org/about-earth-overshoot-day

15 Edward Abbey, 'The Second Rape of the West', in *The Journey Home: Some Words in*

Defense of the American West (Dutton, 1977)

16   George Monbiot, 'The Rich Want Us to Believe Their Wealth is Good for Us All', *The Guardian* (29 July 2014)

17   It's obviously very hard to find solid and comparable stats on this. For the money figure I went with the following: Mitchell Hartman, 'Here's How Much Money There Is in the World – and Why You've Never Heard the Exact Number', *Business Insider* (17 November 2017) www.businessinsider.com/heres-how-much-money-there-is-in-the-world-2017-10?r=US&IR=T. For the debt figure I took a rough median of these two estimates: Marialuz Moreno Badia and Paolo Dudine, 'New Data on World Debt: A Dive into Country Numbers' (17 December 2019), https://blogs.imf.org/2019/12/17/new-data-on-world-debt-a-dive-into-country-numbers; and 'Global Debt Hits Record High of 331% of GDP in the First Quarter of 2020: IIF', *The Economic Times* (16 July 2020)

18   Kate Pickett and Richard G. Wilkinson, *The Spirit Level* (Allen Lane, 2009)

19   As the author, director and systems analyst Peter Joseph says: 'Poverty and economic inequality must end. As noted, this is the engine of fear and dominance keeping bigotry alive more than any other force. Classism is the mother of racism. As long as we have a cut-throat society that forces people into economic competition with each other to survive, with no 'level playing field' to be found as society remains structurally rigged in favor of the rich while the poor continue to suffer, you will never see the racist characteristics of modern society really go away, nor will you see a viable reduction in police brutality anytime soon.' Peter Joseph, 'Systemic Racism in the USA: Origins, Perpetuation and Solutions', *Medium* (13 September 2020)

20   To name a few: Ha-Joon Chang, '23 Things They Don't Yell You about Capitalism' (2010); Paul Mason, *Postcapitalism* (Penguin, 2016); Naomi Klein, *This Changes Everything: Capitalism vs. the Climate* (Penguin, 2015); Yanis Varoufakis, *Talking to My Daughter: A Brief History of Capitalism* (Bodley Head, 2017)

21   Naomi Klein in her book *The Shock Doctrine* (Penguin, 2008)

22   Anna Fifield, 'Contractors Reap $138bn from Iraq War', *Financial Times* (18 March 2013). See also a list of other profiting companies in 'The 25 Most Vicious Iraq War Profiteers', *Business Pundit* (22 June 2008)

23   Often misattributed to Darwin himself; see https://quoteinvestigator.com/2014/05/04/adapt

24   Rob Hopkins, 'Intergovernmental Panel on Climate Change (IPCC) Take-Away: Imagine. Take Action. Repeat.' (8 November 2018), https://transitionnetwork.org/news-and-blog/my-ipcc-take-away-imagine-take-action-repeat

25   See, for example: David Wallace-Wells, *The Uninhabitable Earth* (Crown Publishing Group, 2019)

26   Rob Hopkins, 'Kyung Hee Kim on "The Creativity Crisis"' (20 September 2018), www.robhopkins.net/2018/09/20/kyung-hee-kim-on-the-creativity-crisis. For example, see this study: Kyung Hee Kim, 'The Creativity Crisis: The Decrease in CreativeThinking Scores on the Torrance Tests of CreativeThinking', *Creativity Research Journal* (9 November 2011)

27   Robert M. Sapolsky, 'Depression, Antidepressants, and the Shrinking Hippocampus', *PNAS* (2001), www.ncbi.nlm.nih.gov/pmc/articles/PMC60045/

28   See Mark Blyth, *Austerity* (Oxford University Press, 2013); or, more recently, Tom Kibasi, 'Austerity Is a Zombie Ideology. It's Time to Bury it Once and for All', *The Guardian* (20 October 2020). Or my own discussion from 2015: 'Step Up Podcast With Rou Reynolds – Austerity' (18 November 2015), www.youtube.com/watch?v=snkaJRPHKQ0

29   'Walking in the forest environment may promote cardiovascular relaxation by facilitating the parasympathetic nervous system and by suppressing the sympathetic nervous system. In addition, forest therapy may be effective for reducing negative

psychological symptoms.' Yoshifumi Miyazaki et al., 'Influence of Forest Therapy on Cardiovascular Relaxation in Young Adults', *Evidence-Based Complementary & Alternative Medicine* (10 February 2014), available at www.hindawi.com

30   My free mindfulness meditation podcast may be a good place to start! Search 'Here, Now, Together' on your podcast provider.

31   The 'calm, meditative feeling you get when you're on a hike or canoeing mellow waters, and your mind is completely at ease, taking in the scenery, and maybe daydreaming a little'. Carolyn Gregoire, 'The New Science of the Creative Brain on Nature' (18 May 2016)

32   For further reading, see 'Attention restoration theory', on wikipedia.org

33   '[F]our days of immersion in nature, and the corresponding disconnection from multi-media and technology, increases performance on a creativity, problem-solving task by a full 50% in a group of naive hikers.' Ruth Ann Atchely et al., 'Creativity in the Wild: Improving Creative Reasoning through Immersion in Natural Settings', *PLoS One* (12 December 2012), www.ncbi.nlm.nih.gov/pmc/articles/PMC3520840

34   George Orwell, 'The Prevention of Literature', *Polemic* 2 (January 1946), available in *Shooting an Elephant and Other Essays* (Penguin, 2003)

35   Rob Hopkins, 'Dr Larry Rosen on Activism and Imagination in the Age of the Distracted Mind' (23 January 2018), www.robhopkins.net/2018/01/23/dr-larry-rosen-on-activism-and-imagination-in-the-age-of-the-distracted-mind

36   James Ashton, 'Reading Is in Sharp Decline – That's Bad News for the Future' (8 March 2019), https://reaction.life/reading-sharp-decline-thats-bad-news-future

37   Danielle Cohen, 'Why Kids Need to Spend Time in Nature', available at https://childmind.org/

38   Brian Sutton-Smith, *The Ambiguity of Play* (Harvard University Press, 2001). For further reading, see Bernard L. De Koven, 'We Study Play Because Life is Hard', *Psychology Today* (8 September 2015)

39   Sutton-Smith, *The Ambiguity of Play* (see note 38 above)

40   For example, see Peter Gray, 'The Decline of Play' (13 June 2014), available on https://ed.ted.com/

41   Peter Gray, 'The Evolutionary Importance of Self-Directed Play', https://thegeniusofplay.org/genius/expert-advice/articles/the-evolutionary-importance-of-self-directed-play.aspx#.X7kOlVmny_c

42   Rob Hopkins, 'Talking Play and Imagination with Peter Gray', *Resilience* (30 October 2019), www.resilience.org/stories/2019-10-30/talking-play-and-imagination-with-peter-gray

43   Gray, 'The Decline of Play' (see note 40 above).

44   The American Psychological Association releases a regular survey, 'Stress in America', where they interview people of all ages to assess the degree of anxiety in their lives. See 'Stress in America, Are Teens Adopting Adults' Stress Habits?', *American Psychological Association* (11 February 2014)

45   "Machines to 'do half of all work tasks by 2025'" BBC, 21 October 2020)

46   Rob Hopkins, *From What Is to What If: Unleashing the Power of Imagination to Create the Future We Want* (Chelsea Green, 2019)

47   Ted Nordhaus and Michael Shellenberger, 'Apocalypse Fatigue: Losing the Public on Climate Change' (16 November 2009)

48   For example, The H5N1 strain of bird flu has a 60% death rate in those it infects. Luckily it has a very low ability to pass from human to human meaning it has never reached pandemic status. But ... the risks are rising of this strain or others developing. Two studies from 2012 analysed whether a strain of bird flu could overcome its inability to pass from human to human. It was put through a series of tests on ferrets (the mammal commonly used as a model for how influenza affects us). By

the time the disease had got to the 10th ferret, it had become directly transmissible between mammals. We're putting a lot of trust in the security of these labs, not only to stop information getting into the hands of anyone committed to malign intent / bioterrorism, but also in keeping these studied strains secure. For the studies, see: Herfst et al. (2012), Imai et al. (2012), Butler & Ledford (2012). And it is quite fair to question the security at these labs given their history of 'leaked' pathogens. Instances of pathogens escaping labs – everything from Smallpox to Anthrax – have occurred around the world. One particularly ominous example I found was 3 mice infected with Bubonic plague going missing from a lab at the University of Medicine in New Jersey. They were never found. See: Roxanne Khamsi, 'Lab loses trio of plague mice', *Nature* (September 2005)

49   Toby Ord suggests a 1 in 30 chance of existential catastrophe from an engineered pandemic this century. 'There is no watertight case against pathogens leading to the extinction of their hosts'. Toby Ord, *The Precipice* (Bloomsbury 2020) 'The potential for future pandemics is vast. As many as 1.7 million unidentified viruses of the type known to infect people are believed to still exist in mammals and water birds. Any one of these could be the next 'Disease X' – potentially even more disruptive and lethal than COVID-19. Future pandemics are likely to happen more frequently, spread more rapidly, have greater economic impact and kill more people if we are not extremely careful about the possible impacts of the choices we make today.' 'COVID-19 Stimulus Measures Must Save Lives, Protect Livelihoods, and Safeguard Nature to Reduce the Risk of Future Pandemics', *IPBES* (27 April 2020) https://ipbes.net/covid19stimulus

50   Reuters, 'Partly False Claim: Trump Fired Entire Pandemic Response Team in 2018' (25 March 2020)

51   Oliver Milman, 'Trump Administration Cut Pandemic Early Warning Program in September', *The Guardian* (3 April 2020)

52   Each country has their strengths and weaknesses of course. The neoliberal or individualistic countries seem to have fared far worse than others, though, in part due to their lack of preparation. Over the past two decades the UK drastically reduced the capacity of its infection-focused laboratories. They are now fragmented and unconnected to local public health and GP practices. Other countries have provided better financial support, more information, medicines and food, and accommodation for those who need to isolate away from vulnerable family members. For a balanced analysis see the BBC Radio 4 *Inside Science* podcast, 'Test and Trace – How the UK Compares to the Rest of the World'

53   Jane Dalton, 'Coronavirus: Pandemics Will Be Worse and More Frequent unless We Stop Exploiting Earth and Animals, Top Scientists Warn', *The Independent* (1 May 2020), www.independent.co.uk/environment/coronavirus-pandemic-virus-disease-wildlife-environment-farming-infectious-a9487926.html. 'Climate change means more zoonotic emergence risk [...] even if we stay under 2 degrees', reported Colin J. Carlson et al., 'Climate Change Will Drive Novel Cross-species Viral Transmission', *bioRxiv* (25 January 2020), www.biorxiv.org/content/10.1101/2020.01.24.918755v1

54   Or read Michael Lewis's book, *The Big Short: Inside The Doomsday Machine* (W. W. Norton, 2010)

55   Jean-Jacques Rousseau, *Emile, or On Education* (1762)

56   Martin Fellenz, 'Theresa May Is Right about One Thing – it's Time Politicians Worked Together on Brexit', *The Conversation* (21 March 2019)

57   Jose Miguel Sokoloff, 'How We Used Christmas Lights to Fight a War' (8 December 2014), www.youtube.com/watch?v=0Fi83BHQsMA

58   Human Rights Watch, 'World Report 2014: Colombia', www.hrw.org/world-report/2014/country-chapters/colombia

59   'Profiles: Colombia's Armed Groups', *BBC News* (29 August 2019)

60 Sokoloff, 'How We Used Christmas Lights to Fight a War' (see note 54 above).

61 Tom Vanden Brook, 'Propaganda that Works: Christmas Decorations', *USA Today* (13 August 2013)

62 Sokoloff, 'How We Used Christmas Lights to Fight a War' (see note 54 above).

63 Emily Reynolds, 'How Jose Sokoloff Demobilised Guerrillas with Advertising', *Wired* (15 October 2015)

64 Nicholas Casey, 'Colombia Struck a Peace Deal with Guerrillas, but Many Return to Arms', *The New York Times* (18 September 2018)

Epilogue

1 The survey took place in four developed nations: the US, UK, Canada and Australia. Melanie Randle and Richard Eckersley, 'Public Perceptions of Future Threats to Humanity and Different Societal Responses: A Cross-national Study', *Futures* (September 2015)

2 Regarding a more meditative mindset, see, for example, Peter Aspinall et al., 'The Urban Brain: Analysing Outdoor Physical Activity with Mobile EEG', *British Journal of Sports Medicine* (January 2015). Regarding creativity, happiness and generosity, see, for example, Jill Suttie, 'How Nature Can Make You Kinder, Happier, and More Creative', *Greater Good Magazine* (2 March 2016)

3 Buckminster Fuller, *Guinea Pig B: The 56 Year Experiment* (Critical Path Publishing, 2004)

4 Carl Sagan, 'The Quest for Extraterrestrial Intelligence', *Smithsonian Magazine* (May 1978), www.bigear.org/vol1no2/sagan.htm

5 Quoted in Marshall Frady, *Martin Luther King, Jr: A Life* (Penguin, 2005); or see Gary May, 'A Revolution of Values: Martin Luther King, Jr and the Poor People's Campaign', *Moyers On Democracy* (18 January 2015), https://billmoyers.com/2015/01/18/revolution-values